In the Beginning Is the Icon
A Liberative Theology of Images, Visual Arts and Culture

Sigurd Bergmann

Translated by Anja K. Angelsen

LONDON   OAKVILLE

Published by Equinox Publishing Ltd.

UK: Unit 6, The Village, 101 Amies St., London SW11 2JW
USA: DBBC, 28 Main Street, Oakville, CT 06779

www.equinoxpub.com

First published in Swedish under the title *I begynnelsen är bilden* by Proprius in 2003. This English edition first published 2009. Translation: Anja K. Angelsen, Trondheim.

British Library Cataloguing-in-Publication Data

A catalogue record for this book is available from the British Library.

ISBN-13   978 1 84553 172 0   (hardback)

Library of Congress Cataloging-in-Publication Data

Bergmann, Sigurd, 1956-
  [I begynnelsen är bilden. English]
  In the beginning is the icon : a liberative theology of images, visual arts, and culture / Sigurd Bergmann.
      p. cm.
  Includes bibliographical references and index.
  ISBN 978-1-84553-172-0 (hb)
  1. Art and religion. 2. Spirituality in art. 3. God—Art. 4.
Aesthetics. I. Title.
  N72.R4B39813 2009
  246—dc22
                                        2007038491

Typeset by S.J.I. Service, New Delhi
Printed and bound in Great Britain by Antony Rowe Ltd, Chippenham, Wiltshire

In the Beginning Is the Icon

Contents

Contents

List of Images

Foreword

Sigurd Bergmann's *In the Beginning Is the Icon* is a breakthrough in theological aesthetics, or as he sometimes calls it, art theology. Most writers on theological aesthetics have their eye on high art of the West, some of this being art that originated in the West, some of it art that we in the West have appropriated from other societies for our own purposes. The writer then reflects on the theological significance of this art, employing his or her own theology in doing so. It is of little or no interest to the writer how those who originally made and engaged the art understood what they had made and how they were engaging it.

In place of this way of doing theological aesthetics, Bergmann proposes, and begins to practice, what he calls *contextual art theology*. Bergmann frames his proposal in terms of images; but the significance of his proposal extends beyond images to all the arts.

Contextual image theology is contextual in two respects. It is, for one thing, contextual in its approach to images. Of course, traditional theological aesthetics is also, in a way, contextual in its approach to images. The point is that it limits its concern to just one context, that which consists of what Theodor Adorno called "engrossed contemplation." Fundamental to the approach that Bergmann is proposing is that we liberate ourselves from our myopic concern with this one context and open our eyes to the diversity of ways in which human beings engage images – not just the diversity of ways in which modern Westerners engage images, but the diversity of ways in which human beings in general do so.

This proposal leads Bergmann into an informed and very helpful summary of the various approaches by anthropologists to the role of images in so-called primitive societies. Though naturally he finds some of these approaches more helpful than others, eventually he concludes that none of them can simply be taken over for the purpose of developing a contextual art theology. All of the anthropological approaches to images are, in the last resort, components within some larger anthropological theory; they are not aimed at illuminating the context in which these images were originally made and engaged. By contrast, "image theology…must always base and centre its interpretation in and around the physical and historical images in their context."

As the corollary of a contextual approach to images, Bergmann proposes a contextual approach to theology. Theology emerges in many different contexts, one of these being the academic context. For those of us who are members of the academy in the modern West, this is our context; this is the context within which we engage in theological reflection. Hence it is no surprise that the theology employed by the practitioners of theological aesthetics has almost always been academic theology of the modern West. In proposing a contextual art theology, Bergmann is proposing that we instead attend to the theology-in-context of those who originally made and engaged the images that we are studying. What was *their* theology? How did they understand God and God's activity in the world?

With images and theology both approached contextually, the project of a contextual art theology is then to illuminate how the theological convictions of those who originally made and engaged these images comes to expression in those images and in the way they were engaged. In Bergmann's own words, "How is God represented sensuously –corporeally visually through the image-making and reception processes in the physical works of art? How do these artefacts interpret God? How do we sense and understand God's liberating actions in images?" In his final chapter, Bergmann goes beyond merely proposing this approach and culminates his discussion by taking images from a variety of times and places, and vividly showing what contextual art theology actually looks like in practice.

Nicholas Wolterstorff
Noah Porter Professor Emeritus of
Philosophical Theology, Yale University
Senior Fellow, Institute for Advanced
Studies in Culture, University of Virginia

Preface

"To sense art, to experience art, and to perform art is immensely more important than reflecting over art," exclaims the Spanish painter Antoni Tapies.[1]

Why write about visual arts? And why write about images and art in relation to religious belief, a world that traditionally has been ruled by the written word, both within the church and academia?

Based on the assumption that human beings create and carry the world through external and internal images, it is hard to understand why reflections on the creation of images are not a central component of reflections on humanity and religion. Is the Western culture[2] – in spite of the flood of mass-produced images – still antagonistic to images?

Tapies' positive valuation of creative art did not render it a devaluation, but rather a revaluation of art reflection. The origin of art is the work of art itself. Aesthetics should not be a normative theory that restrains the freedom of creation.

The aim of this book is to contribute to the development of a sensitive theory that supports and preserves the intrinsic value of image creation and creative power. To provide a contrast to the traditional narrow focus on language within religious studies and theology, the main focus will be on the challenge of visual culture for "life interpretation."[3]

A narrow methodological approach would be a presumptuous and, for the purpose of this book, destructive pursuit. The encounter between visual arts and religion must necessarily take place in an open space with room for development, and thus the reader will have to accept a number of loose ends. A certain element of unpredictability and reluctance toward developing a unified theory is part of the author's conscious analytical method, even though some researchers, in order to protect the integrity of their academic discipline, may argue that this methodological approach is in fact a "lack" of method.[4] The aim of iconology is not to establish universal truths, but rather to be a tool for articulating and interpreting visual experiences. Therefore, in this book I urge for sensibility and a certain critical distance to "the order of things" (Foucault), which hopefully may inspire others to continue creatively the open reflections of the book.

The main objective of the book is to explore a field of research that has yet to come into existence. The discursive space of this field should incorporate and develop perspectives from fields that are unrelated or only remotely related. Reflections from iconology, art theory, philosophical aesthetics, art history, and the fairly recent field of anthropology of art intersect with reflections from systematic theology and religious studies.

Needless to say, this is a vulnerable and haphazard venture, as the author cannot claim expert knowledge within all these fields of study. Nonetheless, in a problematically complex and differentiated knowledge context, I find it of utmost importance to spend one's energy on synthetic enterprises.

The book can be regarded as a kind of literary exhibition of various approaches to the theme of "God in pictures" (in continuity with my monograph on "God in Context," 2003). From the very outset I wish to share the duty of synthesis and integration in this novel field with the observant reader, without whom no picture or book have a function.

In addition to the establishment of an open, interdisciplinary field of study, the current proposal also includes a normative ambition. Unlike the well-established philosophical aesthetics and the intent of the old Western Church to reduce visual arts to an expression of logocentric constructions or to mere illustrations of biblical readings and religious dogmas, the normative intention is developed by an aesthetic of production and reception. Whoever asks whether this book represents a theoretical and methodological innovation should look for the answer in the author's intention to set the discursive interpretation of what is seen in close connection with the visual experience of the image and the memory of this experience. A logocentric projection of the spectator onto the picture will be replaced with a reflection over the dynamics of the relationship between the artefact, its creator, and its spectator, partly in the same and partly in different contexts.

A central question is how God, through human creation and observation of pictures, can have a liberating function in images. Within the context of a liberation theological

approach to the interpretation of God and an aesthetic that focuses on the love of the poor, the final chapter develops a constructive proposal for a contextual art theology. In the globalized mass production of pictures, the pedagogy of art and iconology has a special significance in contributing to the humanization and liberation of men and women.[5] The roles of the hand and the eye for learning make up central and crucial notions within liberation pedagogy.[6] The extended time period that is needed to orientate in the visual sphere is in itself a political counterforce to the violation of natural space and a natural passing of time caused by the acceleration of technological developments.[7]

In light of the impact of both art and religion within a world of geographical and historical relations, and with a critical edge toward Western art reflection and the egocentric, Eurocentric character of religious studies, the chapter about "world art" widens the perspective of the book. Even though the research history of ethnography and anthropology also reflects this ethnocentricity shared by art and religious studies, the newly established anthropology of art offers important perspectives for a cross-cultural theology of art.

In light of the history of religion and church history, there are many good reasons for using passion and foresight in the development of the meeting between the ideas of images and art and the Christian interpretation of life. Some of these reasons are listed below.

• In accordance with the superior position of the spoken and written word over pictorial depictions within in the history of Western culture; religious and Christian studies have also suffered from a biased focus on words and texts. The crucial importance of art for the shaping of the religious worldview, first and foremost among the non-literate religious devout, which was well known among medieval theologians, is no longer appreciated. One important challenge is to regard images as "locus theologicus,"[8] as a place where God acts and where the human experience with God becomes manifest in an autonomous medium.

- With regards to the history of Christianity, the theological interpretation of images has a common ecclesiastical and philosophical ground closely related to Jewish and Hellenistic approaches. While the Western Church developed a more catechetic iconology, in which images generally were perceived as positive, albeit in a reductionist sense as illustrations to the Holy Scripture and the written dogmas of theologians, the Eastern Church developed a more ontological theology of icons, in which the intrinsic value of the visual media is recognized. Within Protestant contexts, a more pragmatic, and theologically less well-founded, approach was adopted, situated between the two extremities of image ban and icon worship. There is an urgent need for ecumenical reflection over the inter-confessional historical similarities and divisions of a theology of images and its future ethical potential in a globalized and secularized world system, although such reflection can only be hinted at in this book.

- The various sub-disciplines of Christian and religious studies alike have spent little effort on establishing a reflection over the importance of image creation and the ideas of images on biblical studies, church history, and systematic theology. The consequences

of this biased text focus is an irresponsible distance to the non-verbal dimensions of belief and the artefacts of everyday culture and the world of the devout. Thus an entire reality dimension remains hidden.

- The history of Christianity has created a huge number of pictures, sculptures and buildings through which artists have interpreted Christian faith, worldview and culture. Not until the nineteenth century did art and theology become disengaged. Theologians retired to an increasingly secluded sphere and public translation of reality was handed over to natural scientists and artists. In modern society, art is created autonomously, even if it retains a living metaphysics, unlike the natural sciences and technology, which believe they operate on neutral ethical grounds.

- Visual arts represent an intuitive *and* rational interpretation of reality, which deserves the designation science.[9] In Western society, art studies are included in academia, even though its epistemological potential is far from being adequately examined.

The visual arts express perspectives on the context of culture, environment, and society in a way that makes visible and transcends prevailing patterns of perception. Art elucidates and illuminates problems and processes reflexively. Furthermore, it involves a great deal of experimental urge and play, and hereby art earns a normative frankness which functions as a constant corrective to the threatening cultural rigidity.

The expressions of art, and especially the expressions of pictorial art, visualize life- and worldviews. They shape the system of norms and signs, often with a surprisingly sophisticated level of religious wisdom, knowledge, and consciousness.

- Within hermeneutics and theology, F. Schleiermacher, for example, assumes that images are part of all thinking.[10] In the tradition from Augustine, every insight is manifested through signs. Images cannot be dominated by words. Augustine made a distinction between, on the one hand, the original relation, for example equality (*aequalitas*), and, on the other hand, similar nature (*similitudo*). In a religious philosophical perspective, images can be perceived as having a dual function. The image can bear certain similarities to something (*similitudo*) and it can be exactly like something (*aequalitas*). The image both partly refers to, and partly bears an inherent resemblance to, something that goes beyond that to which one may establish a reference. In modern times, the religious philosophical reflection over the significance of image has obviously lost the historical continuity.

- Pictorial works of art visualize the inevitable problem of their contemporary context, to which the Christian life interpretation with its special preconditions should contribute.[11]

- Visual arts offer alternative courses of action that can make a strong contribution to the Christian Church. In a society dominated by an instrumental goal-orientation, the futile creativity of art represents a critique of this rationality and makes a contribution to a new, balanced form of rationality. The creation of art can be perceived as an expression of a practical-aesthetical and

critical common sense. The freedom of art is an essential component of art, a feature it shares with theology.

- In the so-called Third and Fourth Worlds, ever since the breakthrough of modernity in the First World, visual arts have had a very important role in arts' critical perspective on the way of life of the industrial world. World art is at present in a very dynamic development chain within which a new sign system for communication between artists in the different worlds is emerging. A natural question is how this inter- and transcultural art process relates to the dynamic contextual theology.

The book is organized according to the discourses introduced above.

What is an image? This is the first issue to be discussed. Through a selection of iconological perspectives, the reader with a background in religious studies and theology will be introduced to an interpretation perspective that focuses on the intrinsic power of the image. The selection here is not exhaustive, but by no means is it arbitrary.[12] There is no way by which a theological approach to art can do justice to the visual aspect of human nature, if the theologian does not first acquire a well-reflected attitude and methodology in relation to the world of images and to the creation of images, its gaze and interpretation which is intrinsically related to the experience of images.

What is art? This is the topic of discussion in Chapter 2, where a brief outline of the treatment of art within the context of the Western history of ideas is presented.[13] The philosophical-aesthetical programme of the eighteenth and nineteenth centuries, which presents the dominating view of fine arts in the Western hemisphere, is discussed in more detail. Finally, there is a critical comment on the breakdown of theo-aesthetics, that is, art theory in which the nature of art is fundamentally based on a theological metaphysic.

The third chapter takes close stock of the view of art within the twentieth-century history of religion and theology. Following an exposition of four crucial elements that pose a challenge of a well-founded theology of visual art, nine different approaches within theology and religious history are presented. The nine approaches are subject to critical examination, and the weaknesses and strengths of the various approaches are presented in light of four models for art theology.

Chapter 4 includes an inventory of approaches to the nature and function of art in culture within cultural and social anthropology. A retrospective view on the incorporation of the art expressions of so-called primitive people in the modernist tradition of the early twentieth century is followed by a comprehensive and critical discussion of three different traditions within the anthropology of art. The question of how anthropology relates to the issue of the cultural function and the autonomy of art is the common denominator for these three approaches.

Finally, the loose ends from the first four chapters are woven together to form a proposal for a contextual theology of art. The literary style of this chapter differs from the rest of the book by apportioning the art reproductions and readers' encounters with the images, as well as allowing the author's interpretation and mindset a more autonomous role. Different criteria for a contextual art theology are outlined in seven steps – an art theology which develops the requirement to contribute to an aesthetic of liberation in harmony with the new contextual paradigm of theology. The ancient Eastern Church's enlightened reflections about God's trinity and the life- and space-giving work of the Holy Spirit embed this theology in the continuity and harmony of the classic Christian tradition.

The aim of this book is to contribute to raising awareness about the intrinsic value of images and image perception among those who wish to reflect over God and over pictorial expressions of different experiences from encounters with divinity in earthly and historical situations. It is my hope that the book will appeal to the eyes, intuitions, and thoughts of theologians and academics within religious studies and theology. But I also hope that artists and researchers within art and culture studies may benefit from the religious perspective on visual arts, and that the openness connected to the target audience of the book may in itself contribute to a further cultivation of the expanded, open field of study.

The fruits on the tree of knowledge have not ripened in isolation. I express my heartfelt thanks to everyone who has contributed in a critical and constructive manner to the growth of the tree: students at courses on aesthetics/ visual arts and theology at the Department of Religious Studies in Göteborg, where the two first chapters of the book developed; the research seminar in Social Anthropology at Lund University; the research seminar in Religious Studies at the Norwegian University of Science and Technology in Trondheim; the Department of Teacher Training at the University College of Arts Crafts and Design, Stockholm; Per Erik Persson, Lund, and Carola Envall, Åbo, for a critical examination of the entire text; Anja Angelsen, Trondheim, for translating it into enjoyable English; Ingela Bergmann, Trondheim; Jan von Bonsdorff, Tromsø; Renate Banschbach Eggen, Trondheim; Manfred Hofmann, Lund; Geir Tore Holm, Oslo; PO Holmström, Höör; Arne Martin Klausen, Vesterøy; Tage Kurtén, Åbo; Lena Liepe, Tromsø; Jørgen I. Lund, Oslo; Bengt Molander, Trondheim; Elisabeth Stengård, Stockholm; Birgit Weiler, Lima; and Torsten Weimarck, Lund. Finally, I wish to express my gratitude to the former Head of the University, Emil Spjøtvoll, and the Faculty of Arts at the "Norwegian University of Science and Technology" in Trondheim for grants for producing this book, to Proprius Publishers (Stockholm) which published the Swedish manuscript ("I begynnelsen är bilden", 2003), and to Equinox Publishing which have showed a unique sensitivity for the purpose of this work.

CHAPTER 1

What Is an Image?

"In the Beginning Was the Image..."

"In the beginning was the image..." is the title of a painting by Asger Jorn. The painting was made outdoors in Munich in 1965.[1] (See colour plate section, Image 1.)

Colours pour over the image. The colour flow deforms the figures. The eye hollows, cheeks, and the wing stroke still appear in our vision. There is no external structure – only the fish, the human, and the mask. To the right, we see within the plaice a plastic face with protruding eyes and fat lips. Centre and left, two flying figures glide towards the fish-shaped body. At the bottom, we see three masks with deformed but still recognizable expressions. At the far right, there is a slightly astonished spectator to the event.

The painting lacks symmetry; it places great demands on the viewer, who must create unity and inner structure. The colour shades and the eruptive movements tie the seemingly opposing and random parts together.

It seems futile to approach this painting through words. The image works independent of language. It exists *prior* to language. "Images are created before words and are independent of words," Jorn wrote in another context.[2] The painting illustrates how vision unquestionably must precede all thinking and all interpretation. To the extent that it is at all possible to extract any meaning from this very expressive painting, one cannot transfer this meaning to an imaginary world beyond the visual world. The interpretation of an image of this sort will always be based in its lucidity and sensuous nature. It will not let thought escape the power of vision.

The title of the painting is not arbitrarily chosen. In his powerful civilization criticism, Jorn in part attacks science's conception of nature's rationality – which he contrasts to the natural order of artistic intuition – and in part the renaissance conception of the decisive meaning of geometry and symmetry.[3]

His images do not come from the real, external world but from a subjective experience of an inner world. It is this inner world that is directly expressed in the eruption of colour and light from which the shapes slowly emerge.

Jorn does not regard the subjective as individually autonomous, but he keeps searching for the collective universal phenomena that arise across different cultures. He calls this search "comparative vandalism."[4] The painter's adaptation of the primitive masks does not only involve the import of a visual technique but also, even in the image of creation above, an integrated "total assimilation"[5]: the masks' gaze and expression become ours.

In Jorn's picture coherence arises from asymmetry. Deformation is the premise for the creation of meaning. Intuitive vision and experience precede the linguistic interpretation. In the beginning was *not* the Word, contrary to the Gospel of John. In the beginning, however, was the icon, creation, expression, the visual inner experience, the order in chaos.

We do not need to accept Jorn's view that the ranking of image over word was a typical feature of Scandinavian culture, which he called "Gothic" to separate it from "Germanic" and Central European culture, in order to grasp the central issues of the painting. As a representative for all visual arts this image raises the provocative question about the lack of balance between word and image, "logos" and "eikon" in so-called Western culture.

Are we suffering from a cultural deformation because of the written word's historically superior role in our minds and thoughts? Can visual arts, both its creative and reflective aspect, rectify this deformation and perhaps abolish it? How does the Christian believer relate to the challenge of meeting God in images? How can one visually experience God acting in a context that is ruled by words?

One may interpret Jorn's great painting as a complement to the genesis in the Gospel of John, which reads "In the beginning was the Word, and the Word was with God, and the Word was God" (Jn 1:1),[6] and continues: "and the Word became flesh" (Jn 1:14). When the Word became flesh, that is, when God took on a human form, the sensuous, visible world became divine.

It is not clear whether John was mainly influenced by the early Stoic's veneration of "logos," of reason, or whether what he had in mind is the Hebrew genesis of God's creative speech, or possibly the book of Proverb's imaginative narrative of the Wisdom of God, "Sophia," which preceded and took part in the creation of the world (Prov. 8:22f.). What is clear is that he rejects the independent existence of the Word outside God as well as logos' emanation from the divine with the thesis: God *is* logos.[7]

Presumably all these Jewish and Hellenic traditions converge in his brief confession that God was the Word in the beginning.[8] However, the conclusion that the nature of God is literally connected to words of the Bible and the interpretation of these words is a severe mistake of the biblical exegesis.

Obviously, the problem of the symbiosis of faith and the written word was already known by Paul, who stated that "...the letter kills, but the Spirit gives life" (2 Cor. 3:6).[9] God was never word in the sense that God was in nature equal to the letters of the Bible. However, the creative power and the wisdom were with God in the beginning.

It is clear that the authors of the Bible always have conceived of creation as a visually perceptible reality. The Spirit of God sweeps or hovers over the waters (Gen. 1:2). Wisdom plays like a child of God before his face and on his earth (Prov. 8:30f.). The word becomes flesh (Jn 1:14). According to the biblical texts, God is experienced bodily.

It was only in the iconoclastic period that God was restricted and understood as word in the human verbal sense and as the Creator distanced from his/her creation – as if the free work of the Creator could be tied to letters, scripture, texts and interpretations. God was "deposited" in the letters of the Scripture. However, the main insight in the prologue of the Gospel of John is God's incarnation, the belief that the Creator had become flesh and had fully become a corporeal being.

The Jorn painting critically questions how we should understand the word's power over nature. How does the imagined, spoken, and written word dominate the physical nature and its visible representations? The painting brings to mind the faith of the Hebrew scriptures of a sensuously and bodily present Creator.

Does the God who creates others in his own image (Gen. 1:27) counter Jorn's thesis that in the beginning was image? Can one – in agreement with the Eastern theologians of Early Christianity – reflect further on the title: "In the beginning was image, and the image was with God, and the image was God"?

Is it possible for believers to arrive at the insight still preserved in the Eastern Orthodox Church that the entire world can be seen as an icon of God from Jorn's painting? Can we, with the help of art, expand the perspective of theology beyond the confinements of language to the perception of an open creation where God meets humans in images? How does Christ as "the image of the invisible God" (Col. 1:15) meet us in a world in which the image was in the beginning and *is* in the beginning? How will the believer become a "renewed self" and "the image of its creator" in a world where the divine-human Creator "is all, and in all" (Col. 3:11f.)?

After Jorn's painting has manifested the intrinsic power of the image and its visual presentiveness, this first chapter will discuss the term "image," about the new attention brought to how we reflect over and see images, and about the method of picture analysis.

It is my opinion that the theologian should develop a well-reflected attitude towards and a good method for analysing images. Without such a basis, s/he will not be able to do justice to the visual dimension of humans and of image-making. A theological approach to creativity and to visual arts should be grounded in the creation and reality of images, and picture analysis should always be connected to the actual experience of seeing the image.

The Concept of "Image"

The English word "image" incorporates many layers of meaning stretching over a wide semantic field. These layers overlap as well as differ from the German word "bild" rooted in the old Germanic "bilidi," which refers to the result of a creative plastic process of shaping.

The Latin word "imago" was by Cicero used to refer to – as in a mask – the similarity between a portrait and its model, but later on Varro used it in the sense "artistic picture," which in contrast to its living model was considered dumb.[10]

Western theologians of Early Christianity used the word "figura" to denote the living transference of something. According to Tertullian, for example, when the Eucharist was instituted, Christ's words "this is my body" at the beginning of the Eucharist refers to the "image" (figura) of his body. For Tertullian the bread as image (figura) is in essence connected to Christ's corporeal body.[11] In Hellenic antiquity "imago" also referred to cultic and divine images, and thus it was similar in meaning to the graven images rejected by Christians, the idols (eidolon).

Historically, the concept of image thus has both practical and epistemological significance. The image is an object that is formed physically in relation to an extant object and to epistemological and symbolic acts of transference. Religiously, the image has a magic, god-given or even divine power. The image concept has both a visible exterior layer and an interior, partly hidden and sometimes even focal, spiritual layer.

In addition to signifying an artefact, an object made and created by humans, the image also denotes an inner idea which, somehow, is related to our emotions and our thinking, and even more so to our abilities to remember what has taken place and to predict what will happen. Reminiscence and vision, which in antiquity were captured in the term "intuire," to see, is equally as much part of the meaning of the image concept as the concrete physical objects.

Mental imagery, in contrast to verbal language, mainly relies on spatial processes. In his theory about intuition and visual presentiveness, the art scholar Sven Sandström talks about the "creation of spatial meaning," which with its spatial visualization is characteristic of all human cognition and which is radically different from linguistic meaning.

Ludwig Wittgenstein summarizes the epistemological aspect of pictures and defines picture as a "model of reality."[12] For Wittgenstein, a picture simply expresses its subjective meaning: "What a picture represents is its sense."[13] However, later on Wittgenstein adopts a more nuanced view and introduces the notion "family resemblance"[14] that can be used to explain how one entity can resemble another entity without sharing all characteristics. The picture can represent something different from what it is.

Gernot Böhme has a much wider understanding of images. According to Böhme, images exist in a peculiar and special way that does not correspond to the existence of objects. For Böhme, aesthetics is a reflection over this specific way of being (Seinsweise), human perception of images (Wahrnehmungsweise), and how humans practically relate to images (Umgangsweise).[15]

"He who would know the world must first manufacture it," says Immanuel Kant.[16] An idea must first be manufactured before reason can acquire knowledge of the world. Some kind of model, a construction, a draft is needed. If we do not manufacture a model of the world, we cannot create an image that claims general validity for the world. The drafts are dependent on the world, as they are ideas of *something in* the world. It is vital that there is correspondence between what is imagined and how it is imagined if the draft is to be used in the knowledge process.

Nelson Goodman perceives pictures as a world of representations that appears as a coherent system.[17] For Goodman, art and science are not converses where one would appeal to emotions and the other to reason, one to pleasure and the other to knowledge.[18] Aesthetic experience is for Goodman a form of knowledge on a par with an experiment or a deduction. Both art and science re-categorize symbols and thus create order in the world.

Umberto Eco presents a synthetic definition which – with the exception of the religious meaning – unites the practical, knowledge-creating, world-making and intuitive dimension, when he defines image as "a perceptual model...that is homologous to the model of perceptual relations that we construct when we recognise an object or remember it."[19]

The image is here primarily a model of relations; it is connected to an external context of relations. Secondly, this model is in turn connected to our mental image-making, which is active when we recollect and acquire knowledge about something. The practical aspect of the picture is connected to its intuitive and knowledge-creating aspect.

Eco's semiotic understanding of images is based in the ancient western idea, recognized from Augustine onwards, that human knowledge is created using signs. In this tradition, Friedrich Schleiermacher saw human rationality as a "signifying activity" and the theologian Rainer Volp following Schleiermacher sees sign relations as some kind of behavioural model and worldview.[20]

Volp refers to Augustine's strong emphasis that both the equality (aequalitas) and likeness (similitude) belong to the image and that only Christ himself, God's Son, inhabits these two qualities as the perfect image of God (imago Dei).

The semiotic interpretation of images should not be defined by the word, according to Volp, and this is a widely-held view, especially in the narrow interpretation of the prologue to the Gospel of John. From a religious theoretical viewpoint, one should not reduce images to becoming a tool for transferring symbolic or coded meanings, which with necessity would lead to a magical view of images as vehicles.

The Middle Platonic and biblically inspired theologies of late antiquity, contemporary visual semiotics, and modern theories about perception and cognition contribute to and expand Asger Jorn's awareness of the power of images. Insights from these disciplines challenge theology to pay much more attention to pictures and their autonomy. "God is the creator because he creates certain images."[21] In the beginning *is* the image.

"The Pictorial Turn" – the Return of the Images

Images in twentieth-century modern philosophy there has been a growing focus on the autonomous role of language in relation to the construal of our apprehension of reality. Language acquisition and usage have a significant impact on our perception as well as on how we think and act. Some people believe that all the important philosophical issues essentially can be traced back to language and language rules. Philosophy has "converted" to language: "the linguistic turn."[22] Neither the self-consciousness of the subject, a higher being, nor the ultimate potential of knowledge is the central purpose of philosophical reflection – language is in itself the purpose.

However, making language the subject of investigation on the quest for knowledge did not lead to the irrefutable insights that one had anticipated. Wittgenstein's criticism of his early quest for clear objectivity led him to revalue the life-world of everyday language and to the invention of "language games" based on the semantic family resemblances of the different meanings of the concepts.[23] Language can no longer fulfil the demand for unambiguousness and logical clarity; quite the contrary, characteristic of language is the overlap and semantic diversity that bind together and create communicative spaces in our everyday language.

In our context it is important to take note of the fact that Wittgenstein, like all "hard" theories of nature and knowledge, made use of metaphors to develop the language-game idea. The "game" metaphor is an expression of the freedom, unpredictability and creativity of the speaker and the listener as well as of language as a tool. The family metaphor denotes the cohesion and unity of language, which exist despite all subjective and contextually versatile meanings. In this respect, Wittgenstein's choice of metaphor refers to the somewhat evasive character of everyday language.

In parallel with philosophy's conversion to language, "the linguistic turn," is it feasible to talk about a "pictorial turn," a conversion to pictures?

Art scholars and philosophers have in recent years given a positive response to this question.[24] The revival of pictures can be seen on different levels already in the twentieth century, and Wittgenstein's idea of "language games" has been a major influence on contemporary art and picture theory. If cognition and language are reliant on metaphors, as shown in Wittgenstein's language philosophy, then the question of the nature of images becomes even more important.

The turn towards pictures is, however, not only related to the image in itself but equally so to seeing and vision. The phenomenologist Maurice Merleau-Ponty is one of the many scholars that have reflected on the mutual relationship between vision and what is seen. Merleau-Ponty uses Paul Cézanne's artworks to study pictures as an imaginary projection surface that offers us the possibility to see through things. When I see something I always perceive it both outside me in the place where it exists and at the same time as something present within me. "The eye is in the world, the world is in the eye."[25] Merleau-Ponty underlines how the gaze crosses when looking at a picture, how vision and what is seen are intertwined, and how Cezanne's painting is not a reflection of what is seen but creates the premises for representing something that one can look at.

Verbosely the psychoanalyst Jacques Lacan theologizes on Merleau-Ponty's ideas and he talks about the "gaze *behind*" the gaze. In accordance with his theory about a double, overlapping relation between subject, image and "tableau,"[26] Lacan claims that the Byzantine icon – through its double meaning – both represents the God and arouses the deity's desire to look at the picture: "the significance of the icon is that the God it depicts also looks at the icon."[27] According to Lacan, the icon reveals that behind the gaze of humans another gaze is always hidden. What is seen is not congruent – as we commonly assume – with the viewer, just as the person that is seen cannot see her/himself in the other's gaze. Between the subject and the gaze there is always a third element, which Lacan speculatively rewrites with the term "tableaux."

The Swedish art scholar Torsten Weimarck uses Roland Barthes' distinction between "studium" and "punctum" in picture analysis.[28] While studium is the interpretative description of the similarities, meanings, and uses of the object, punctum refers to that which in the object does not have similarities, that which cannot be represented. In connection to the ancient notion of the duality of the image, between the inherent qualities of the image and its external connections, it seems pertinent, even in a postmodern context, to investigate the punctum sphere of images, that is, their inherent double character. Facing the challenge of the "poetics of visual materiality" the dimension of subjectivity becomes particularly important as our mental imagery is subject to a dynamic dialectic between continuity and change in the inner mental spaces of time and memory.

When we talk about the "pictorial turn," we may, on the one hand, refer to the mass media's massive image production, bombarding us with an increasing amount of images, claiming some kind of validity in the relation between reality and the depicted. However, on the other hand, we may also refer to the development of visual arts and the reflection over that which represents something and at the same unveils the preconditions and methods for the making of the picture and for the viewer's gaze. The conversion to pictures is very much ambivalent.

The art scholar Gottfried Boehm justly points out that the media industry is characterized by a distinct iconomachy or hostility towards images. This hostility presents itself not through bans and restrictions but through the overwhelming inundation of images which, along with the principle of simulation, disbands the border between reality and fiction. In this context, visual arts must, almost inevitably, assume an iconoclastic, hostile attitude to images. Visual arts must counteract the reduction of the image to an "as-if-object." Its double task is to both display artworks and at the same time provide the premise for seeing what the artwork represents. The visual work of art is special in that it protects the visual medium's ability to contrast and visualize, and to sensuously create meaning.

Furthermore, Boehm clearly shows how an understanding of the independence of the visual medium, which is based in the perception and art theoretical insight about the contrast and difference of images, cannot reduce the image to an expression of an historical and social context.[29] This view involves a dramatic reduction of images and it does not take into account the fact that the image has an independent ability to create meaning. This inherent autonomy of images to create meaning in different viewers at different times and in different cultures should not be undervalued by reducing the image entirely to its context, even if the context insolubly is related to the making and reception of each individual object.

In the context of the swamping image production which threatens to drench our ability to see pictures and experience their expression and meaning, reflection over the intrinsic value of images becomes imperative.

Is it really the case that many people prefer to consume pictures superficially rather than become profoundly engaged in the picture? What are the consequences of an uncontrolled flood of images which claim to represent reality? Does this flood of "as-if-images" together with a prevailing ignorance of the nature of vision and picture analysis generate an image fundamenta-lism which is just as threatening as the religious fanaticism that construes definite norms from texts that are defined as unambiguous?

The questions related to the return of images and cognition's conversion to images are many, and answering them demands a significant effort. Theology's challenge is to contribute to a more reflected attitude to the autonomy and mystery of pictures and of vision. If the image in the beginning was with God, then theology is called upon to guard the autonomy of the independent medium. The image is a part of the creation whose diversity one should not reduce.

Interestingly, as a part of the pictorial turn, in Sweden theology changed its conceptual apparatus at an early stage. Without any real discussion or investigation, the earlier concept of "idea of God" and "concept of God" have been replaced by the term "image of God," on the initiative of the theologian Gustaf Aulén from Lund. It seems that the new concept "image of God" has been readily accepted in the games of everyday language as a focal term in the religious worldview. A more extensive reflection over the question of whether God exists and acts in and as image has, however, not yet taken place. Hopefully, this book can provide a basis for such reflection to take place at some point in the future.

The Iconic Difference and the Spatial Presentiveness

What is characteristic of what we hitherto have referred to as the intrinsic value of images? What is it that distinguishes the autonomy of the visual medium? Boehm's and Sandström's theories may provide us with an answer. Characteristic of images is their special ability to create meaning partly sensuously and partly spatially and visually.

Boehm's interpretation of the essential property of images relies on the term "iconic difference."[30] A distinct property of pictures is their duality which consists in the corporeal sensuousness and the conceptual, semantic aspect. Images are characterized by an interaction between contrasting and unifying effects and make visible both the profusion of diversity and the wholeness of totality at the same time.

The pictorial expressions involve a special form of autonomy which is impossible to translate into verbal language. Presentiveness can be interpreted, and the visual medium can be subject to theoretical reflections, but a theory that does not connect the abstract reflection to the sensuous experience of the artwork is misleading. Just as an artwork opens up for the analyst, it will close again.

Studying an artefact is different from looking at ordinary phenomenon because the picture surface is limited for the viewer. The frame of vision is set. There is a difference between the surface of the manufactured piece of art and perception's visual surface. The gaze moves freely through the image and is marked by simultaneity, while the picture composition constitutes several successive processes. According to Boehm, the process of seeing consists in an interaction between simultaneity and succession. Simultaneity and succession interact and together they give the premises for attributing meaning to the picture. Boehm emphasizes that this interaction should not be regarded as an abstraction; rather it is essential to the act of studying pictures.

The interpretation of the meanings of images is made possible through this iconic difference. A direct transference to verbal discourse is not possible as verbal discourse cannot comprise the same contrasting and uniting effect. "Between succession and simultaneity we find the iconic difference that only can be measured by means of productive imagination."[31] The difference is thus, if it is consciously reflected upon, not a hindrance for mutual support and elucidation between the image and the word.

Just as Boehm, Sandström offers a theory of visuality and perception. While Boehm emphasizes the difference of images, Sandström focuses on the spatiality of meaning-creation in his theory of intuition and visual presentiveness.

Sandström assumes that the picture is analogous to our mental image, and that humans' special way of perceiving reality creates analogies with reality.[32] Further, he shows how thinking in images is a meaning creation process in a semantic space.[33] When we look at something, an image appears within us. It is this image that exists as the "image in all images."[34] Thinking in images is not next to and equal to linear discursive thinking – it is structurally and qualitatively different from it. As "presentiveness," visual thinking appears as a spatial constellation, while "discursivity" takes place as digital confrontation, in Sandström's words. Understanding in vision does not necessarily entail hermeneutic understanding; primarily, it is a spatial process of orientation.

Sandström shows how the iconic, experiential meaning-creation and the intuitive reminiscences are the preconditions for natural, verbal language, because verbal language does not "contain" anything but it only works in relation to meanings. The spatial process of creating meaning in images is characterized by a multi-dimensionality that builds on spatial structures. What creates meanings is according to Sandström different aspects of and encounters between meanings in what is seen.

To think in images and intuitively to process and understand is thus not an alternative to the logical discourse; rather, verbal thinking should be seen as a fulfilment of visual thinking. Linguistic and conceptual thinking presuppose the creation of mental images. As a consequence, one cannot presuppose language but one must assume that the creation of meaning and sense take place in a complex process relying on experience and mental imagery. Without these images as a point of reference, the linguistic processing would be impossible.[35]

Following the biologist Jakob von Uexküll, the linguist Thomas A. Sebeok explores the same insight in his semiotic approach to language in the wider human biological context.

Von Uexküll's theory about the functional circle sheds light on the organism's relation to its environment – the term "Umwelt" was by the way invented by von Uexküll – in light of an interplay between the organism's "Merk- und Wirkwelt," that is, between its perceptual surroundings and operational context.[36] In analogy to this distinction Sebeok develops the semiotic relation between "code" and "message."[37]

With the help of von Uexküll's ecology, Sebeok connects the sign system to the biological reality and he regards "semiosis" – the exchange and interpretative processes of signs – as a basic amalgamation of verbal and non-verbal signs, and as fundamental to human life. The integration of the two different forms of function, also referred to as "zoosemiotic" and "anthroposemiotic," is seen as a special characteristic of human life.[38] In our context we may see Sebeok's view as yet another confirmation of the significance of mental imagery and the visual interpretation process for the specific human aspect of our existence.

Asger Jorn's introductory insight into the almost god-given autonomy of images receives further support from the theories of Boehm, Sandström and Sebeok. The image that meets our vision is a unique event, providing the ontological basis for visual arts as well as humans' inherent capacity for orientating in complex surroundings and attributing meaning to and finding a place in their environment. The production of mental imagery and memory-images and the making of external visual representations are part of the existential conditions of humans. Our thesis that the image is in the beginning is thus not primarily an attempt to make an historical claim about the origin of humans and images; rather, it refers to the existential continuum of images through different cultural and historical eras.

Methods for Picture Analysis

An academic approach to picture analysis demands a comprehensive and carefully considered method. Picture analysis is a highly advanced field of study, like hermeneutical theories and methods are for text studies. However, bearing in mind the unique character of the visual medium it is obvious that picture analysis cannot be developed in simple analogy to text analysis; it must continuously make way for the special nature of pictures.

Even if we seek religious and spiritual meanings and implications in pictures, it is not sufficient to identify themes or motifs in the chosen picture; it is equally important to consider the practical and technical expression before we devote ourselves to the meaning that arises from these expressions. The three methods do not oppose each other; they complement each other.

A constructive attempt of a qualified picture analysis was developed by the Swedish art scholar Jan-Gunnar Sjölin, whose approach was inspired by semiotics.[39] According to Sjölin there is a fundamental difference between the expression and the meaning of the picture. This distinction replaces the common but highly problematic division between form and content. In accordance to the antique Aristotelian worldview, where the spiritual and material worlds were clearly distinct, the form was assumed to carry the content. The form belonged to the world that could be perceived by the senses, while the content belonged to the invisible spiritual world.

Sjölin maintains that form should not be confused with expression. Expression is what is given; it is not a container for the content of the image but an inseparable part of the content. Expression and content presuppose each other. The two aspects of the image, the expression and the meaning deriving from the expression, are always present. However, these two aspects of our perception cannot be perceived simultaneously. In accordance with Boehm's theory, in the process of seeing we can alternate between either seeing the physical expression or contemplate over its content and meaning. Picture analysis must therefore account for both if we are to do justice to the artwork.

Sjölin distinguishes between the plastic and the iconic meaning of pictures.[40] In this regard, the concept of form is closely connected to the formation of meaning. It encompasses a spatial and a plastic dimension and a dimension that is related to the collective expression of the picture. Form is, according to Sjölin, all relations and oppositions characteristic of any sign system that make meaning-creation possible. For picture analysis this entails that one should put great emphasis on understanding and describing the plastic and physical structure of images. The interpretation of the picture's plastic dimension is essential and necessary for understanding the different layers of meaning of the image.

Furthermore, historical awareness is fundamental to picture analysis, according to Sjölin. The purpose of analysis is not an ahistorical search for one single, constant truth; picture analysis should always be mindful of its task of translating from one medium to the other. Awareness of the ambiguity of the picture, which enables a plethora of possible and apt interpretations, is an essential tool for the interpreter. This awareness helps secure the integrity of the pictorial medium and enables the viewer to take part in a continual process of interpretation. Meaning does not arise simply because the picture exists; meaning emerges from the process of seeing and interpreting.

This becomes obvious when we look at and try to interpret one of Oscar Reuterswärd's so-called impossible figures. Try to do the impossible, to see the meaning of both heights in the same form at the same time!

Sjölin's method demands four stages in a good picture analysis. The process is focused on: (a) the material meaning of the image, its choice of natural elements; (b) its plastic meaning; (c) its iconic meaning; and (d) its verbal meaning, for example, what is said in the title or words used in the image.

To summarize, the task of picture analysis is to interweave the overall expression of the picture, both in its parts and wholeness, in a close and insoluble relation to its meaning production.

Art historian Oskar Bätschmann developed an historically more diversified method. For Bätschmann the figure of the interpretation process can be summarized in the "undetermined surface," where the interpreter must go through all parts without necessarily having to start in a specific point.[41]

Bätschmann carefully distinguishes between different tasks in the interpretation process which all are connected to each other. The interpretation must always refer to the artwork. However, it is neither immanently nor exclusively concerned with the artwork as a reflection of its time. The reconstruction of the artwork's expression and context approaches the object as an open, productive artwork.

The medium of interpretation is language and thus fundamentally different from the object. The understanding of the interpretation is based in the loss of the iconic function of the work and requires awareness of this function. A good start, according to Bätschmann, is to start with one's own lack of ability and formulate questions to the object.

If one follows "the undetermined surface" as a figure of interpretation, this activity can be subdivided into smaller tasks. Bätschmann has a rough threefold division: analysis, creative abduction, and assessment.

In the analysis one gathers information about the artist, the artwork, and the context of both the artwork and the artist. Potential iconographical connections to texts or other themes are investigated. The genre, style and history of the artwork are examined, along with its cultural reception and visual and literary references. One may even search for possible historical explanations in the form of commissions or other functions.

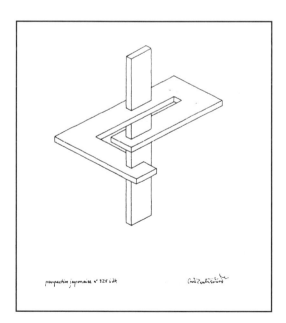

Image 2. Oscar Reuterswärd, *Perspective japonais.* Drawing, © DACS, London 2006.

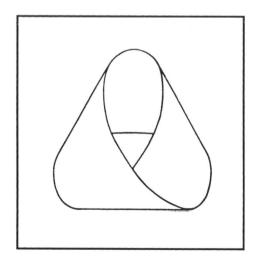

Image 3. *The Undetermined Surface as a Figure of the Process of Interpretation.* In Bätschmann (1988: 198).

With the term "creative abduction" Bätschmann refers to the process where one creatively unravels and creates connections in the picture's meaning production. The final evaluation refers to an argumentative grounding of the collective results that other people must accept or reject. In this context examples of guiding questions are whether the artist her/himself will agree to the evaluative interpretation and if this interpretation is possible in relation to the historical context of the artwork. Inter-subjective, testable arguments will be part of this third step of the analysis.

A third method for picture analysis is based in the artwork's composition and process of production. Before one focuses on – in accordance with Bätschmann's undetermined surface – all the fields that surround the picture

one must interpret and understand the picture's special character with great caution. This method allows the interpretation to follow closely the making of the picture. The movement of the hand through space in time leaves a trace in the form of a line that we can follow with our eyes, and the nature of the line creates an expression that we may attribute meaning to. Without understanding the line's expression the interpretation process cannot preserve its basic connection to the artwork. "The hand that creates educates the seeing eye."[42]

The interpretation reconstructs how the artist went about creating the picture. The aim is not only to understand the technical aspects of the making of the picture; the interpretation aims at unravelling how closely connected the

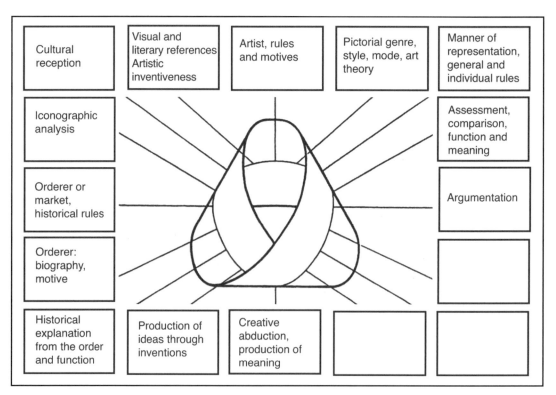

Image 4. *The Figure of the Interpretation with its Single Operations.* In Bätschmann (1988: 218).

meanings of the picture are to the physical expression of the creative process of production. Meanings arise when matter is moulded, and understanding how this happens is in itself a necessary prerequisite for understanding the meaning of the image.

Exploring all the nuts and bolts of image-making in detail is beyond the purpose of this book. The comprehensive handbook "Art Fundamentals" distinguishes six different basic elements of image-making: space, line, form, colour, value, and texture. These elements can be pedagogical instruments for reconstructing the making of a picture in retrospect. If one chooses to develop this scrutinizing model for picture analysis, one ought to be able to give a detailed account of all these different elements in the artwork in question. Rather than providing a general description of this method, I will show how it works by analysing an older painting.

In 1803 Joseph Anton Koch painted "Landscape with Noah's thank-offering." (See colour plate section, Image 5.) A balanced space, consisting of three parts, appears on the surface of the picture. In the foreground we see a meadow, verdant with sprouting grass; behind this space a second space with playing animals, and in the background we see mountains against the sky, still unsettled after the storm. The sea, where the ebbing water is withdrawing after the flood, delimits the space of the foreground and the background. Far right the sea opens to the horizon.

Diagonally the picture shows a valley landscape with a marked elevation in the landscape towards the water. An open space arises around the group of figures, people, and animals at the front. At the centre of this space we see the altar made of stone blocks and the smoke from the sacrificial fire. Another image space opens up behind the first space where the animals playfully move about in a new nature. The two spaces are separated by shadow and are harmonically connected through the colour harmony and dispersal of light. A third image space consists of the cold, jagged mountains with the ark that is run aground. The vaulted rainbow over the scenery binds together the close and distant elements, the bygone time of catastrophe and the hopeful promise of the future. Far away the sign of the warrior, the bow, sinks into the ocean.

Just like the boulder at front left and the mountains in the background, the shapes of the shooting, verdant trunks are repeated at the right and at the left. The repetition of form in the trunks, the filigree, and in the clouds and the smoke from the fire and the stone surfaces both in foreground and in the background create a strong, harmonious and coherent expression and accentuate the sense of depth and space.

This feeling is further strengthened by the colour temperature. The light is dispersed evenly with warm, green-yellow and brown tones in the foreground while the cooler blue-grey colours define the part of the landscape that is still devastated by the flood. The different colour tones create a contrast between the old and the new, between violence of nature and its structured, life-giving energy.

The contrasts in the colour play are reinforced also by the three scenes of the picture. Against the background of the cold dark blue-greyish life-threatening scene, waning in the background, the new life unfolds in warmer colour tones in the yellow foreground and green middle-ground. There is a succession of past and future, life and death, cold and warm as the eye meanders from the background to the middle-ground and foreground, enabling the viewer to attain a liberating distance to the horror-filled history behind the scene, and allowing her/him to return to the close, earthly and unique experiences of the meadow.

Even the persons in the group of figures express unity, primarily through the expressive movements of arms and hands. Some of them lift their faces towards the rainbow in the sky; a woman is lost in prayer. The sons of Noah with the goat and the ox and the woman in white are looking at the others. The colour tones of their clothes are incorporated in the colour harmony of the ground. The meadow, the people and the animals are made part of the same warm, revitalizing light.

Koch is one of the most powerful painters of the Enlightenment. His painting is marked by strong symbolizing features. In his famous depictions of the water plummeting down the mountain side ("The Schmadribach Falls", see image no. 14 in the colour plates section), the water connotes the wild and liberating primordial power of reason and enlightenment.[43]

Koch's depiction is related to the biblical narrative, and he chooses to portray the time after the devastating flood has withdrawn to its original confinements.

The promise of a new future is represented in the colour scheme in the sky and in the dispersion of light. Above the ocean at the right a light blue, sunny sky appears, in contrast to the storm clouds at the left. The light dispersion above the pasture in the foreground is evenly and warmly distributed.

The play on the farthest meadow refers to the atonement vision found in the book of Isaiah in the texts about "new heavens and a new earth" and about the heavenly meadow where the wolf plays with lambs, and the lion and the ox eat grass, and panthers lay next to chickens. "They will not hurt or destroy on all my holy mountain; for the earth will be full of the knowledge of the Lord as the waters cover the sea" (Isa. 11:9, cf. 65:25).

It is possible that Koch, who is well versed in the literature of antiquity, also refers to one of Virgil's rural poems (*Eclogues* 4) from the century before Christ. *Eclogue* 4, Pollio, speaks of the birth of a boy that will put an end to the age of iron and who marks the beginning of the "golden race"; "…and with his father's worth reign o'er a world at peace…while flocks afield shall of the monstrous lion have no fear."[44]

Koch's painting is a technically brilliant depiction of Isaiah's vision of God's rainbow promise. The different parts of salvation history are integrated into a tight, visual unity. The peacock – because of its dryness and the belief that it could not decay and die[45] – is an ancient symbol of resurrection and of Christ, and the couple at the right bottom abandon the surface of the picture; perhaps they are on their way from the Old to the New Testament.

The art historian Eberhard Roters interprets the symbol of the rainbow in romantic landscape painting as a sign of the tension in the relation between human and nature.[46] If one interprets the text literally, the light phenomenon is only possible after the flood. Through the clear light the human becomes capable of recognizing things based on their inherent properties. S/he develops a rational visual awareness. "With Noah the development of human individuality commenced."[47]

The landscape, according to Roters, thus becomes an external image of humans. The distinction between the external and internal world of humans takes shape. For painters, the rainbow is the primordial image of the corresponding place in nature where the internal world interacts with the external world. It is like a bridge extended between the two worlds, but it is a bridge that only the gods can tread on.

In other words, the rainbow has both a divine and meteorological natural meaning. The rainbow is not physically present in the distant heavens; it only emerges at the point where the viewer is situated, and only in the visual field of that position. The rainbow confirms the point of the I in the meeting between its internal and external world.

If we look at the ecological meaning of the painting, another hermeneutical angle emerges.

In relation to Koch's famous waterfall paintings I can interpret landscape painting and landscape with an ethical dimension.[48] The abrasive edges of the mountains are formed with a distinct tectonic and rhythm. In this painting, the exaltation/elevation of the mountains is contrasted to the idyllic meadow. Nature's inherent power with its alternation between life's beginning and its end, visualized in the tree as a symbol of both life and death, is contrasted to human culture. The rainbow bridge vaults over the tension between the soft and hard style elements, between the heavy and the light elements of the lighting, between the rough and the refined and between nature and culture. Only the gods can cross this bridge and it gives humans an individual and painful insight into their world.

Is the sacrifice of thanksgiving in Koch's painting only related to the biblical narrative – a thanksgiving for the Creator's promise to never again devastate the world, or is it also a thanksgiving for reason's gift to human kind, symbolized by the illuminating power of the rainbow?

Even if our example can hardly do justice to the richness of Koch's brilliant and detailed painting, it has hopefully demonstrated how important it is that picture analysis develops awareness of the plastic and physical expression of image-making, such that the iconic loss, integral to a verbal translation of the image's expression to hermeneutic meanings, is seen in its right context. The loss of the specific expression of the pictorial medium may thus be transformed to a stable dock that directs our mind to the experience of what is seen. The interpreter thus remains as a viewer *within* the painting.

Summary

- The presentive image has a unique intrinsic power. The theology of art should grant the visual medium a special autonomy. A critical reading of the prologue to the Gospel of John and its assertion that in the beginning the Word was with God, along with a scrutiny of Asger Jorn's painting "In the beginning was the image," may inspire us to ask if the image *was* in the beginning. Was the image with God? Image and Word, *eikon* and *logos*, should not stand in opposition. Reflection over images and the experience of pictures prevent theology from confining the revelation of God to word, scripture and text.

- The concepts of image and picture cover a wide semantic field. They refer to artefacts, artworks, mental subjective reminiscences, and ideas that are shared with other people. Images have both a practical, operational dimension and a theoretical epistemological dimension. The view of contemporary semiotic that the image is an open relation of signs, intuition research's emphasis on the function of spatial meaning creation for cognition and for language, and ecological-linguistic semiotic's understanding of the relation between environmental and human aspects further emphasize the importance of discussing the visual medium's autonomy. Based on insights from Platonic Christian philosophy of late antiquity, one may further protect images and visual perception's openness to tendencies of subordinating the image to the word or reducing the image to a magic container for religious faith.

- Similar to philosophy's conversion to the fundamental nature of language, "the linguistic turn," and its "aesthetic turn" from reflections over content to reflections over expression, we can observe an ongoing conversion to images: "the pictorial turn." Ludwig Wittgenstein's reflections over the significance of family resemblance and the semantic polyvalence of the "games" of everyday language have also influenced views of the image and the ambivalence of images. A phenomenological view emphasizes the connection between the subject of seeing, its gaze and the object. The world and the eye become one. However, in the context of the economically motivated industrial mass production of a massive amount of image, the very notion of the "pictorial turn" becomes ambivalent. The flood of "as if" images provokes an image fundamentalism and challenges visual art to a reflective iconoclasm; a critical awareness of the misuse of the visual medium. Naturally, creation theology's reflection over the "image of god" (G. Aulén) should contribute independently to this awareness.

- What is the distinctive character of art? Gottfried Boehm summarizes his view in the concept "iconic difference." The image is characterized by its dual nature, with corporeal sensuousness on the one hand and cognitive meaning creation on the other. Intrinsic to the image is the interaction of contrasting and unifying elements. The image both visualizes the richness of diversity and the wholeness of totality. It is not possible to fully translate into words the expression and autonomy of the image. Sven Sandström shows how thinking in images is a "process of creating meaning" in a "semantic space." Thinking in images is not the same as linear, discursive, linguistic thinking. The former is structurally and qualitatively different from the latter. The understanding in vision is primarily an orientation and not an understanding in communication.

- I recommend three methods of picture analysis for the theologian and scholar of religion; methods that will preserve the distinctive quality of the visual medium and remain conscious of the iconic loss of linguistic interpretation. A semiotically oriented method separates between the expression of the image and its meaning and content. The method involves four levels of interpretation – the physical, plastic, iconic, and verbal dimension of the object. A second art historical method follows "the figure of the undetermined surface" and treats different aspects of the picture's expression, artist, and context to co-evaluate these elements argumentatively and in terms of their value. A third method is employed in relation to the process of creating the picture and investigates – in terms of the picture's space-dimension, line, form, colour, value, and texture – the basic, physical layers of the picture from which its meaning arises. The analysis of Anton Joseph

Koch's "Landscape with Noah's thank-offering" showed an application of this method with a close comparison of what is physically seen and cognitive construction of meaning. Any picture analysis must keep the channel open for a mutual flow between the physical and cognitive aspects of looking at pictures.

CHAPTER 2

What Is Art?

The question of what art is and how one can define and distinguish art has been a source of debate at all times. For some unknown reason, the question of what art is seems to be just as provocative discussion subject as is issues related to sex, crime, punishment, and God.

– What on earth is this? the Sami artist Iver Jåks asks in this object.

One needs to bear in mind that the concept of "art" has undergone quite a few transformations through the course of history and that our Eurocentric conception of art is by no means the only possible view.

Australian aboriginals, for example, acknowledge the meaning of manufactured artefacts in the form of paintings and sculptures in their life-world without ever constructing a word or concept denoting "art."

The Sami people have, in their cultural history, developed the term "duodji" for skilled handicraft and symbolic artworks, but it was not till the 1970s that they invented a term for

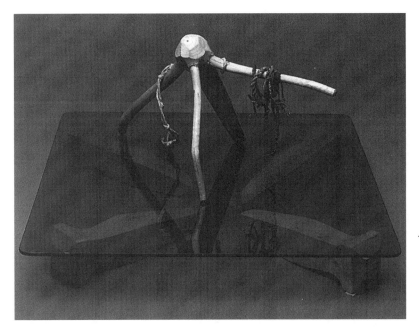

Image 6. Iver Jåks, *hva for noe (What on Earth Is This)*. 1994, wood, coloured glass, reindeer skin rope. Photo: Petter Hegre, Stavanger, © DACS, London 2006.

art, "dáidda." It is not at all clear to what extent the term "art" with concomitant theories corresponds to the practical making and seeing of art.

Umberto Eco identifies another problem related to this issue, and he justly claims that one cannot "define" the ultimate structure of a work of art. If that were the case, it would not be art. An "open work of art" contains, according to Eco, an "ultimate structure" that remains hidden, inconceivable and unstructured and thus capable of creating new experiences.[1]

The concept of art is an abstracting and thus variable linguistic construction, and in this chapter we investigate the question of what is art in the perspective of art history, history of philosophy and art theory. We pay special attention to the displacement from the normative requirement of philosophical aesthetics to the object focus of art theory. Finally, we focus on the controversy pertaining to the relation between the nature and context of art.

Glimpses from the History of Reflecting about Art

From the Antique Problem of Pictorial Depictions of God...

Plato was the first person in history to define art; however, according to him, only music and poetry were counted among the liberal arts (Greek techne), and the visual arts were seen as inferior. In the philosophy of antiquity art was divided into one superior liberal and one inferior mechanic sphere, where the "artes liberales," the liberal arts, were contrasted to the "artes mechanicae," the mechanical arts. The rationale was the conception that manual work belonged to the domain of slaves, while free men would devote themselves to spiritual activities.

In the early days of art philosophy, visual art was very much rendered suspect; ostensibly visual art was merely capable of reproducing primal images and thus the assumption was that visual art was some kind of appearance of appearance. The object of visual art created confusion rather than increasing knowledge and understanding. Nevertheless, it is an interesting fact that this period, when the sensuous was subject to criticism and suspicion, was also a golden age for image-making, the evidence of which we see in vase decorations and death masks. In other words, the schism between art theory and the making of art is evident already in the early days of art philosophy, and this relation is also reflected in the iconomachy and image worship of Early Christianity; however, this scepticism never seriously impeded on the visual art's expression. It is as if the *discourse* on art in a peculiar manner is not connected to the *expressions* of art.

However, Plato's attitude was not the only possible view. The philosopher *Dio Chrysostom* (born c. 45 CE) – who also developed a strong ethical compassion for his coeval poor people and women, whom he regarded as nobler humans – contrasts the reductionist view with an extensive and nuanced support for art and artists. In his "Olympic speech" (c. 97 CE) Dio developed – receiving massive criticism from his contemporaries – a diversified argumentation for idols and common people's right to worship these images. The idols would not necessarily lead to an identification of god and image; quite the contrary, they could bring about the most profound knowledge possible of god, namely experience of and insight into the semblance of gods and humans, deriving from the beginning of time when humans and gods co-existed on earth.[2] Dio's view is the first known promotion of a positive view of the autonomy of art in Western culture.

Aristotle developed a refined view of art, placing the human "poietic" ability, artistic creativity (Greek *poiesis*), next to theoretical and practical activities. For Aristotle, art was based in the human desire to portray – to imitate – nature, and artistic depictions were not mere copies but representations of the true nature of the portrayed entity. Aristotle was the founder of the influential mimesis theory of art (*mimesis*, Greek for imitation) which was rediscovered in the Renaissance and since then it has been highly influential on Western art philosophy.

In antiquity, it was the philosophers that reflected over art, but in Early Christianity and during the Middle Ages art reflection was the responsibility of theologians.[3] During the first six centuries of Christianity, the use of images did not raise any major theological issues. In the source material we find both reserved-critical attitudes to the cultic image veneration in Hellenistic culture and sketches for iconodulic programmes.[4] In these early days, the term "icon" does not exclusively refer to the sacred image for cultic veneration – which is the conceived sense after the Iconoclasm up till modern time – it simply refers to "image" with its full meaning potential.[5]

According to Acts 17:29, Paul rejects the possibility of "imagining" the divine as "an image formed by the art and imagination of mortals," referring to man being "God's offspring"[6] and alluding to the Jewish criticism of idols or graven images (Isa. 44:9ff.). Later on we find in Acts (19:21ff.) the narrative of the silver reproductions of the temple of Artemis with an image-critical purpose, when Paul is said to pose a threat to the craftsmen's income and business and to discredit the goddess

Artemis and her temple "by saying that gods made with hands are not gods" (19:26).

A more positive view of the creative artist is found in Hebrews 11:10, describing Abraham's Promised Land and Abraham's reflection over God the Creator: "For he looked forward to the city that has foundations, whose architect and builder is God."

Just like the image concept is used in Genesis to redefine the relation between God and the human as "the image of God" (*imago Dei*), the relation between the Father and the Son in God's creation is also identified with the use of image: "He is the image of the invisible God, the firstborn of all creation" (Col. 1:15). The concept is also used (e.g., Col. 3:10, cf. Gen. 1:27) in an ethical sense referring to an increasing renewal "in knowledge according to the image of the one who created it" (i.e., the image of God and the Son).

Although Paul, on the one hand (according to Luke in Acts), criticized the confusion of the physical icon with God himself, he did, on the other hand, develop the image concept theologically and soteriologically in 2 Corinthians 3:17f. where he, in the continuation of the thesis of the relation between the Sprit and freedom, lays out the vision of liberation, in which we are "being transformed into the same image from one degree of glory to another" as "with unveiled faces, seeing the glory of the Lord as though reflected in a mirror." Glory comes from God, the Lord and the Spirit. When we see this glory, we do not only become similar to God, we are "transformed into the same image." However, the question is, with Dionysius and against Paul, whether it is absolutely necessary to subordinate the reception of a human-made physical artefact to a verbal sermon-based spiritual perception of God. Is it not possible – in compliance with the iconophile theologians of the eighth century – that the artefact works together with God in, for and through the liberation of creation? Is it not possible to see and meet God through the veil of art?

An important milestone for the Christian art view is the iconoclasm that commenced – for reasons unknown to us – in 726 CE.[7] A growing opposition to image cults eventually became official policy through Emperor Leo III. A long-lasting battle between the throne, the church and the monastic system led to destabilization of the church and the empire, but this conflict also brought about a deepening of the theological view of images.

With support in Neo-Platonic philosophy and Plotinus's doctrine of the connection between primal image and icon, John Damascene developed the theory of how matter is a carrier of divinity and invisibility. In icons Christ and the saints become present; however, there is an essential difference between icons and the persons portrayed. In order to accommodate the iconoclasts' argument about idolatry, John introduced the distinction between the "veneration" which befalls God and the "reverence" that befalls images.

The theologically most important support for the iconoduly was related to the mystery of the Incarnation. Because God had become human, made of flesh and blood, material nature must also be acknowledged greater

Image 7. *Icon Procession (Akathistos) on a Serbian Fresco in Markov Manastir.* Fourteenth century. In Belting (1991: 63; H. Belting´s archive, with kind permission).

21

Image 8. Giotto di Bondone, *Expulsion of the hucksters from the temple* and *Pentecost.* 1302–1305, fresco, 200 × 185, Capella degli Scrovegni i Padua.

Image 9. Masaccio, *Trinità ai Monti.* C. 1428, Sta. Maria Novella, Florence.

Image 10. Pontormo, *Depositio.* C. 1525, Sta. Felicità, Florence.

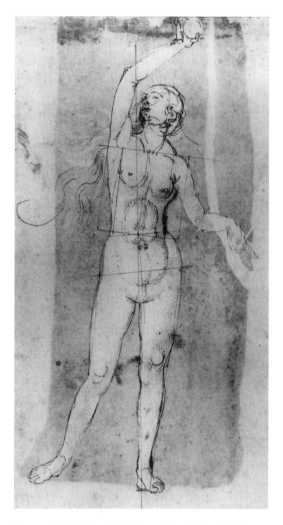

Image 11. Albrecht Dürer, *Eva, Konstruktions-zeichnung*. Pen in bister, © Albertina, Vienna.

value. Incarnation theology departed from the Platonic depreciation of materiality and provided the basis for a positive Christian theology of the image. The Second Council of Nicaea in 787 CE restored the position of icons, but the Constantinople Synod of 815 reintroduced the suppression of images by imperial edict. Only in 843 CE was iconoclasm brought to an end, giving way to a more iconodulic sentiment.

After John of Damascus, Nicephorus of Constantinople and Theodore the Studite developed the view of images christologically. The contention of iconoclasts, that it is not possible to depict the uncreated God without reducing him, was contested – with support in Aristotle and departing from John's Platonic-influenced mysticism – through the doctrine that images did not depict God but formed a relation which was based on likeness. According to Theodore, the icon did not portray God's nature but Christ's person.

In a Trinitarian theological perspective it is also noteworthy that Nicephorus claimed that icons are a witness to Christ's "enduring humanity," that is, even after the resurrection and the ascension Jesus kept his body in the triune godhead. In this way, the image became icon in Early Christianity. The Aristotelian mimesis doctrine was relativized through the Christian theology of the image and the icon as a created expression of the uncreated nature of God and Christ's human nature in the Godhead.

...via Renaissance Measurements of Art and Humanity...

During the Renaissance a new view of art emerges; however, it is not clear when exactly this transformation took place. In 1550 the founder of art history, Giorgio Vasari (born 1511), published his main work in Florence, identifying the childhood of the new independent art with Giotto (born c. 1267), its blossoming with Masaccio (born 1401) and its mature life with Michelangelo (born 1475).

Characteristic of the Renaissance is the emphasis on the creation of autonomous independent works of art. Art was liberated from the Platonic reduction to handicraft. The first academy was established in 1462 in Florence, superseding the traditional guilds.

Parallel to the portrayal of beauty the scientific exploration using the tools of mathematics and notably geometry comes to the foreground. Artists, alongside theologians, now take an active part in the reflection process. The works of art, which up till now have been containers for divine substance, become objects of knowledge for the understanding of the sensuous world.[8] The Pentecost scene in Giotto's fresco and Masaccio's construction and three-dimensional space around Jesus' cross are structured allegorically in accordance with the newfound geometric knowledge. The artist becomes an erudite and spiritually enlightened intellectual, a "pictor doctus." He would create, not expressly to honour God, but for the liberal, independent, knowledge-seeking art.

The mathematical concepts of "perspective" and "proportion" take the place of religious terms, but they are interpreted as the divine qualities of creation. The Aristotelian mimesis doctrine in relation to nature has regained its position. Leonardo da Vinci effectively departs from the antique classification of art into mechanic and liberal arts. Mathematics, geometry, the creation of volume and the central perspective, which is immensely important for Western seeing, are the primary tools of the new art. The artist as a person becomes significant, and artists put their signatures on the work of art.

However, we have every reason to wonder to what extent the artistic creation and art view of the Renaissance really has brought about a liberation, or whether it has also coerced our way of seeing. The mathematical power over visual perception and our geometric shaping of our natural surroundings were firmly and lastingly established through Renaissance art. Even today the measuring gaze that creates a grid pattern on our life space still exists.[9]

...to the Modern Art Interpretation of "God" in Every Kind of Detail

By introducing the "history of styles," J. J. Winckelmann (born 1717) opens a new chapter of art history. Winckelmann was interested in the particular art expression that evolved in different time periods, independent of individual artists. By exalting the artworks of antiquity (the Roman version) as the touchstone of all art, Winckelmann wished to refute the contemporaneous art expression. Despite the fact that he had never personally encountered any of the artworks of antiquity in the original, he developed the influential conception of a "style" that distinguishes every historical epoch. Modern art historical research criticizes early scholars like Vasari and Winckelmann for their unsubstantiated, normative ideology that defines one period as a golden epoch without studying its artworks in detail. A common criticism today is that reception aesthetics should not supersede the study of production aesthetics and the examination of the contexts of the artworks.

With Konrad Fiedler (born 1841) art history makes a pronounced shift towards the object. The study of the artwork and contact with artists shift the research focus from reception to production. Fiedler, in agreement with Aristotle, bases his theory in visual arts' depiction of reality, although this portrayal is no longer related to nature in itself but to our perception of nature. With reference to Plato's idealism, the perception of art may bring about contemplation on a higher metaphysical level. Paul Klee says that Fiedler takes art beyond portrayal and to knowledge; art is "no longer only a science but a philosophy."[10]

Benedetto Croce (born 1866) moves in the opposite direction – within the frame of his comprehensive Philosophy of the Spirit – by emphasizing emotion as the basis for his reception aesthetics. Croce concurs the only thing we have access to is the art object, but he makes the viewer's intuition the primary tool of art analysis. The identity of intuition and expression is focal in Croce's aesthetic. "The intuitive knowledge is what gives art expression."[11] Croce postulates the artwork's "insularità" – its likeness to a desert island – whose qualities are accessed only by individual intuition. There is a convergence in the art object's and the art scholar's island-like claim to validity when it comes to defining what art is. The aesthetic judgment pertains to the spiritual reproduction and not to the physical expression of the work of art.

It is only with the so-called Vienna school that academic aesthetics fully adopts the primacy of the object. Franz Wickhoff (born 1853) and Alois Riegl (born 1858) investigate works of art without normative pretences and view artefacts as periodical expressions of the "will of art." The concepts of taste and beauty abandon art studies. Heinrich Wölfflin (born 1864) develops his approach with the concept of "basic shapes" to study the unicity of art expressions in different periods.

The opposition between Croce's subjective approach and the objective approach of the Vienna school is an expression of a conflict that has pervaded Western art history since the Renaissance. One the one hand, there is the view that art is essentially autonomous, and on the other hand, there is the insight about the historical dependency of art-making. It is the autonomy of art versus the autonomy of humankind and of history.

While the concept of form was one of the pillars of the Vienna school, the Warburg school placed iconography in a cultural-historical context. There is an increasing focus on the general history of ideas context and iconography is given a more pretentious name, "iconology."[12] Interdisciplinary contacts with psychology, ethnology, and linguistics enrich this approach, culminating in Erwin Panofsky's seminal work "Studies in Iconology" in 1939. Art is not studied as a subjective expression of emotions; art is "the struggle between realisation and objectification of a creative force and a pliable material that leads to a valid result."[13] Of the academic art history one may critically conclude that it – in its relatively brief history, squeezed between literary studies and history generally – has operated with a universal concept of art and yet it has limited its focus to objects of art of European origin, and primarily objects that are somehow related to the Christian faith.[14] Despite the fact that Franz Theodor Kugler in his art historical encyclopaedia of 1842 treated art as a universal phenomenon, pertaining to all times and all peoples, and programmatically sketched arts' world history, there was a Eurocentric reduction of academic art studies and art historical education already by the end of the nineteenth century. The world history of art has during the twentieth century been reduced to the art of the Western world.

In accordance with this geographical, historical, and methodological reductionist view, the art historian Hilde Zaloscer, amongst others, argues that only the art concept of the Renaissance can provide a suitable basis for an objectivist, academic art study, while she classifies premodern artefacts as "visual incantation" and late modern objects as "ideographs," that is, visual carriers of ideas.[15] However, it is highly questionable whether it is academically tenable to maintain the exclusion of expressions from non-European cultures and from premodern times.[16] It is also questionable to categorically define a concept of art that rejects the self-perception of active artists.

The Warburg school offers a new direction by which production aesthetic and reception aesthetic are not opposites. The huge influence granted the subjective and trained eye of the researcher summarizes this tradition in the famous saying: God is in the details. Style and philosophy, expression and meaning must be studied as related qualities in a dynamic field where the artistic creation interacts with various dimensions in its context. Therefore, in contemporary art history there is agreement among approaches that convey expressions and meaning functional-theoretical framework. Reception aesthetics does not discard, as do its predecessors, its continuous connection to the artwork, but seeks the "viewer that is in the picture."[17]

Art history today is characterized by a methodological diversity that supports the primacy of the object without ignoring its subjective, geographical and historical contexts. What art *is* remains unanswered; however, this should not stop us from studying artworks in contexts. The question about the essence of art has to be secondary to the question of the concrete work of art: "What on earth is this?"

Nevertheless, the relation between art production and interpretation has become more complex as art critics as well as curators today also act as "commissioners" of "exhibited art."[18] The need for a diversified model for the relation between work and context thus becomes even more pressing.

Theo/aesthetics

It was not until the eighteenth century that aesthetics became an independent discipline of philosophy, with increasing importance. Philosophically it was decided as a reflection over art with a special concern for beauty.[19] Although the Greek term "aisthesis" refers to perception and sense impressions, philosophical aesthetics has been more interested in art, and more interested in the conceptual and epistemological aspect of art than in the artist and the artwork. Historically two paradigms emerge. While one is dominated by the epistemological aspect and art as a lucid way of interpreting life, the other paradigm accentuates art as a process and art as a special type of act.[20]

With the Enlightenment and focus on reason, aesthetics developed into a separate branch of philosophy. For René Descartes (born 1596), aesthetics was an impossible discipline on the grounds that any assessment of beauty would depend on subjective judgments and would not fulfil the requirements of a scientific, objective method. Gottfried Wilhelm Leibniz (born 1646), on the other hand, ranked aesthetics low on the scale of human knowledge. Leibniz did not distinguish sensuousness from knowledge, but the experience of beauty was for him a type of second-rate knowledge – it was "cognitio clara et confusa." Aesthetic knowledge was perceived as both lucid and conceptually obscure.[21]

The Science of Sensuous Knowledge

Alexander Gottlieb Baumgarten (born 1714) is the founder of aesthetics as an autonomous philosophical discipline. His view of aesthetics is based in Leibniz's acknowledgement of the epistemological potential of aesthetics, but he

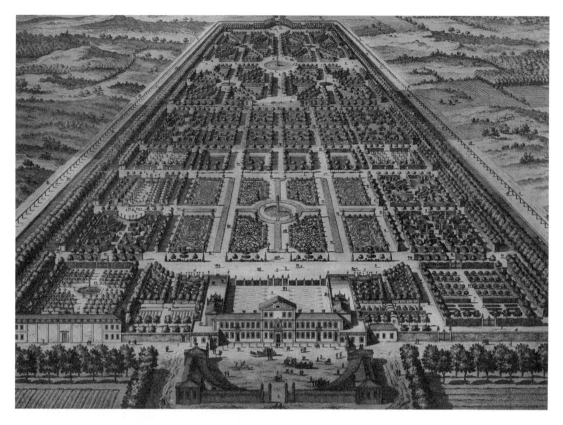

Image 12. *The great garden (Der grosse Garten) of Herrenhausen, in Hannover.* Anonymous, copper engraving, c. 1710, in Dörries and Plath (1967: 26). Leibniz's multifarious interests as a philosopher included mathematics, technology, and the art of gardening.

opposes Leibniz when claiming that art involves a special and independent insight. Aesthetics for Baumgarten is "the science of sensuous knowledge."[22]

In his main work "Aesthetica" from 1750, Baumgarten brings together the theory of art, the metaphysics of beauty and the epistemology of perception. Baumgarten gets his examples primarily from poetry and on this basis he develops his account of how human beings have a special, sensuous intuition which he defines as an "analogon rationis," as something that happens in analogy to reason. Mental imagery is perceived of as "representing" the soul in varying degrees. According to Baumgarten these representations embody an "abundance" of many different mental perceptions from which the soul creates mental images.

Baumgarten coined the term "aesthetic truth," which states that the experience of beauty is based in a subjective cognitive ability and an object-related, clear idea about the multifarious qualities of the object of beauty. In order to unite the logical and aesthetic dimension of knowledge, Baumgarten invented the term "aestheticological" truth. Baumgarten sees sensuous knowledge as an essential dimension of all types of knowledge.

Image 13. *The Fountain in the Baroque Garden of Herrenhausen, in Hannover.* Etching by Robert Batty, 1829, in Dörries and Plath (1967: 39). The fountain in the baroque garden of Herrenhausen which was constructed by Gottfried Wilhelm Leibniz 1718–20, was the tallest conceivable and practically possible in Leibniz´s time, with a water column of 67m (today 81m).

Baumgarten's philosophy is based on the same theological metaphysics as Leibniz's ideas. Metaphysical truth is a "conformity of existence and its principles," which presupposes that God is the ultimate form of reason whose principles are laid down in creation. In this sense Baumgarten's aesthetic is theo-aesthetic, that is, it lays out the doctrine of the artistic experience of beauty as a road of knowledge leading to God via sensuous knowledge. Any philosophical aesthetic of the Enlightenment is in one way or the other theoaesthetic: theoaesthetics presupposes God as the ground for aesthetically true experiences.[23]

Through Baumgarten's positive establishment of aesthetics in relation to epistemology, aesthetics has developed an independent and knowledge-critical function whose tradition up till the present remains unbroken. With the help of aesthetics, Baumgarten relativized the analytical-logical understanding of knowledge and introduced subjective experience as an objective-metaphysical knowledge form. Thus, an independent aesthetic element would become a critical corrective to formalistic and structuralist models of knowledge that claimed unfounded universal scientific validity at different times.

For Theodor W. Adorno, in agreement with several later postmodern thinkers, aesthetics is salvage from or a confirmation of the non-identical, that is, of what escapes abstract, conceptual knowledge but which we still try to fathom with reason. After Baumgarten, the human analytical logical ability is only one of several possible paths to knowledge which, by necessity, must be complemented by subjective sensuous experience.

Experiencing the Sublime and the Autonomy of Reason

Immanuel Kant (born 1724) also sees aesthetics as a reflection of the human epistemological ability.[24] In his early works, Kant works on the problem of taste and how human taste can lead to a reliable judgment. Are there any general principles for valuing beauty? How can one develop the subjective principle of taste as a principle for the power of judgment (*Urteilskraft*)?

Kant's later development of aesthetics as an independent part of his critical transcendental philosophy focuses on the epistemological conditions of subjectivity. In contrast to Baumgarten, Kant rejects an ontological foundation of beauty which claims that representations of the human imagination depict beauty's existence in Being. According to Kant, aesthetics, rather than being grounded in metaphysics, should investigate the conditions for the relevance of the judgments of beauty.

Kant's theory of beauty is a theory of the taste's judgment of beauty. The judgment of taste is both distinct from and develops in analogy to the judgment of reason. Kant emphasizes, as does Baumgarten, the objective and the subjective dimensions of aesthetics.

Kant sketches four different functions for the judgment of beauty and the sublime: the judgment is without self-interest; it is not based in concepts; the judgment agrees with emotions but does not have a purpose; and the judgment is made out of necessity. Aesthetics claims its independence in Kant's view of knowledge in that the "productive power of imagination" functions together with reason. This means that aesthetics also in Kant's approach maintains a knowledge-critical, corrective function.

In Kant's days, the idea of the sublime (*das Erhabene*, that which is elevated) evolved into a synonym of beauty. Great natural phenomena like steep mountains, wild seas, or endless plains were regarded as landscapes that would inspire a flood of overwhelming emotions that would challenge reason.

Kant emphasizes how these experiences of grandeur and powerfulness do not subdue people; rather, people become elevated, as the experience of the natural infinity refers people to the infinity of ideas, to the things that we can think of but never express, for example, the World, the Soul or God. Reason and imagination interact in this experience, and reason is confirmed through the experience of the independent and unrestrained experience of nature.

It is crucial for Kant that reason is not controlled by the heteronomy of the empirical laws but that it is possible to experience the independence and autonomy of reason emotionally. In this way, aesthetics becomes a way of sensuously liberating people by referring to the independent power of enlightened reason.

The painter Joseph Anton Koch embodies the free, unruly nature as an appeal to the natural freedom of humankind. Through the sublime, serene landscape the water plummets down as a symbol of the unrestrained power of freedom. (See *Der Schmadribachfall*; in the colour plates section, Image 14.)

Even if one may pose serious objections to Kant's version of aesthetics, which does not pay heed to art itself; to its cognitive content and its historical context, Kant's ideas are remarkably germane. The paradoxical relationship between the disinterested interest of taste in the experience, between ugliness and beauty, spirit and nature, reaction and reflection represents a tension field relevant for many modern artists of today.

Even the subjective process of experience related to art reception is a critical problem. Through Jean-François Lyotard and his interpretations of Bernett Newman's paintings,[25] the experience of something that cannot be represented has contributed to a vitalization of Kant's aesthetics, which concedingly was more concerned with the dialectic of aesthetic judgment than with art itself.

Art as a Spiritual and Historical Phenomenon

Georg Friedrich Hegel's (born 1770) contribution meant a focal deepening of art theory.[26] Hegel's definition of art is: "…the beautiful is defined…as the sensuous appearance of the idea."[27] Hegel focused on the role of art in the "system" that embodies truth. The system in turn is characterized by historical change. Art does not have a supernatural, super-historical role; it is in itself a phenomenon in the historical process in which the world spirit gradually emerges.

Art history, according to Hegel, is divided into three eras: the classical, the symbolic and the romantic. He corrected both Aristotle's view of art by emphasizing art's departure from nature and Plato's art view by making knowledge of truth dependent on the awareness of sensuous experience. As art makes the idea shine sensuously, the sense

experience is valued higher in Hegelian aesthetics.

In connection to his interpretation of Christianity as a model spiritual religion, Hegel highlights art's dependency on religion as another spiritual phenomenon. Despite the fact that the Renaissance had separated autonomous art from religion, and despite the fact that the Reformation had reinforced this distinction, art was ultimately defined by its religious connotation in Hegel's view. He saw the autonomy of art as an impoverishment that bereaves art of its obligations. Hegel observed that the contemporary art of his time had been reduced to a scientific object of knowledge without faith and he evoked an archaic synthesis of religion, truth and art.[28]

Hegel has often been interpreted to have predicted the death of all art, and hence one has criticized Hegel's view on the grounds that art-making is vital and blooming. However, one may positively interpret Hegel to have described the transformation process that art underwent in his time and that his thesis about the death of art referred to the end of a religiously determined art view, which would not necessarily stop the development of new views on and ways of expressing art.

The Critique of Alienation and the Utopia of Freedom

Friedrich Schiller (born 1759) agrees with Kant but he develops Kant's aesthetic theory by focusing on action rather than knowledge.[29] For Schiller, art is a necessary part of the historical process of change. The liberating potential of art is in its lucid representation of the beautiful act and its potentials in the context of human alienation. The central function of art is, for Schiller, the critical aspect which develops the human facility for rational

Image 15. *Goethe-Schiller-Denkmal*, Ernst Rietschel. 1857, Weimar, photo: author. F. Schiller with (his patron and friend) J. W. Goethe in front of the "German National Theatre," where the famous "Weimar constitution" was worked out as the first democratic one in Germany and made public on 11 August, 1919.

thinking and acting freely and with authority. In situations where people are deprived of freedom art represents the potential for freedom of action. Art helps us see freedom.

The question about the significance of art is closely connected to the question about life in a humane future world. For Schiller, nature's purpose with humans is their happiness, and the task of art is thus to foster human beings to a free and responsible life. Art becomes a mediator of happiness. Aesthetics should thus not be a theory of duty; it should be a theory of pleasure, of the pleasure that cultivates a responsible use of reason.

Schiller defines beauty as the "the freedom that emerges." In contrast to Kant, Schiller does not confine his definition to natural beauty, but states that beauty is "nature in its refinement." Artistic creation brings into existence art objects and these objects are subjected to a rule that is not determined by the nature of the object but by free, human actions. Schiller thus defines the autonomy of art as "heautonomy," that is, autonomy that has been given to the object through an acting subject.

The aesthetic education has, for Schiller, an important political function; however, art should not be confused with freedom itself. Schiller makes the important distinction between, on the one hand, art that visualizes ideas and, on the other, the potential for action that does not yet realize freedom. Fiction and reality are kept separate.

This is a potential weakness of Schiller's aesthetic, as it provides a diversified reflection over the cultural function of art but does not say anything about how and why its representations actually can contribute to making this liberation happen. Does art remain a critique without works to criticize? Does it offer utopias without helping realize these utopias?

Marcuse brings us one step closer to the answer in his essay about the permanence of art ("Die Permanenz der Kunst"). The sources of art's radical potential is, for him, partly the "erotic quality of beauty" that represents the principle of pleasure and thus also a "political

Eros" that rebels against a repressing reality principle,[30] and partly arts ability to retain "the promise of happiness together with the aims that has not yet been reached." Art represents in this way the ultimate goal of revolution: freedom and happiness for the individual.[31]

Aesthetics and Art Theology beyond Theoaesthetics?

Can Being Be Good and Beautiful in our Time?

The aesthetic conceptions from antiquity to the Enlightenment briefly outlined here rest on a theoaesthetic foundation. The assertions about beauty, the sublime and ethically liberating presupposes an idea of being that is based in the antique worldview. Even if the image of God – with the exception of Hegel's concept of spirit – was not central to the Enlightenment conceptions of aesthetics, we may describe these approaches as theoaesthetics as they, just as the Christian faith, presuppose the notion of a metaphysical basis of reality.

Even though Kant rejected metaphysics as the basis of aesthetics, his transcendental-philosophical epistemology was based on a cogent philosophy of religion which, like the apophatism of late antiquity, presupposed God's existence as the ultimate goal of the practical and theoretical use of reason.[32] In Hegel, the ties between religion and art are made explicit and Hegel also interpreted the death of art. Friedrich Schleiermacher (born 1768) developed a well-argued theological conception of art, and just as Schiller, Schleiermacher advocated freedom as the essential nature of art, and theologically Schleiermacher interpreted this freedom positively in light of God's open creation.

Philosophical aesthetics' view of the essence of art was supposed to support the introversion of the thought system.[33] Epistemology was normatively superior, perhaps not to artistic creation, but at least to the concept of art.

Common to enlightened aesthetics of the eighteenth and nineteenth centuries was the vision of a possible reconciliation and liberation to which art could contribute. Aesthetics thus made a special contribution both epistemologically and in terms of action to "enlightenment," which Kant defined as "der Ausgang des Menschen aus seiner unverschuldeten Unmündigkeit" (release from an undeserved minority).[34] Theoaesthetics defended the connecting power of religion that could counteract fragmentation and disintegration. Together, art and religion would advocate the integration and unity of humankind, society, and the world.[35] At the same time, theoaesthetics also was sensitive to the soaring power of menacing pictures, something which is particularly obvious in Hegel's philosophy.

The transition to the later phase of the Enlightenment, so-called modernity, does, however, shake the foundation for theoaesthetics by challenging the basic assumption of the beauty of existence and the harmonizing and unifying power of art and religion. The twentieth century sees the collapse of theoaesthetics. The devastating experiences from World War I and II, anti-Semitism and the violence of nationalism, Auschwitz, Hiroshima, and more recently Chernobyl, Ruanda, Bosnia, Kosovo, Afghanistan, and Iraq, shatter the basic principle of the goodness of existence in theoaesthetics. Neither theology nor aesthetics can remain unaffected by "Modernity and the Holocaust."[36]

Image 16. David L. Bloch, *The Last Stop.* © DACS, London 2006.

Image 17. Hannah Ryggen, *Drømmedød.* 1936, textile weaving, 225 × 272, Nordenfjeldske Kunstindustrimuseum, Trondheim. Photo: Nordenfjeldske Kunstindustrimuseum, Trondheim, © DACS, London 2006.

Image 18. *Burial of an Unknown Child and Victim in Bhopal.* The image shows the remains of an unknown child and victim. Photo: anonymous, at http://www.tribuneindia.com/2004/20041128/spectrum/main1.htm (21.1.2007). In the poison gas catastrophe in the Indian city of Bhopal, the death of a great number of innocent people, among them also children, was caused by the recklessness of a greedy international company and by an equally irresponsible government.

Image 19. Marcel Duchamp, *Bicycle Wheel*, 1951 (third version, after lost original of 1913). Museum of Modern Art, New York, © Succession Marcel Duchamp/ADAGP, Paris, and DACS, London 2006.

From Aesthetics to Art Theory

By the turn of the twentieth century, sensible artists already questioned the validity of the old aesthetics and challenged the established art view, provoking art in order to replace the established art view with a completely new view of art.

Marcel Duchamp's so-called ready-made objects are brilliant examples of this provocative art. By bringing together different elements from daily life in an unusual combination the viewer is challenged to redefine their view of what art is. The old explanations no longer apply. Duchamp's work caused a landslide which led most of twentieth-century art and aesthetics to a transformation process which still goes on. Even the mystery of the Incarnation can be seen in a new light in Duchamp's art: Christ as a "readymade god among gods," a god that no longer can be separated among other human beings.[37]

Other reasons for the demise of theoaesthetics are found in the natural sciences detachment from metaphysics and in art's autonomy in conflict with the established religious institutions. Feminist and semiotically oriented art critics' scepticism towards defining the nature of art was philosophically important.[38] The normative claim of philosophical aesthetics was also weakened in art history's turn to the object. A theoretical evaluation could no longer be done using abstract, constructed conceptual systems; and a theory of art must have some consideration for the actual art object.

Modern art theories shun the idea-based normative instrumentalization and instead ponder over experiences of art.[39] The *experience* of art precedes the *idea* of art. The main focus shifts from essentialist definitions to interpretations of the function of art.[40] The tide has turned compared to what was the case with aesthetics: from function and reception to reflection over phenomena. Today only metaphysical and Marxist art theories maintain comprehensive theoretical frameworks for art reflection. Art theories of the twentieth century are instead about "translating the work of art to discourse."[41]

The purpose of art theory is not to conceal aesthetics, but to terminate it in public such that it provokes an increased need for interpretation that cannot be covered by the theory but demands that one returns to the phenomenon, the work of art itself. Theory and method are intertwined. The purpose of theory is to continuously refer the interpreter to a close face-to-face encounter with the object. Thus the theory creates the method of analysis rather than explaining the meaning of the work of art.

Aesthetics in-between Truth, Action, Criticism and Aestheticization

However, philosophers have not passively accepted this displacement of art reflection and they continue to heed the completeness of philosophical systematicity and the function of aesthetics in this system. Annemarie Gethmann-Siefert claims that the two paradigms of aesthetics as epistemologicy and action-oriented art theory, respectively, can be united in understanding art as a mode of experiencing truth (Weise der Wahrheitserfahrung).[42] In other words, she goes back to a logocentric conception of art that defines and determines the nature of art based on one single concept: the truth.

Aestheticians that operate with a sharp distinction between form and content in the Aristotelian tradition risk overlooking the dual interaction between object and viewer that is particularly crucial in contemporary conceptual art. Indeed, conceptual art is based on ideas and uses physical expressions as mediators of ideas. But the interpreters' meeting with the expression of the installation changes these ideas and profoundly influences on the meaning of the work of art.[43] The relation between idea and expression is far from static; rather, it is highly changeable and, in addition, highly dependent on reception in a way that is not picked up by the old distinction between expression and meaning. The semiotic distinction between expression and meaning, however, offers a more fitting analytical tool.

Brigitte Scheer proposes another direction for philosophical aesthetics, and she highlights the epistemological perspective that was present already in the philosophy of early antiquity. Scheer is positive to art theory's critique of the logo-centric rationality characteristic of theoaesthetic conceptions, and she interprets "the aesthetic turn" as a positive analogy to "the linguistic turn."[44] Scheer claims that philosophical aesthetics can only be understood in contingency to prevailing views of knowledge which it either will confirm, oppose or complete. Aesthetics is, for her, one of the core disciplines of philosophical epistemology. The claim to power is not abandoned in this programme, but the claim for normative validity is expanded – not to include artistic creation but to include the prevailing views of power and knowledge. Thus reflections on experience in art theory may gain relevance for (philosophy´s) epistemology.

Yet another possible development beyond theoaesthetics is found in the philosopher Wolfgang Welsch, who develops aesthetics as a reflection on the challenging coeval aestheticizing processes.[45] Welsch rightly criticizes art theory for confining art to a detached artistic realm, which may lead to a process of ghettofication if aesthetics does not contribute to making art analysis relevant for the understanding of other aestheticizing social phenomena.

The fact that art is liberated from the philosophical view of knowledge as well as the theoaesthetic foundation does not entail that artistic creation has lost its metaphysical and religious dimension. Rather, it is the opposite that has happened. The liberation from the predominant normative aesthetic interpretation has also brought about the liberation of the spiritual dimension of art, which without doubt is a major part of the foundation of the history of modern art.[46]

Towards a Soteriological…

Even art theology must somehow relate to the displacement from theoaesthetics to art theory,

from the essence of art to the artwork. Art theologies that assume an ontological juxtaposition of beauty, goodness, being, and God are no longer viable. Just as the linguistic turn has involved a challenge to theology – which has been handled amongst other in the "God-is-dead theology" and in the hermeneutical theology as well as in the criticism of theism's conceptually fixed faith – the aesthetic turn also challenges theology.

What are the consequences of the fact that we do not perceive the world visually as it is but meet it intuitively in our internal and external realms? What is the impact of the aesthetic turn on Christian theology which mainly has based its interpretations on examinations of the word? What do the established churches relate to their art critical attitude at the turn of the new millennium? How do they relate to art's criticism of established religion?

In my opinion, after the liberation from the ontological foundation of theoaesthetics, we need a soteriological definition of art theology, that is, a definition that is related to how God in his creation handles sensuous liberation. George Pattison aptly points out that theologians' discussion about art through the course of history mainly has taken place within the discourse of natural theology and he pleads for an interpretation of works of art "in the context of redemption."[47] The experience of art is in itself a soteriological inception in the form of a potential experience of God. The focal question for a soteriological theology of art is: how does God perform acts of redemption and liberation with humankind and nature through art?

A first demand on the theology of art is that it should retain a positive attitude to the displacement from aesthetics to art reflection. An art theory should not stand in opposition to the basic intention of art theories, namely to bring the theory to a close with an openness that enables continuation of the interpretation processes, directly related to the experience of the object.

A second demand is that art theology avoids the concepts of art and knowledge of philosophical aesthetics that give norms for art-making and reception.

A third demand is that the theology of art must legitimize the freedom of art, not at any cost but in a responsible commitment to different communities of interpretation.

Finally, art theology should abstain from a putative universalistic ontological approach to the essence of art. Just as contextual theology demands a reflection over "God in context", art theology also forms its interpretation as a reflection over God-at-work-in-art. The final chapter of this book gives a comprehensive account of how this can be approached.

...and a Contextual Theology of Art

In the choice between an essentialist and contextual foundation for the theology of art, I favour the latter. If the theology of art is to adhere to an essentialist theory about the nature of art it will end up in the furrow of theological metaphysics and consequently it will interpret the phenomenon of art normatively based on certain given conceptual systems.[48]

Theologically, an essentialist definition of art is just as problematic as defining God's nature, as it breaks with the apophatic epistemology of classical theology. According to this view, human beings cannot have knowledge about the nature of God, but only about God's work in the creation. An art theological metaphysics which is based on an assumption of the nature of art is in danger of confusing assertions pertaining to the nature of God and the nature of art and from this deriving universal claims of validity and power.

Against a contextualist foundation of art theology one may profess that this approach tends to promote context to a determinative factor of art-making. Consequently, it threatens to put the autonomy of art above the autonomy of art, and it uses the social interpretation as a tool for standardizing art-making and reception.

However, bearing this risk in mind, the contextual theology of art may accentuate the subjective dimension of art-making too, which in turn will have an altering influence on the context. For example, patterns of perception may change when we look at a work of art. An art object may relate to contextually given elements and at the same time be capable of changing these elements. Similar to theology's relation to context,[49] the interaction between art and context can be described using the form of the functional circle:

In this representation, the focus is partly on the image's relation to its context of production and reception and partly on the autonomous capacity of the image to influence its contexts. The autonomy of art and of context in this approach is not in opposition to each other; they complement each other. They make each other complete in a circular movement. The theology of art should be

the work of art

influence   influences

contextual dimensions

developed contextually with awareness of the iconic difference and the unique quality and autonomy of the visual medium.[50]

Summary

- The question of what art is and how one can define and distinguish art has been a source of debate at all times. There is not a necessary link between this overarching question and the question "what on earth is this?" in connection to the perception of a unique object.

- There is, from antiquity onwards, in the history of ideas of aesthetics in Western culture a peculiar gap between the thinking about art, on the one hand, and the creation of art, on the other. While Plato saw visual art as subordinate and rendered it suspicious, Dio defended image-making and image cults, especially in a social and theological perspective. Aristotle saw the human inclination to mimic and copy, *mimesis*, as the basis of art.

- For reasons unknown to us, the 700s saw the beginning of the long-lasting iconoclasm and battle between the throne, the church and the monastic system, which led to destabilization of the church and the empire; however, it also brought about a deepening of the theological view of images. The theologically most important support for the iconodulic theologians was found in the mystery of the Incarnation. Because God had become a man, made of flesh and blood, material nature must also be acknowledged a greater value. Incarnation theology departed from the Platonic depreciation of materiality and provided the basis for a positive Christian theology of the image.

- The Aristotelian mimesis doctrine was relativized through the Christian theology of the image and the icon as a created expression of the uncreated nature of God and Christ's human nature in the Godhead.

- During the Renaissance a new view of art emerges. In this novel take on art the emphasis is on the creation of autonomous independent works of art, and art is freed from the Platonic reduction to handicraft. The mathematical concepts "perspective" and "proportion" take the place of religious terms, but they are used to interpret the divine qualities of creation. The Aristotelian mimesis doctrine in relation to nature has regained its position. Mathematics, geometry, the creation of volume and the central perspective, which is immensely important for Western seeing, are the primary tools of the new art. The artist as a person comes to the foreground.

- In the eighteenth century, J. J. Winckelmann introduces the concept of "style" and this marks the start of the history of style. Konrad Fiedler founds modern art history by a critical turn to the object. There is a shift in focus in the research from reception to production, as there is a shift of focus to the artwork itself and contact with the artists increases. Benedotto Croce emphasizes taste and the notion of the artwork's "insularità" as a basis for reception aesthetics, while the Vienna school promotes the primacy of the object. Where the concept of form was one of the pillars of the Vienna school, the Warburg school focused on iconography. There is an increasing focus on the general history of ideas context and iconography is given a more pretentious name, "iconology." Art history today is characterized by a methodological diversity that supports the primacy of the object without ignoring its subjective, geographical and historical contexts.[51] The need for a diversified model for the relation between work and context thus becomes even more pressing.

- With the Enlightenment and the focus on reason, aesthetics developed into a separate branch of philosophy. Philosophically, it was defined as a reflection over art with a special concern for beauty. Historically, two paradigms emerge; one dominated by the epistemological aspect and the other accentuates art as a process and art as action.

- G. W. Leibniz ranked aesthetics low on the scale of human knowledge. Aesthetic knowledge was perceived as both lucid and conceptually obscure. A. G. Baumgarten is the founder of aesthetics as an autonomous philosophical discipline. His view of aesthetics is based in Leibniz's acknowledgement of the epistemological potential of aesthetics, but he opposes Leibniz when claiming that art involves a special and independent insight. Aesthetics for Baumgarten is "the science of sensuous knowledge." He creates a theoaesthetic, that is, it lays out the doctrine of the artistic experience of beauty as a road of knowledge leading to God via sensuous knowledge. Any philosophical aesthetic of the Enlightenment is in one way or the other a theoaesthetic: theoaesthetics presupposes God as the ground for aesthetically true experiences.

- I. Kant also sees aesthetics as a reflection over the human epistemological ability. In contrast to Baumgarten, Kant rejects an ontological foundation of beauty. According to Kant, aesthetics, rather than being grounded in metaphysics, should investigate the conditions for the relevance of the judgments of beauty.

Kant's theory of beauty is a theory of the taste's judgment of beauty. The judgment of taste is both distinct from and develops in analogy to the judgment of reason. Kant emphasizes, as does Baumgarten, the objective and the subjective dimensions of aesthetics. In Kant's days, the idea of the sublime (*das Erhabene*, that which is elevated) evolved into a synonym of beauty. Reason and imagination interact in this experience, and reason is confirmed through the experience of the independent and unrestrained experience of nature. Aesthetics becomes a way of sensuously liberating people by referring to the independent power of enlightened reason.

- G. F. Hegel focuses on the role of art in the "system." Art does not have a supernatural, super-historical role; it is in itself a phenomenon in the historical process. Hegel highlights art's dependency on religion as another spiritual phenomenon. Despite the fact that the Renaissance separated autonomous art from religion, and despite the fact that the Reformation reinforced this distinction, art is ultimately defined by its religious connotation in Hegel's view. He sees the autonomy of art as an impoverishment that bereaves art of its obligations. Hegel observes that the contemporary art of his time is reduced to a scientific object of knowledge without faith and he evokes an archaic synthesis of religion, truth and art, and from this the provocative thesis of "the death of art" emerges.

- F. Schiller develops Kant's aesthetic theory by focusing on action rather than knowledge. The liberating potential of art is in its lucid representation of the beautiful act and its potentials in the context of human alienation. The central function of art is, for Schiller, the critical aspect; in situations where people are deprived of freedom art represents the potential for freedom of action. Art helps us see freedom.

- Common to enlightened aesthetics of the eighteenth and nineteenth centuries was the vision of a possible reconciliation and liberation. Theoaesthetics defended the connecting power of religion that could counteract fragmentation and disintegration. Together, art and religion would advocate the integration and unity of humankind, society, and the world. The transition to the later phase of the Enlightenment does, however, shake the foundation for theoaesthetics. The twentieth century sees the collapse of theoaesthetics. The basic principle of the goodness of existence is shattered.

- At the turn of the twentieth century, sensible artists question the validity of the old aesthetics and challenge the established art view, provoking art in order to replace the established art view with a completely new view of art. In M. Duchamp's ready-made objects the viewer is challenged to take a completely new view of what art is. The natural sciences detachment from metaphysics, art's autonomy in conflict with the established religious institutions, and art history's turn to the object further contributed to the demise of theoaesthetics. Any theory of art must now show some consideration for the actual art object. Modern theories of art shun the idealist, normative instrumentalization and instead ponder over experiences of art. The main focus shifts from essentialist definitions to interpretations of the function of art. Theory and method are intertwined. The purpose of theory is to continuously refer the interpreter to a close face-to-face encounter with the art object.

- Philosophers do not passively accept this displacement of art reflection and they continue to heed the completeness of philosophical systematicity and the function of aesthetics in this system by seeking new paths for aesthetics, either as "modes of experiencing truth," as critical reflection on actions, or as reflections on aestheticizing processes.

- The theology of art beyond theoaesthetics is challenged to develop a soteriological (history of liberation) definition within a contextual paradigm. Theologically, an essentialist definition of art is just as problematic as defining God's nature, as it breaks with the apophatic epistemology of classical theology. According to this view, human beings cannot have knowledge about the nature of God, but only about God's work in the creation. An art theological metaphysics which is based on an assumption of the nature of art is in danger of confusing assertions pertaining to the nature of God and the nature of art, and then from this deriving universal claims of validity and power. Just as contextual theology demands a reflection over "God in context," art theology also forms its interpretation as a reflection over God-at-work-in-art.

CHAPTER 3

Theological Views of Art

Images are spaces for theological discoveries. Despite the fact that modern visual artists throughout the twentieth century struggled deeply with the problem of spirituality, the established Churches have hardly accepted the ability of the artistic picture to visualize God. Although Early Christianity offers a cogent theology of the icon based on the mystery of incarnation, the Church still lacks, ever since Friedrich Schleiermacher developed his aesthetic,[1] a functioning theological tool for meeting art and seeking theological insights in images.

The present chapter firstly proposes four aspects of visual arts' challenges to theology. Further, ten different notable attempts to meet this challenge by theologians and historians of religion are presented. For each individual approach I discuss to which extent the four aspects of the challenge have been met. Finally, four ideal models for a theology of art are presented.

The Challenge of Modern Visual Arts to Theology

The Autonomy of Presentiveness

In the first chapter of this book, we focused on the special expressive quality of the visual medium. The concept "iconic difference" summarized how the domains of sensuousness and the creation of meaning inextricably interact in images. Every image is an independent visual expression. The autonomy of presentiveness cannot be interpreted in words; one can only ponder it using theories that refer to the openness of the work of art. The visual presentiveness of the image must not be translated into linguistic discourse; rather, it should make us aware of a loss. The visual spatial expression cannot be reduced to word-bound, discursive linear forms of language.

Works of art are characterized by their inherent hermeneutic constitution. They produce their meanings in relation to the viewer. The artworks in themselves constitute the very context of meaning that later makes their interpretation possible. Modern objects of art also presuppose a multitude of different concepts of art that should not necessarily be imposed on the artwork from the outside. Only in the encounter with a specific work of art will the concept of art which attributes meaning to the object arise.

The special influence of space on the creation of meaning makes images markedly different from texts. Additionally, they cannot be read as texts as the discursive, linear way of approaching texts reduces the diversity of spatiality. The primary tool of picture analysis is therefore intuition, which should not be regarded as secondary to linguistic analysis.[2]

The connection between production and reception aesthetics is crucial for any picture analysis which aims at retaining the precedence of the object. In order to be able to interpret something one observes, one needs to consider the making of the object of observation; how it has come into being. It is inevitable to view the physical structure of the image as a carrier of meaning.

Theology is thus challenged to accept the autonomy of the image as a special medium for God and worship. Through the autonomy of expression, the image has an independent revealing capacity, but this obviously does not entail that all art objects contain religious expressions. Rather, this is related to the recognition that the specific capacity of the visual medium to express independently, with clarity, and spatially both ideas about and experiences of God and religious faith and worldview. Sometimes images are even regarded as direct mediators of encounters with God, for example in the theology of the icon of the Eastern Church. Images create different spaces for theological discoveries. There is no doubt that visual art is a "locus theologicus."[3] Its pluralistic capacity for creating new meanings, in addition to creating alternative concepts of art, could prepare the grounds for new and challenging concepts of God and religion.

The Spiritual in Art

Although art has developed into an independent realm and emphasized its independency and autonomy, art has never stopped wrestling with the problem of the Sacred. Despite the fact that modern man's conception of reality becomes increasingly distant from religious worldviews, modern artists have deepened and developed religiosity in their artistic creation. Concepts like "transcendence" and "spirituality" may be used to characterize a fundamental, continuous feature of modern and late modern contemporary art.

The art historian Wieland Schmied says that the wrestling with spirituality is of such a magnitude both qualitatively and quantitatively that the problem of spirituality goes right to the heart of all art and especially of modern art.[4] Without an interpretation of the spiritual element, we are incapable of understanding modern art, according to Schmied's view.

Hence theology is obviously challenged to rehabilitate the artist as an equal discussion partner with a unique competence in the discourse pertaining to the content and expression of religious belief. It is a fact that many artists have understood themselves in religious terms as, for example, prophets, shamans, preachers, sages, and so on, and that the elites of the established church communities have not at all recognized their claim to recognition. The most compelling support of Schmied's thesis is found in the two comprehensive exhibitions that Schmied organized in Berlin 1980 and 1990,[5] in addition to the 1986 New York exhibition "Spiritual in Art."[6] A hindsight view on the exhibition activities of the late twentieth century reveals that a huge number of artists display a stylistic rather than semantic interest in religion, and that in this regard especially the dimensions of space and place are developed creatively.[7]

We find further support in the modernists' diverse expression of Christian iconography as a social-critical metaphor and their liberation of the Christian iconography from closed, dogmatic traditions for interpretation. Art meets the scientific-positivistic reduction of spirituality at the turn of the twenty-first century with the making of images as direct mediators of God.[8]

In art, the individualization of worldview and religious conviction becomes equally obvious as is the need for and longing for a direct experience of God and the presence of nature. The pictorial world goes through a comprehensive transformation process which also challenges the conceptions of God to undergo a similar and equally comprehensive metamorphosis.[9]

Artists also interpret – using carefully selected metaphysical elements from, for example, theosophy – the dissolution of figuration as a spiritual process. Several of these artists come from Eastern European regions deeply rooted in Orthodox Christianity. The apophatic view of the human inability to understand the nature of God but still the ability to approach God's work is interpreted in several of the visual programmes of these abstract artists. However, this aspect of the history of ideas and theology of art is only given scant attention among art historians.[10]

Many artists interpret their own life struggle in light of the passion of Christ and express an analogy or identification with the suffering God-human.[11] Karl Schmidt-Rottluff engraves the condition of the German people after World War I in Christ's face. The created space is by Max Beckmann primarily conceived of as a holy space, which his pictures portray in a marked and lucid manner. The artist Walter Pichler voices in a provokingly clear manner the displacement of religion to art: "Today religiosity is only possible within art."[12]

The Conflict between Faith, Reason, and Society

In his book *Kunst und Mythos* the German philosopher Georg Picht describes how modern art reveals premodern mythical views that help religious movements to a ritual breakthrough.[13] Artists, according to Picht, monitor like seismographs the breakthrough of a mythical thinking that feeds on the prehistory of our culture. For Picht, art objects and myths are historical powers in which universal content is manifested and which neither aesthetics nor religious studies can subdue. Picht interprets art in light of its conflict with faith, reason, and society.

The conflict with faith has an historical basis as the enlightened theology, which is in harmony with rationality, feeds on the synthesis of Greek and Christian philosophy, for which art and myth were regarded as superstitions. Rational theology mistakenly assumes that it is emancipated from myth.

Art theory and aesthetics also reduce the artworks by making them objects of aesthetic experience and interpretations. The work of art is in this respect robbed of its meaning and function. Picht maintains that the light of revelation becomes invisible if one evades the world of myth.[14] If one denies the experience that the gospel presupposes, then one rejects the gospel itself as the gospel necessarily must be the opposite of this experience, according to Picht.[15] This is why the content of faith has abandoned the Church and theology and we need to seek it elsewhere.

Because the Church and theology have not realized the universal power of myth, the conflict between art and faith has been

Image 20. Karl Schmidt-Rottluff, *Ist euch nicht Kristus erschienen.* 1918, woodcut, 50.1 × 39.1,
© DACS, London 2006.

Image 21. Max Beckmann, *Kreuzabnahme*. 1917, oil on canvas, 151 × 129, The Museum of Modern Art, New York, © DACS, London 2006.

Image 22. Kurt Schwitters, *Die Versuchung des heiligen Antonius*. 1918, crayon on paper, 17.7 × 11.2, Kurt Schwitters Archiv im Sprengel Museum Hannover Nr. 355. © DACS, London 2006.

displaced to art itself. The gospel is therefore preached by godless artists outside the Church. For Picht, art has remained Christian from late antiquity up till present time through its self-apprehension as sometimes "only art" and other times "absolute art." From this self-conception springs its freedom. It seeks to dissolve itself and can therefore constantly reinvent itself.

Furthermore, art is in conflict with philosophy's scientific truth concept. Ever since Plato's academy, art has been placed in a spiritual, obscure world which is suspect and which does not represent any form of knowledge. It was only with the aesthetic of the enlightenment that this axiom was dismissed by regarding "productive imagina-tion" as a basic component of cognition.

Kant, Schelling and Hegel, according to Picht, hold the opinion that s/he who does not understand art is not capable of understanding the meaning of a word like "God."[16] The good is revealed in the beautiful together with the one, the true.

However, Hegel and Nietzsche see the contradiction of this synthesis and how art stands in contrast to truth. The will to art is also a will to the lie that makes life possible. Therefore modern art must embody the opposition between truth and art.

Art causes helplessness in relation to beauty. For Hegel, beauty was the revelation of gods. However, modern art discloses the outward show and thus also reveals who is taking on this facade. Neither aesthetics, metaphysics, game theory, nor sociology are universally valid philosophies of art but they all must concede that art leaves behind and transgresses academic and philosophical reasoning. In art, thinking in itself becomes the objective.

The third conflict point of art is, according to Picht, its relationship to society. Modern

humans are convinced of their supremacy in and over nature. Whatever questions this authority is banned; reason and faith and even nature's intrinsic value are disrupted.

Picht's thesis presupposes the philosophy of Adorno which sees art as a mirror reflection of conditions of production and works of art as a tension between autonomy and heteronomy. "Theory" is for Adorno only possible as a "negative dialectic" that transforms harmony to dissonance. Picht develops Adorno further with regards to the conflict between society and production in the Industrial Age. For example, the tension between production and reproduction illustrates in a fundamental way the breakdown of the foundations of modern society. Reproductions' hold on production transforms art into a commodity and is the equivalent of nature's submission to the reduction of time in physics.

However, the production of art divulges another view; it does not only reflect the conditions of production but it also visualizes, as does nature, a deeper power. All art is appearance and still it cannot lie. Art remains the most sensitive tool for criticism, not so much because of its content but for its form. Art is in different cultures in harmony with the political order which is the equivalent of the order of production, while it contrasts the political order when the latter serves the demands of reproduction.

Picht's view of the conflicts of art challenges theology. Theology needs to ponder over art's ability to embody holiness, power, and mythical reality, and also over its ability to dispel the veil of myths in accordance with the message of the gospel. Picht's assumption that today it is art that controls the gospel's ability to reveal the myth and not a rationalist Church and theology is a bitter pill to swallow in all the talk about a revived spiritual movement. Picht's view of art challenges theology to take art's ability to embody the gospel seriously.

The Global, Social, and Subjective Processes of Aestheticization

According to the German philosopher Wolfgang Welsch, a central characteristic of the development of modern society is processes of aestheticization. Welsch distinguishes between shallow and deep aestheticizing.

Deep aestheticizing refers to a material change in the production process, while shallow aestheticizing turns the world into an arena of experience. Our understanding of reality relies on aesthetic elements and is subjected to "Verhübschung," an exterior beautification. This does not entail an expanded definition of creativity, as we see, for example, in Joseph Beuys and his view that "every human is an artist"; quite the contrary, the old conception of art and its value of beauty are transferred to everyday life.

In shallow aestheticizing, hedonism becomes an ethical ideology and advocates pleasure without responsibility for its consequences. Advertising uses aestheticization as a commercial strategy. Form and "styling" become the independent and dominant values of a new type of currency.

In parallel to the aestheticizing of our exterior there is a corresponding aestheticizing of our inner world and of our apprehension of reality. Today the construction of reality is strongly influenced by the media, and the aesthetic reality is becoming increasingly global. The emergence of a "homo aestheticus," who manufactures her/his appearance, personality and life to a *lifestyle,* is according to Welsch a critique of Kierkegaard's and Foucault's notion of aesthetic existence.

The concept of aesthetics is, according to Welsch, semantically polysemous and its many different semantic fields overlap each other. The many meanings of aesthetics have a family resemblance. Welsch separates amongst others between aesthetics in a sensuous, an elevated (artistically inspiring), a perception theoretical, a poetic, a hedonistic, and a cosmetic sense.[17] The different meanings of the concept of aesthetics are held together through overlapping senses and a loose coherence.

Further Welsch argues convincingly for not delimiting the concept of aesthetics to art in order not to isolate art, as in a ghetto, trapped by its own autonomy.[18]

While the ideas of autonomy in the enlightenment made a clear distinction between the realms of ethics and aesthetics, today there is obviously a conflation of these two realms. One important question is to which degree aesthetics already contains ethic elements.[19] Welsch wants to develop Adorno's notion of aesthetic justice. Adorno accentuates the importance of justice in relation to heterogeneity when he critically opposes political understandings of justice that tend to obliterate the differences because of a formalized idea of equality. The art world, on the other hand, already employs the diversity of paradigm and the awareness about the significance of difference.[20]

Welsch's approach widens aesthetics from the world of art to other lifeworlds. A decisive cause for this expansion is found in the globalized aestheticization and in the transformation of our perception of reality governed by aesthetic values. Unlike the theoaesthetics discussed above, Welsch advocates an expanded concept of aesthetics which takes into account the autonomy of art and its capacity for expressing diversity and difference.

The challenge to the theology of art is therefore to heed the context of aestheticization when analysing contemporary artworks. A theory that exclusively reveres art's capacity to display beauty is hardly a sensible theory in the context of beautification. Quite the contrary, the artists of today seek to relativize and counteract the power of shallow aestheticization.

Welsch's philosophical aesthetics is informed by the plurality of art making and argues for a reflective "aesth/ethics," that is, for a self-critical and ethically significant awareness of inherent dazzlements and for justice through sensitization for what is unknown and different.[21] Can theology also learn from these insights?

Yet another central question arises in the encounter with Welsch's analysis of society. If art and deep aestheticizing can counteract and transform the shallow aestheticizing processes, how can art making and "faith making" interact with each other in a late modern, critical alliance?

One final question for theology is whether the ambiguity of the concept of aesthetics is any way analogous to the concept of religion? If this is found to be the case, how can we develop the concept of God in the array of overlapping meanings of the word "religion"?

Different Approaches to the Challenge

The reflection over art and aesthetics is not among the key areas of theology. Quite the contrary, ever since Schleiermacher presented his comprehensive account, the dialogue with art has been sadly neglected.[22] The theology of art has lived a shadowy existence at the periphery of theology. The present section provides an inventory of approaches in theology and the history of religion that seek

to develop an alternative concept of God with a clear art and religion profile, and whose reflections over the relationship between art and faith are based in analyses of individual artworks. The selection is restricted to authors from the twentieth century after the age of theoaesthetics.

The Revelation of the Sacred

Mircea Eliade (born 1907) in his theory of religion develops Rudolf Otto's key concept "das Heilige" (the Holy) and talks about "the Sacred." For Eliade, the sacred reveals itself in different shapes in different historical contexts. Cultural history and ontology conflate in Eliade's theory. Eliade was both a scholar and a writer of fiction and he regarded these activities as two sides of his spiritual life. Religious phenomena and artistic creativity spring from the same well.

It is not clear whether Eliade means that the sacred has an ontological or phenomenological quality. Does the sacred exist or does it arise for worshippers in the "hierophancies," in the revelation of the sacred? Eliade relates art and religion primarily through his symbol theory.[23] Symbols have, according to Eliade, a "trans-conceptualizing" dimension; they express the lived spiritual element; they have a numinous aura; they are "modalities of the spirit" and "manifestations of life." In this respect, the symbols carry an array of meanings and also refer to the unity between different levels of reality.[24]

In a later article about contemporary art Eliade notices a certain "symmetry" in the development of art and philosophical theology.[25] In the insight that God is dead, both art and philosophical theology conclude that religious experience no longer can be expressed in a traditional religious language. God's death is the destruction of an idol. Art in this sense can no longer create religious art; it will no longer venerate idols. The sacred, according to Eliade, is now beyond recognition. Although artists are not conventional believers, Eliade assumes the presence of the sacred in their work.

The Rumanian historian of religion often bases his analyses in the art of (Rumanian) Constantin Brâncusi and believes that in our contemporary society, because of some kind of second fall (of man), religion has fallen into oblivion while the sacred remains intact. Because of Christianity and science, sanctifying revelation or hierophanization and cosmic religiosity have fallen into oblivion. Art on the other hand, says Eliade, follows the tracks of the two and discovers the sacred, as for example Brâncusi does in a stone. In this respect art is devoted to a ritual destruction and re-creation of the world.[26]

One may criticize Eliade's tendency of ontologizing, that is, making unfounded claims that the sacred resides in being itself. Where is the boundary between the sacred and the profane? How can one determine what aspect of the art expression it is that holds the sacred?

Eliade is still seeking, in the spirit of theoaesthetics, a comprehensive and universal view of the connection between art and religion, and his approach becomes so wide-ranging that is it hardly useful as a tool for hermeneutical, art theological investigations. However, a positive feature of his approach is the focus on the multivalence of symbols, which entails a positive judgment of art's ability to make the variety of life manageable. On this point, Eliade agrees with aesthetics inspired by Wittgenstein, although it is based on a more static metaphysical and dualistic interpretation.

Eliade's analyses of specific works of art are fairly limited; paintings by Chagall and sculptures by Brâncusi are selectively used as support for his ideas. The first challenge is in relation to the autonomy of presentiveness. Through his symbol Eliade theory; however, without reflecting over the special qualities of the visual medium. The theoaesthetics of the nineteenth century is obviously not the basis of his approach although Eliade shares its ontological view of knowledge. However, there is no space for the concept of God in his general theory of religion.

The opposite is the case in Gerardus van der Leeuw's approach.[27] Leeuw, in accordance with Eliade, highlights the sacred as the basic category of art. For Leeuw God is revealed through the mystery of faith. The task of theology is not to be descriptive but proclamatory; it should bring attention to the alterity of revelation.

For Leeuw, faith is a numinous power and the tension between art and religion should not be neutralized leading to an instrumentalization of the two in relation to each other. There is often a relation of rivalry or subordination between art and religion. For Leeuw, numinous dimensions are often found in different art expressions – in dance, writing, pictures, architecture, and music. All forms of art express an interaction between God and human beings. Beauty and sacredness are closely connected. Even if art and religion are different Leeuw argues for an essential unity of the two. Leeuw meets the challenge of regarding expressions of art as autonomous, and for religion and faith, important phenomena, but the same criticism that was raised against Eliade pertaining to universal validity applies also to Leeuw's biased approach.

For Paul Tillich (born 1886), it is not beauty but the expressiveness (Ausdruckskraft) that is the defining property of art. Art is an indication of the discord, meaninglessness, and despair associated with different areas of life.[28] It does not mediate anything definite but through the doctrine of the Holy Spirit it can be interpreted as an expression of historical, unique qualities of life that only art can embody.

Religion should not control art or prevent it from reflecting contemporary society and new trends. This should refute the principle of truthfulness in art. For Tillich the autonomy of art and the theonomy of culture presuppose each other. The theologian's job is to mediate between cultural worldviews through creative individuations.

One major objection against Tillich is that his solution to assign the autonomy of art to form and faith to the content of art contributes to maintaining a normative concept of religion, in spite of the seemingly unbiased approach. Through the contention about theonomy, the theologian reserves the right to interpret everything culturally in light of divine revelation. Besides, in relation to modern art one cannot analyse the form-content relation statically, as in Tillich's approach. Even though Tillich develops the distinction between content (Inhalt) and substance (Gehalt) to overcome the notion of the supremacy of a "pure" faith over a culturally mediated belief system,[29] the question remains unanswered when it comes to the impact of art for the substance of faith.

Historically Tillich develops a schema for the relationship between five religious types that corresponds to five stylistic elements of art history.[30] Sacramentalism is connected to the magic realism in, for example, primitive art and in Paul Klee. The mystical religious type is connected to non-figurative painting, as for example in impressionism. The prophetic-critical pious type corresponds to realism, as for example in Dennis Hopper, George Grosz, and Otto Dix. The fourth religious type is religious humanism, which corresponds to idealism, as for example in Poussain. Finally, the fifth type is ecstatic-spiritual and corresponds to expressionism.

Expressionism had its breakthrough and became the most prominent art movement in Tillich's time. It is fascinating to observe the sensitivity with which he approaches the analyses of expressionism, at the same time as it is problematic that he grants this one style among many other styles a superior role in relation to the spiritual element. We may conclude that despite the universal pretension of Tillich's theological system, it remains just as bound to the tendencies of the period in which it emerged as the cultural phenomena it describes.

Tillich interprets the relationship between art and religion using the concepts of symbol and expression in accordance with his definition of God as the ultimate reality: "If art expresses reality in images and religion expresses ultimate reality in symbols then religious art expresses religious symbols in artistic images (as philosophical concepts)."[31] The content of faith is for Tillich first expressed in religious symbols and then these symbols are expressed in art.[32] Does the concept of symbol entail that the content still is superior to form, and are the ideas of religion also seen as superior to the expressive power of art? Or does Tillich believe that art images not only express but also embody and create religious symbols? How should one interpret the relationship between symbol and image? Tillich meritoriously challenges us to understand the implications of the question of whether both the image-making in art and the cultural expressions of religion are independent dynamic interpretations of existence and the mystery of the Creator.

Beauty and Holiness

The idea of an essential unity between beauty and holiness is deeply embedded in our culture. Even after the era of theoaesthetics, theologians have attempted to preserve this tradition.

The North American philosopher of religion, James Alfred Martin, takes the approach that the value of beauty controls the application of general conceptions of art and the view of holiness in the same vein controls the application of the concept of religion.[33] However, Martin does not present any ontological claims on the existence of beauty and its given value, but he applies the concepts of beauty and holiness as categories in his analysis of various historical models.

In his criticism of Arthur Danto's end-of-art thesis and W. C. Smith's end-of-religion thesis, Martin recommends a critical position and argues for the deconstruction of the subject paired with a dialogical principle. Martin uses John Dewey's concept "inquiry" and Michael Bakhtin's dialogical principle as methodological concepts for promoting the discussion between art theory and the theory of religion.[34]

Although the concepts of beauty and holiness mainly serve as historical categories for analysis, one must ask why Martin ascribes such high status to these two categories in particular. How is holiness related to the concept of God? Can the concept of beauty

shed light on art theories and works of art that do not conform to the metaphysical view on art's commission to embody beauty?

A merit of Martin's proposal is its intention to further the open discourse between art theory and the theory of religion; nevertheless, because of its conceptual fixation on beauty and holiness, it tends to become a logocentric conclusion to the dialogue which puts his own demand for openness at risk. If the dialogue is to remain open, the concepts and perspectives that dominate approaches to art and religion must also be subjected to trial and alteration. An exclusive focus on the concept of beauty and holiness will reduce the autonomy of art and religion to a far too great extent.

Another attempt, albeit not equally justified, to unify faith and beauty is made by the English bishop Richard Harries in the book *Art and the Beauty of God*. Contrary to Martin, Harries bases his approach in the careful analysis of a number of artworks. Harries develops an eschatological view on the objective of art. The new heavens and the beauty of the new earth in the coming age are already reflected in the beauty of the world and in works of art.[35]

For Harries, God is the God of beauty and we are called upon to share this beauty by taking part in his work to transform the world. Harries provides an ethical, eschatological and even theo-ontological definition of beauty which attributes an independent power to the spiritual element of art. However, the basis of his proposal is subjected to the same criticism as is theoaesthetics. The theologian presupposes that beauty exists in being and that it is ontologically connected to God's existence.

Art is surrounded by the basic assumptions of faith and it is reduced to a tool for the knowledge about the beauty of this and the coming world in relation to God. The concept of God controls the concept of art. The problem with Harries' approach and many other approaches is that they confuse the discourses of art and of theology. The German theologian Horst Schwebel has for good reasons demanded that the theological discourse is singled out as some kind of "second discourse."[36] Harries' intriguing perspective on the eschatological function of art would thus not have to be an argument for the eschatological nature of art – that is, in the first art discourse – rather, reception aesthetically one may interpret art objects in light of, for example, Christian eschatology, that is, within the other discourse. Approaching modern works of art with an open eschatological questioning seems to be a valuable approach; however, claiming that art in itself already contains an eschatological element is quite a different story.

A similar mistake is made by the Swiss theologian Matthias Zeindler in his comprehensive dissertation on the beauty of God. Zeindler seeks to highlight the beauty in God's salvation, creation and in God's nature.[37]

Zeindler recognizes the challenge that one cannot exclusively approach beauty as an ethically positive category. With reference to the theology of the cross, one must also acknowledge the repulsive aspects of art.[38] Zeindler rejects the assertion that beauty has lost its significance in modern art, but his argumentation is rather weak. For him beauty is not the materialization of truth, but it has preserved its position as a form in which the truth may be expressed.[39]

It is beyond me what this shifting from the thesis that "beauty is truth" to the thesis that "beauty expresses (in its form?) truth" really entails. Does not Zeindler end up in the same dilemma as Tillich when he tried to distinguish between the form and content of art such that

the form was acknowledged an autonomous role while content remained open to an ideological heteronomy?

Spirituality and Creativity

Another approach to the relation between art and religion was developed by the North-American philosopher and scholar of religion Earle J. Coleman in his "religious aesthetic."[40] In Coleman it is not ideas of "beauty" that define aesthetics; it is the concepts of "spirituality" and "creativity." Coleman rejects both the thesis about the similar identities of art and religion and the thesis that they are fundamentally different. Instead he argues for complementarity and claims that art and religion "are complementary responses to the quest of self-realization."[41] In a cross cultural oriented study Coleman devotes himself to the analysis of classical religious texts – Taoist texts and texts by Saint Teresa of Avila, in addition to texts by artists and a selection of scholars. The project of religious aesthetics is redefined as an interdisciplinary and multicultural undertaking.

According to Coleman, there are five observations that support his thesis about complementarity and convergence of art and religion.[42] First, both are found in all societies. The pluralism of art reflects the diversity of world religions, all of which have some form of conception of truth. Second, religion enables us to grasp the revelatory potential of art. Third, art gives religion a mode of expression without which it would have been destined to silence. Further, art and religion share some common fundamental existential experiences, and fifth and final they are both, just like ethics, "axiological spheres" that produce values and criteria for valuation. Moreover, according to Coleman, all religion is artistic.[43]

There is also a strong resemblance between saints and artists, according to Coleman, and he draws an analogy between the mystical experience and the artist's creative power, in which divine creation is regarded as "the model for artistic creativity."[44] In response to Martin Buber's relational philosophy Coleman poses a basic requirement for the creativity of religion,[45] and later he develops a four-part schema for creativity, going from "inception" to "incubation" to "inspiration" and finally "work."[46]

While in the introduction to his book, Coleman proposes equality between art and religion, he develops a somewhat different view in the concluding theoretical discussion: "Art is after all a part of religion," he says, and further he claims that art is "a means to the ultimate end of religious fulfillment."[47]

In the conclusion Coleman summarizes his view of the relation between religion as spirituality and art seen as creativity in the assertion that religion relies on art to create unity and self-integration and that great religious art always springs from a personal completeness.[48] Spiritual awareness itself is according to Coleman aesthetic in its nature.[49]

Similar to a number of other accounts, including that of Martin, Coleman also offers a logocentric definition of the relation between art and religion, albeit with other implications than the conventional beauty concept. Nevertheless, this means that his theory is subject to the criticism and objection that it is based on reductionist conceptions both in relation to art and religion. Is religion really just spiritual mysticism? And is art really mostly an expression of religious experiences? Although Coleman meritoriously sheds light on one – among several other – obvious dimension in the relation between art and religion, it is simply not possible to accept his attempt to develop a universal definition of the relation between the two.

In Light of God's Alterity

One of the most comprehensive and profiled attempts at a (post)modern theology of art is offered by the North American theologian Mark C. Taylor. He discusses theologians' general suspicion towards art and criticizes, in particular, Karl Barth and his commentary on the Epistle to the Romans for rendering suspect all cultural advances and for regarding art as a sign of human corruption.

Taylor justly stresses that too much emphasis on God's transcendence may lead to a nihilism that drains all worldly matters of spiritual qualities. If God is completely different from all, every discourse on God will remain empty. The emphasis on transcendence leads to God's death. The sign of alterity becomes a sign for nothingness. Taylor asks, "How to refigure disfiguring by figuring nothing?"[50] For Taylor the interaction between religion and aesthetics is not important; rather, it is the interaction between religion and visual arts that matters.[51] Thus he leaves the theological constraint with philosophical aesthetics and makes visual arts the key dialogue partner for theology. His book is distinguished by its comprehensive and detailed analyses of art objects in light of the makers of art and of the context. Theology, in compliance with the postmodern Zeitgeist, Taylor wishes to develop as an "a/theology," that is, as a venture that both relates to the negative tradition of classical theology and to a theology beyond debates on theism and of the type god-is-dead.

A constructive and reconstructive exploration of contemporary art opens an alternative space of theological imagination for Taylor.

Taylor bases his theory in Kierkegaard's tripartite division with an aesthetic, ethical, and religious phase, and he wishes to put greater emphasis on the aesthetic stage. With reference to Hegel he presents an approach to the three eras of modern art, but without interpreting these periods evolutionary.

"Disfiguring" is a main concept in Taylor's analysis. He identifies three different strategies of disfiguring in modern art: (a) the abstract non-figurative art, (b) the figurative revival in for example pop art, and (c) something in-between abstraction and figuration in contemporary art. Taylor affiliates with the postmodern ideology and defines the goals of art and religion as redefining their goals after the destruction of modernity.[52]

Taylor also presents an appealing account of the parallels between the discourses of art and of theology. The pioneers of abstract modernism are interpreted in light of iconoclasm, and Le Corbusier and van der Rohe are analysed in light of the comprehensive belief systems of Barth and Thomas. Art's transformation to a commodity and its self-critique, especially in Kurt Schwitters, Taylor places in relation to the criticism of the instrumentalization of the image of god in the god-is-dead theology.

Taylor is particularly influenced by the German artist Anselm Kieffer, and he demonstrates convincingly how this artist struggles with the same problems that have been a recurring theme in the Jewish-Christian tradition for a long time, for example, the relation between God's presence and absence, between emergence and disappearance.

Similarly, Taylor argues convincingly that there is a remarkable agreement between art history and the history of theology in the twentieth century on common issues.[53] Artists come across as important contributors to the theological discourse. It is quite clear that Taylor sees a great potential for developing the theological discourse on the premises of art analysis.

In the chapter "A/Theoesthetics" Taylor repeats his pun with "a/theology" and indicates his rejection of theoaesthetics as metaphysical basis for art theology. "A/Theology" is for Taylor "a nonnegative negative theology that nonetheless is positive."[54] Instead, what is important is the experience that the things we know nothing about are concealed behind a boundary. God remains the absolute difference but he is still present through his absence.

Taylor uses the double negation to avoid a purely positive definition of God and at the same time to be able to continue developing the theological discourse. The dream of the utopia of hope and the possibility of salvation should be abandoned by the theologian, paving the way for a better justified "ethic of resistance." Taylor considers both oppression and struggle as eternal processes. The text of art becomes an "allograph," a writing of the "other"; it writes in the other but cannot represent the other.[55]

Despite the fact that Taylor displays an open-hearted sensitivity for modern visual arts – which he gives a meritorious methodological interpretation in a "second" discourse in relation to theology's challenging discussion beyond the struggle with God's existence – there is room for some criticism.

Why must Taylor's "a/theology" reject all soteriology and eschatology for his theological analysis of twentieth century art? Will this rejection not defeat the artists' clearly expressed visions and driving forces in the hope of a different world and new humankind? Does Taylor drain art of its moral power[56] and ethical potential?[57]

Personally I would rather make use of all of the loci of systematic theology in order not to reduce the diversity of artistic expression. From a theological perspective one should object that Taylor's abandonment of soteriology, and his categorical refusal to reflect on God´s liberating work, hardly solves the disparity between the doctrine of creation and the doctrine of salvation. Rather, the problem is dislocated to a vague idea of the eternal and obscure alterity of God and of being.

Similar to the criticism directed against the philosophy of alterity based on the concept "otherness"[58] – which eventually only makes the other to a reverse projection of the self – one may question whether in Taylor's alterity concept the concept of God is too closely tied to the perspective on humanity. If God is "the other," is s/he not then tied to us, that is, to our conceptions about what the one is, which in turn controls our conception of what the other is in relation to the one?

Thirdly, some objections based in the tradition of classical theology, which Taylor wishes to affiliate himself to, are also in place. According to apophatic theologians of late antiquity it is the awareness of the unattainable in God's nature that enables and advises us to talk positively about God's work, that is, about God's worldly and historical acts of salvation. The classical apophatic and negative theologies necessarily end in a positive reflection over God's economy, God's liberating work.

However, according to Taylor, postmodern theology should desist this reflection. Hence he reduces theology's interpretative task to seek God's disappearance-appearance traces in a hopelessly abandoned universe. The feeling oscillates between absence and presence, the dialectic experience of a zigzagging gesticulation becomes a self-fulfilling goal. There is not really a trace of a God who acts in the scenery of the floundering Taylor. It is therefore relevant to ask whether Taylor's a/theoaesthetic eventually only falls back on an ancient theo-ontology in a modern alterity philosophical disguise and without ethical relevance.

Art and Transcendence

The German Protestant theologian Günter Rombold uses a more conventional conceptual apparatus based in art's transcendental quality. For Rombold all experience has a sensuous and a spiritual dimension, including the production and reception of works of art.[59] A work of art is, according to Rombold, a sketch of the world, a "Weltentwurf" (literally a draft of the world).[60] In his comprehensive study of the importance of opposition in modern art,[61] Rombold represents the thesis that art ever since the Enlightenment "expresses a deep disturbance over and a state where humankind is emancipated from the world as it is."[62] In art making it is divine qualities of humankind that constitute the *homo creator*. Rombold highlights three quality measures for a work of art. It must be embodied, ingenious, and intensive (tight).[63]

The transgression of art points, according to Rombold, in three directions: an anthropological, a cosmological, and a theological direction.[64] Works of art contain, he claims, drafts of views of humanity and of worldviews, and they also refer to absoluteness. Transcendence is not a finite but an open concept in Rombold. Transcendence identifies what religion and art share. While art offers creative proposals for outlooks on life, religion seeks the purpose of existence and the ethical actions of the individual. Both develop a claim of absoluteness and may come into conflict with each other.

56

Rombold discusses how modern art visualizes the incomprehensibility of absoluteness. Imageless pictures of an ultimate reality come into existence. Rombold argues that the theology of art must let go of the idea of a predominantly Christian symbolism.[65] Symbols are not ontologically static but contingent on the context and variable according to conventions. The idea is that some symbols should be more Christian than others seems unreasonable in this context. Just like Tillich and Rahner asserted that religion equals transcendental experience, Rombold now wants to give art the same definition.

Like Rombold, the Catholic theologian Friedhelm Mennekes seeks to base the intersection of faith and visual arts on the search for the meaning of existence. For Mennekes, myth and art are different primitives for the mediation of meaning. Both art and religion seek to expand the concept of experience, and there is, according to Mennekes, a special artistic way of understanding the world.[66] While religion for Mennekes is a contemplative form of self-transcendence, art is an embodying type of self-transcendence.

The benefit of using the concept of transcendence in the theology of art is that one may approach a substantial share of the objects of modern art with an open mind. Hence one may describe the diversity and extent to which artists have dedicated themselves to spiritual issues, either through spiritually laden form experiments or direct iconic references. The catch, however, is that this approach makes almost everything subject to theological interpretation with regards to the search for existential meaning.

There is a risk that reception aesthetics controls production aesthetics and that the art objects are incorporated into a view of Christianity that interprets everything in light of a vague concept of faith and divinity. Is there a risk that the specificity of art and of Christian theology will subside if one interprets art in general words as existential, and existentiality just as generally in the light of faith? Is the theologian of art keeping the door open in order to sneak in a confessional concept of God in the guise of general transcendentalism?

Art as the Language of Religion

In contrast to Rombold and Mennekes, the German Protestant theologian Rainer Volp argues for a semiotically oriented view of the theology of art. Volp regards the metamorphosis of the visual realm in modern art as an important challenge to religion to which so far too few scholars of religion have paid attention. The visual sphere is transformed; the minds undergo a revolution.[67]

The religious challenge of visual art is summarized in the three concepts *aisthesis*, *poiesis*, and *mimesis* (perception, creation, and imitation).[68] Visual art creates an unpredictable sign relation which we try to perceive. It expands the expressive potential of creativity and produces experiences. Religion needs art, Volp asserts. Without art the living rite evaporates and becomes mere convention.[69]

Volp bases his argumentation in a quote from Schleiermacher and regards art as a language of religion: "Like language relates to knowledge art relates to religion."[70] Volp describes how many artists are disappointed with the established Churches and with "religion having lost its power to produce metaphysical horror."[71] Therefore they have taken over the areas and tasks of religion.

In addition to interpreting art as a semiotic phenomenon and as a medium for religion,

Volp also highlights the power of art to embody ideas.[72] According to Volp, the ethical dimension of art is found exactly in this ability to create. Art contributes to widening the scope for decisions.

As long as one regards Volp's conception as a tool for raising interest for the encounter with visual arts in Churches and in theology it is unproblematic. However, if we understand his approach in relation to general validity claims as regards the nature of art, the issue becomes more complex. Is all art a language of religion?[73] Why should the art theory of semiotics in itself be the most suitable ground for a theology of art?

Art and Theology as Interpretations of Life

While older theoaesthetics and even some art philosophers of the twentieth century, for example Adorno and Picht, used the truth concept to investigate the relation between art and religion, this approach is completely rejected by the German theologians Wolfgang Erich Müller and Jürgen Heumann.[74] They believe that the idea that art is a tool for expressing revelations of truth limits the freedom of art and continues to maintain the power of rationality over creativity.

Instead Müller and Heumann refer to Hegel's insight about the subjectivity of art, Nietzsche's critique of metaphysics and Eco's thesis about "the open work" of art which is characterized by a diversity of different potential interpretations. Müller and Heumann use the state of secularization as a point of departure and observe the demise of religious interpretations as the favoured explanation of all lifeworlds. In the modern, secularized, pluralist society, religion cannot intersperse with art claiming precedence in relation to finding the meaning of existence.[75]

In agreement with Ernst Cassirer's symbol theory, Müller and Heumann regard art and religion as separate symbolic forms of culture which both interpret reality. And both express views of life in a multitude of different perspectives.

The art objects may in this approach not be used to support theological dogmas. Instead the same reality is analysed but within different frames of reference. Art and religion are "vermittelte Rede," mediated talk about reality.[76] An important feature of contemporary art views is the positive attitude to the wide range of interpretations. Hence, a uniform understanding of theology's view of art in general becomes problematic. In addition to expanding the dialogue between art and theology, Müller and Heumann are eager to clarify theology's relation to the world and its importance for the interpretation of life.[77]

The English theologian George Pattison assumes that the role of religion in modern society has changed. He seeks a theologically informed view of art which can help theology to accept visual art "on its own terms as a unique and irreplaceable interpretation of reality and, as such, of great human and religious significance."[78] Also in this context art is a form of interpreting life and reality which builds on its own specific premises. As such, according to Pattison, it also has religious significance, which obviously presupposes the – not entirely uncomplicated – assumption that reality itself one way or the other has a religious dimension.[79]

Pattison concurs with the postmodern criticism of the great ideologies, the metaphysical assertions, and the history of progress, and he regards the open-mindedness towards new perspectives and ideas as an asset, especially for theology.[80]

Pattison demonstrates how the history of theology, especially in the West, is dominated by the hostility to images of iconoclasm. Augustine's ambiguity in relation to matter and beauty influenced medieval thinkers and later also Calvin, and it contributed to the negative theology of the image of the Reformation. This tradition stretches even into the twentieth century to Karl Barth's corroboration of Calvin's idea that images and symbols did not have a place in a house of Protestant worship.[81]

It was only with Romanticism that a positive Christian view of art became possible. Kierkegaard, however, joined the iconoclast tradition when he restored religion's pre-eminence over aesthetics. However, the issue at stake was not to condemn art but to develop a critique of civilization based on the iconoclast tradition. In a complacent time of "commercial self-gratification" which elevates art to a fundamental value, Pattison concludes, based on Kierkegaard, that faith must direct attention to the total emptiness and humankind's existential reliance on the grace of God.[82] All the same, Pattison pertinently questions whether Kierkegaard's view of the relation between art and religion as conflict is the only possible view.

The neo-Thomistic interpretation based on the vision of a Christian culture is also rejected by Pattison, as it is grounded in philosophical claims about knowledge that no longer seem reasonable and reliable. Plainly Pattison establishes that the story of natural theology in the classical tradition is not a good foundation for the establishment of the relation between art and religion, as it maintains faith's heteronymous claim to power over art.[83]

Pattison shows how the Western Christian tradition is characterized by a continuous distrust of visual elements which has its roots in classical Platonism. Further, he shows how the theological art discussion throughout has been located in the discourse of natural theology, where the dominance of faith over art has been justified as it has come to be seen as an expression for knowledge about the Creator and of creation.

Pattison develops his approach under the label "Restoring the Image." He maintains soteriology as the theological discipline most appropriate for a theology of art. For Pattison, the processes of seeing are of inevitable importance in people's lives, and therefore the theology of art must reflect on how these processes relate to redemption.[84] Consequently, the main focus shifts from metaphysics and philosophy of art to a reflection of embodiment and vision – art and theology put the focus on people's corporeality. The theology of art does not belong with natural theology but with a "theology of redemption." In accordance with Küng, Pattison claims that art forestalls God's Messianic kingdom.[85]

In the context of globalization and the dialogue of religion, Pattison ascribes art with a positive significance as it visualizes the specific religious tradition in a very lucid manner, which enhances the dialogue. Further, it is important for people's apprehension of their religious tradition that they become aware of their seeing.

The task of art theology is, according to Pattison, to cancel the sharp distinction between nature and grace which has been characteristic of interpretations of Western Christianity. "Christian secularity" should be perceived as a "total transformation of our relation to nature, to the visible, material world and to our carnal, bodily involvement in the world."[86] Redemption is thus not liberation *from* this world but *to* this world. The knowledge about God's liberation enables us to recognize the beauty and goodness of nature.

An asset of Pattison's approach is that he assigns to art and the visual realm the independence and autonomy which, in my opinion, is paramount for any trustworthy theology of art today.

Additionally, Pattison clearly identifies the reasons why it is impossible to claim faith's supremacy over art through various iconoclastic or image-controlling theo-dogmatic systems. I completely concur with his plea for a soteriological definition of the theology of art, but I am not entirely convinced that Pattison ultimately lives up to his own demands for the theology of art beyond the natural theology.

If theology's view of art means that it will sharpen its focus on the beauty and goodness of creation because of an increased awareness of seeing, could it not still become an instrument for theology's own purposes? Is it not possible that works of art may make visible the pain, the agony, the meaninglessness, and the repulsiveness of creation? Is it not the case that Pattison ultimately presupposes that nature in itself is good, that is, that the Creator and creation on some level are ontologically united? If this is, indeed, the case, then Pattison's theology of art will dim the vision that it sets out to sharpen of the need of salvation among humankind and in creation.

It is hardly sufficient to formulate the objective of the theology of art as "recognizing" God's beauty in nature. A theology of art should also aim at visualizing the agony of creation under the powers of evil, its hope of liberation from these powers, and God's liberating actions. Pattison's argumentation is a helpful guide to a future theology of art developed on a soteriological principle.

Widening the Sensibilities of Theology

In his book *A Theology of Artistic Sensibilities* the North American theologian John Dillenberger asks whether theology in its discourse may cover other mental modalities.[87] Dillenberger discusses both theologians who give visual arts a place in theology and theologians who deny its importance. Karl Barth, Rudolf Bultmann, Schubert Ogden, and Gordon Kaufman are criticized for undervaluing art, while Edward Farley, Langdon Gilkey, George Lindbeck, Paul Tillich, John Cobb, and Mark C. Taylor regard art as important. Dillenberger also shows how some theologians perceive art as a model for the work of theology (viz. Balthasar, Rahner, Hart, Tracy), and he highlights, in agreement with Müller/Heumann, the benefits of pluralism also in theology.

Dillenberger's own approach is based on theology's need to widen its sensibility and move away from the limitations of the linguistic dimension. He pleads for a "theology of wider sensibilities." Dillenberger claims that in the West, language has been deprived of the power of imagination and language has won dominance over the visual expression of reality.[88]

Therefore, artists may help theologians with a "reappropriation of the visual." In order to turn the narrow focus on linguistic expressions Dillenberger demands that the visual and artistic dimensions are integrated into the theological education programmes.

Dillenberger's theology of art is more practically and theoretically oriented. Quite simply, it is based on the notion that looking at art will cause a well of experiences that widen people's mental capacities. Hence, it widens the horizon of the theologian who is overly concerned with text and language, enabling him/her to embrace other forms of expression; expressions that materialize visually in nature and optical phenomena that are processed by the artist. Together with his wife, the art historian Jane Dillenberger,[89] Dillenberger has given a number of courses and created educational programmes in the borderland between visual arts and theology, and the Dillenberger couple are regarded as the most influential representatives of an applied theology of art, although this theology – on purpose (?) – is not backed by art philosophical or systematic-theological reflections. The Dillenburgers' pedagogical demands for a sensible and open, interpretative approach to art is a focal component of a dialogically competent theology of art. It is the entrance requirement for any theology that wishes to approach the works of visual art. Theoretically, however, I understand Dillenberger's word and image rich contribution mainly as an argument for theologically qualified – and sorely needed – art pedagogy.

The Symbolism of Beauty – the Theology of the Icon in the Eastern Church

"Beauty will save the world," says a Dostoyevsky quotation often cited by Orthodox theologians. The relationship of the Eastern theological tradition to image-making, icon paintings and the design of church space deserves a chapter, if not a book, on its own.[90] The reason why I include it here is that this very strong and influential part of the history of the theology of the image should not be forgotten or ignored.

Because the theologians of the icon of the Eastern Church in contrast to the theologians henceforth discussed are critical towards or blatantly refute the history of modern visual arts and its claim for autonomy, it is pertinent to include them in the group of other theologians who consciously try to develop a visual theology.

In the following, I will first describe briefly some fundamental features of the historically developed concept of the icon as a tool for God's revelation before proceeding to discuss the theologies of the image of the Russian theologian, natural scientist and poet Pavel Florensky and the Russian-French emigrant theologian Paul Evdokimov.

The Historical, Spiritual and Political Dimension of Icons

In the first known Christian visual representations, the artists used the symbol of the lamb and the fish. There were also occasional representations of Christ and Mary. The Christian visual realm was related to Hellenist art and paintings, miniatures, or sarcophagus reliefs were based on a Hellenistic image template. The Christian tradition evolved in the midst of the idol veneration of antiquity and the image ban in Judaism.[91] When the Christian persecution ended the visual representations gained in significance, and during late antiquity an independent Christian image realm evolved which eventually was accompanied by the reflections of theologians. The Christian theologians also followed the Hellenistic tradition theoretically, and they interpreted the images ontologically as being physical representations of the divine without the implications that the image and its divine model in essence would meld together. The icon was a part of God's reality and gave a visual insight into God's work. For example, in the sixth century Dionysius created a semiotic theory according to which signs that were different from the model were highlighted as the most suitable for apophatically representing God's incomprehensible and unattainable essence.

In several periods, icon veneration was the source of theological and political dissent where the imperial elites, possibly under the influence of Arabic conceptions of images, rejected and banned the use of images for liturgical use. During the second phase of iconoclasm, however, the iconodulic theologians defeated the iconoclasts and they developed a cogent theological defence, primarily through an interpretation of the mystery of the incarnation.

Considering that God himself had taken human shape it was regarded as perfectly feasible also to give God's revelation a physical manifestation in images, although the awareness of God's invisible essence had to be retained. The iconoclasm contributed to defeating the hegemony of the word, and "'logos' and 'eikon' acquired equal magnitude" in Eastern Christianity.[92] In Western Christianity, however, the image remained subordinate to the word and primarily served as a catechetical tool, a pedagogical method for presenting biblical interpretations and theology, an attitude that was adopted by the Lutheran tradition without questioning.

From late antiquity through the Middle Ages, icon painting was developed both in the East and the West, and it became an important element first and foremost in the life and teachings of the Eastern Church. After the collapse of the Byzantine Empire the heritage was developed further in the tradition of the Russian-Orthodox Church, and the central codes of the theology of the icon are preserved even today. Icon worship belongs to a special piety that develops a unique sensibility for the symbolic and educational function of the icon.[93] The icon is a window to God's heavenly realm. It gives the devout viewer a part in God's liberating history. The iconic image repeals the distance between image and archetype and brings the worshipper closer to God. The Eastern Church can regard not only the painted image but the entire world as an icon of God. The making of icons is subject to very strict rules.[94] Personal touch is indeed valued but it should stay within the frames defined by the tradition.

At a fundamental level the theology of icons is characterized by a dogmatic symbolism, where the pictorial elements are conceived of as physical signs of spiritual representations of the message dogmatically formulated by theologians. Art and the image have no inherent power or autonomy. It is the belief systems of theologians that control the production, liturgical use and reception of images. The image is subject to dogmatic heteronomy, although it is also perceived as a tool in God's own redemptive actions.

After the sixteenth century there is a decline in the icon painting tradition, even in Russia – which in the context of Russia's encounter with the West is often blamed on the contempt in Italian art of the medieval[95] or the aspiration for mathematical precision in renaissance art[96] – and it is not until the nineteenth century that icon painting experiences a revival.[97] We will meet two of the representatives for this revival shortly. Recently we have witnessed a soaring interest for icon paintings, even in cultures that on the surface are highly secularized. In the context of new religious movements emerging, the spiritual image laden with tradition is an easy way of maintaining material contact with a spiritual, underlying reality. To which extent this new image veneration and contemplative production harmonize with the life and teachings of the traditional conception of the image is, mildly put, unclear and I will not pursue the issue any further.

Another interesting dimension is related to the political implications of icon theology. In a thought-provoking manner, Per Arne Bodin has pointed out the connection between the image programme of the Eastern Church and the symbols used in Russian society after the October Revolution. Even in the Soviet Union the leaders appeared as ideal saints and they were portrayed in huge paintings. Just as in liturgy, the state representatives were carried in visual processions for public display.

One a more fundamental level, the ontology of the theology of the image was in agreement with politics, where the sign was perceived as an essential component of reality.[98] The Russian leaders adopted this thousand-year-old Eastern Church tradition where one visualized the spiritual reality by depiction, and they used ritualization and visualization to express their conviction of the new social order.[99] The spiritual existence of the Soviet state materialized in image processions and in liturgies for the masses in the parades.

What can visual theology learn from the unhappy marriages, first with the Byzantine and later the Soviet empire? Can the awareness about this transfer make the theology of art more self-critical, especially with regard to its claim to the answer to true nature of being? Should one not refrain from claiming the superiority of the religious image – which, moreover, is developed within a specific confession and culture – in relation to the divine origin and the primal image of all things at all times and in all spaces?

The Reversed Perspective

From 1910 onwards Russian philosophers of religion sought after holistic interpretations of the theological, liturgical and aesthetic meanings of icons. This movement was part of a general aspiration among intellectual theologians to recognize and renew the Russian Orthodox heritage, especially among former Marxist philosophers.

One of the most significant attempts at reinterpreting the icon is found in the physicist, mathematician, theologian and poet Pavel Florensky (1882–1937).[100] In connection wi8th the Soviet state's appropriation of the properties of the Russian-Orthodox Church after 1918 Florensky was given a leading position in the "Commission for the protection of monuments and art treasures of The Trinity Lavra of St Sergius." Florensky tried to preserve the valuable relics of the monastery, unfortunately without any success. In 1927, Stalin's occupation of the Patriarchate prompted a wave of protests in which Florensky also took part. Later his refusal to leave his benefice and his continued resistance led to his deportation to the Solovetsky Monastery in northwest Russia, which had been turned into a special prison, and presumably he suffered a martyr's death there in 1937.

The text collection "The reversed perspective" gathers some of Florensky's central texts from the struggle to preserve the cultural environment.[101] The icon is, for Florensky, a revelation of the archetype, which we can experience sensuously in the depiction.[102] The icon has the capacity to "create a new reality"; it makes visible the archetype and opens the unworldly for perception.[103] For Florensky, the icon is of greater significance than written, literary documents.[104]

In a detailed study Florensky investigates the historical and theoretical dimensions of icons. He ascribes great significance to the development of the so-called reversed perspective, the representation of shadows, and the polycentrism of the visual realm. On a fundamental level, Florensky assumes that perspective is inextricably connected to the underlying worldview of the art style in question in its historical context. Florensky points out that the consistent perspective did only appear in the context of the theatrical stage in antiquity to replace reality with illusion. He regarded decoration as a pursuit of verisimilitude, not of the truth of life, as an "imitation of the surface."[105]

Later Florensky identifies an historical decay of the perspective after the fifth century. This is connected with the medieval apprehension of reality as a gift, which he contrasts to the modern subjectivism characterized by illusionism. Florensky regards the theatre perspective as a reduction of space, which he considers as "neither simplistic, uniform nor unstructured," or as a simple category. "But it [space] is in itself – originally reality, thoroughly structured, nowhere indifferent and it even has an internal order and an internal structure."[106] Hence Florensky does not interpret the loss of perspective in the Middle Ages as lack of knowledge but as a conscious refusal to structure the open space.

In this view, the development of perspective in renaissance painting appears as a gigantic restriction. According to Florensky, Giotto produces stage decorations and he replaces liturgy with illusionary art and God's actions with acting.[107]

As regards the icon, Florensky bases his approach on the assumption that all representation is sin and that the perspective can only be understood within the frame of the painting's symbolic objective.[108] Florensky criticizes the view of space as a geometric Euclidian entity and he rejects the belief of the Enlightenment that humans can gain knowledge about the world. Against the reductionist and distorted perception of space and the created, spiritual reality, which finds its expression in Western central perspective, Florensky places the reversed perspective of the icon.

This is far from being misconstrued; it is based on an underlying symbolic metaphysical view of life. The breach of the rules of perspective creates, for example, together with the special colour compositions (*raskryschki*), a special gaze.[109] The lack of focal point is justified by the knowledge about the impossibility of experiencing or knowing anything about the place and nature of God. The absence of parallel lines and the polycentrism of icons create a theologically motivated view of the diversity of the creation.

Art is, for Florensky, "not psychological but ontological," it "is the true revelation of the archetype. Art indeed shows a new and for us hitherto unavailable reality."[110] Theologically, Florensky bases his conception of the image in the mystery of the Incarnation, which for him creates the potential that "the absolute content of life" and "the perfectly good" can become real and corporeal.[111] The technique for making the icon painting embodies concrete metaphysics. The image is God's tool for becoming visible and open to experience in creation.

The Image of Beauty

The life of the Russian-French theologian Paul Evdokimov (1901–1970) was also influenced by the drama of the twentieth century. After the Revolution, Evdokimov emigrates to France, defends a thesis on evil in Dostoyevsky and belongs to the first ecumenically open generation among the eminent Eastern Church theologians. In the monograph, *The Art of the Icon: A Theology of Beauty*,

Evdokimov lays out his comprehensive theology of the icon.

With a number of examples from the Bible and the writings of the Church Fathers, Evdokimov builds up his fundamental thesis that the Holy Spirit of God is revealed in beauty.[112] For Evdokimov, the patristic tradition is the basis for a theology where God allows us to take part in his beauty.[113] The beauty of God is perceived cosmologically, making the entire creation one single visual theology.

Bearing in mind what has been said previously about theoaesthetics' identification of the nature of reality with the nature of God and art's capacity to disclose this true being, both Evdokimov and Florensky and most other theologians of Eastern Christianity appear as late representatives of theoaesthetics.

For Evdokimov, the artist reveals "the reinstated fullness of being and enables us to contemplate over its ideal aspects."[114] True beauty cannot exist in nature itself but only in the revelation of the transcendental; in this sense all beauty is some form of the incarnation of God.[115] The reference to the "logos" of God in the Gospel of John, Evdokimov interprets metaphorically in such a way that the visualization of the word of God is the focus and "the visual nature of the Word" is emphasized.[116]

The artist is, for Evdokimov, together with the scientist and the philosopher, representative of God's clergy on earth, where every piece of work can become a sacrament for transforming the culture to a "theophanic meeting place." The aim of culture is to become a doxology, a song of praise, within the cosmic liturgy.[117]

Similar to Florensky, Evdokimov develops a symbolic understanding of images. For him the symbol itself contains the presence of what is symbolized.[118] The icon creates a movement that leads the viewer to the symbols, so that, for example, even the architecture of a church takes part in the mystery of the liturgy. The liturgy is perceived by Evdokimov as "a visualisation, an iconic representation of the entire salvation history."[119]

Theologically, Evdokimov places the greatest emphasis on the doctrine of the Holy Spirit and he interprets iconography as an expression of the doctrine of the Spirit, pneumatology.[120] The Spirit of beauty identifies, according to him, the semblance to Christ and makes the image an icon, a contemplated beauty of the word of God.[121]

Evdokimov reads the epistemological principle of apophatic theology such that the icon confirms God to be "a meta-icon," or in Dionysius' terms "hyper-icon," an above/beyond-image.[122] Consequently, God is placed beyond all positive confirmation and beyond all negative denial. Christologically, Evdokimov thought-provokingly interprets the humanity of Christ as an image of his divinity: "...the humanity of Christ is the image of his divinity."[123] In the context of salvation history, Evdokimov ascribes huge influence to the icon as it is "a symbolic-personal representation which invites us to transcend the symbol and join in community with the represented person and take part in the indescribable. The icon is a path which one must travel in order to transcend it."[124] In agreement with classical theology, Evdokimov describes his theology of the icon as "iconographic apophatism."[125]

However, because of its dogmatic connection to theoaesthetics grounded in the Hellenistic synthesis of an antique ontology and a Christian worldview, Evdokimov sadly does not manage to bridge his traditional theology of the image and the developments within modern art. Problematically, he seconds Florensky's critique of the central perspective but in a comprehensive and detailed chapter he categorically rejects modern art as a whole in one single sweep.

Already with the illusionism of Giotto, modern art lost its potential to relate to God and the transcendent. Abstract art is, according to Evdokimov, held captive by "dominating forces," it is denaturalized and desacralized.[126] When art attempts to be theurgic it gives itself over to magical powers.[127] Occult symbols are important in the trendy veneration of masks. Art has completely drained God's unattainable image of meaning.[128] Non-figurative art denies reality with its creative energy.[129] Abstract art has nothing that can tell us the Word has become flesh.[130] In the light of a theology of wisdom, art seems in Evdokimov's view to build on an exhausted *sophia* and it only gives us a false sense of the magical moment.[131] The theological correspondence of disfiguration is the demythologization of the Bible.[132]

Evdokimov completely ignores the fact that Florensky's emphasis of the supposedly traditional theology of icons in a national-romantic spirit develops in an historical perspective in parallel with both the Russian-Orthodox traditionalistic theology and not least with the artistic quest for the primitive, for example, in Kasimir Malewitsch's quest for the new absolute icon.[133]

One can only regret that a creative and erudite theologian like Evdokimov resorts to such a rabid and unfounded denunciation of the image-making of modernism. In the history of ideas this side of his theology appears as an ideologically unfounded, anti-modernist traditionalism.

Hopefully, the theme of this book will make a positive contribution to the challenge of formulating a cogent new interpretation of the free spirituality of modern art equally important to the theologians of the Eastern Christianity. It hardly is a value in itself to defend the ancient Hellenistic ontological image programme as the only feasible philosophical foundation for a theology of art that harmonizes with the Christian tradition. Other theologians of the icon, working in the spirit of Florensky and Evdokimov, seem to confuse the task of defending an ancient ontology with the task of developing a soteriological reflection on God's actions in, with and through image-making at different times.

The link to a specific culture- and context-dependent type and style of pictorial representations should not be combined with absolute theological claims. The consequence would be that the mystery of God's autonomous and liberating actions is dominated by theologians who assume that doctrines evolving in a specific context at a specific time have some kind of universal and eternal validity. The theology of art, on the other hand, investigates God's actions in the visual realm at different times. It does not need to defend the image-making of a specific period and one philosophy of art against another. God's actions are liberating through the images of different cultures.

Models of Theology of Art

What is the position of the different theological models of interpretation relative to each other in connection with the challenge of reflecting on the relationship between art and religion?

In this final section I will group the various approaches to the theology of art into four models. A model is an idealization constructed to make a complex reality appear simpler.[134] Volp presents three perspectives of five different models of the theory of art in his overview of the relation between art and religion,[135] while the acclaimed anthology of Henrich and Iser has ten theoretical types in the classification of topical, representative art theories,[136] which makes it possible to relate different theologies of art to their classification. In the following I will use both these classifications and supplement them with examples from the previous historical and systematic sections.

The Ontological Model

A definition of art which is grounded in a reflection on the nature of art leads to an ontologically defined theology of art. "Ontology" is a sub-discipline of philosophy devoted to the study of being. Ontological statements are arguments pertaining to how things "are," in our case, what and how art is. It is the general conception of art that guides the analyses of the individual works of art, which are seen as expressions of art. An ontological theology of art is grounded in the view that art is uniform in nature and that one can have unequivocal knowledge about its nature and being.

Criticism of essentialist approaches, that is, theories of art that focus on the nature of art, has emphasized their failure to account for historical and contextual factors that influence artistic creation. Further, it is pertinent to ask if an ontological determination of what art is could entail a reduction of the autonomy of art and the visual medium. Is an ontological theology of art an authoritarian ideology aimed at construing precedence for definition, as the view of what art "is" is expressed in words and in relation to current and culturally variable value systems? Does art exist at such a level that one may describe its nature with conceptual-linguistic expressions? It seems problematic that an art theology today should choose an ontological formulation similar to that of the older theoaesthetics.

Another theological view of art that leads to an ontological rejection of art is represented by Karl Barth, whose reduction of all reality to the word of God raised suspicion towards visual art. Paul Tillich is subject to the critical question of whether his theology of art is about the dialectic of being between what ultimately concerns us, that is, God, and the forms of expressions of art. Even the theologians of Eastern Christianity are subject to this objection. Does our conception of what the basis of being is control the analysis of the works of art, reducing these to expressions of divine being? Does the ontological theology of art maintain and preserve theology's supremacy over aesthetics?

The Historical Model

In this model the relation between art and religion is determined by a comparison of different historical epochs and concomitant symbolic systems. As we saw, Hegel assumed a development from a lower to a higher stage while Tillich differentiated between different stylistic religious types. Both Hegel and Tillich must answer to the criticism that their interpretation of history is far too contingent upon an ethnocentric understanding of the excellence of our own culture. In Hegel's case, this ethnocentricity manifests itself in the view that the perceived excellence of one´s own culture is the ultimate aim of development, and in Tillich's case it manifests itself in a fascination for contemporary expressive art.

However, it is not necessary to base an historically-oriented theology of art in the notion of a development from a lower to a higher level. Research in art history may naturally, and without a valuation of different epochs, dedicate itself to comparative research focusing on the interaction of conflict and continuity, between preservation and renewal. Both the engravings of Ice Age art, and the political graphic art of the 1960s, and their internal relationship and differences, can be studied in such an historical perspective.

A theology of art that is developed according to the historical model should be capable of working in analogy with art history. Its main objective would be to investigate to what extent the relations between religious expressions and visual, artistic expressions have been subjected to the dialectic between continuity and change.

We find in Tillich and his analogies between religious faith and artistic types an attempt at such an approach, even though these analogies have proved not to be analytically valid. Eliade's category, "the Sacred," also offers the possibility for an historically differentiated analysis. Furthermore, the discourse about the relationship between myth and art has mainly made use of an historical approach, where the concepts from antiquity studies have found a wider application.

The symbol theories have also provided a concept that makes it possible to focus on what is retained through various processes of change. Symbols, on the one hand, change over time and succumb to cultural changes. It is therefore important to be aware that even the content and form of symbols are subject to the dialectic of change. On the other hand, symbols may also have a preserving function in the processes of change, which makes the concept of symbol suitable for an explanation of the alteration between change and continuity.

If symbolization is regarded as the task of art, as Susanne Langer says,[137] then art theology may investigate religious content by focusing on the motifs and iconography of art. The risk associated with the approach grounded in symbol theory, however, is that the expression of the work of art is reduced to a carrier of religious content. The form-content distinction, however, should on no account be made the motivation for a differentiated approach to the theology of art as it counters the insight of the iconic difference of images and creates a twofold division between the spiritual and the material dimension following a typical Western pattern of thinking – abiding by the principle "divide et impera" – divide and rule.

I do not know of any consistent art theological theory that has been developed in collaboration with art history. There are, however, a number of theological analyses of details that connect the history of art and the history of theology research. [138]

The Correlation Model

The concept of correlation stems from history studies and refers to understanding the relation between different historical eras. In theology this concept has primarily been developed by Paul Tillich and David Tracy.[139] In an eco-theological context I have proposed a delimitation of the validity of the concept in order to strengthen the position of correlation theory as one among several tools for constructive and normative theology.[140] Tracy talks about the "mutually critical correlations" between tradition and situation in order to describe the task of theology. Even in his reflections over art's significance for theology, Tracy refers to this basic code. Art provides forms of expression for what is culturally salient in the situation, and the task of the theologian is to relate these expressions to the Christian tradition.

We see here how Tracy partly concurs with Tillich's view of art as an expression of culture and partly art develops a static, ontologically influenced concept of tradition which seems to presuppose the unambiguous nature of tradition.[141]

In an art theological perspective the correlation model develops a perspective for interpretation that focuses on the temporal dimension in the relationship between art and religion. In Tracy's correlation theology it is the relation between eternity and time, between tradition and context that is the focus of attention. In Dorothee Sölle, Hans-Eckehard Bahr, Hans Küng, and Richard Harries it is the eschatological question about the relation between the present and the future that dominates. In the North American pragmatic tradition, even social anthropology has developed a view of art that perceives art as a compensation for the desired, but not yet accomplished, harmonic society.[142]

Common for all these approaches is that they are grounded in a dialectic between the present and future where God's consummation and liberation of creation take place in the future. This liberated future is announced and starts already here and now, and the task of art in this process is to visualize the goal and direction of liberation, to forestall it but yet create anticipation.

This second type, in distinction to Tracy's ontological correlation theology we may refer to as an eschatological correlation. While the former investigates the connection between the past and the present, the latter focuses on the connection between the present and the future. A third type we can designate as a proto-eschatological correlation that studies the connection both between the past and the present and the future and the present.

One may question whether the eschatological position, on the one hand, places too much weight on the myth of progress, that is, a view of history which involves an objective of history which is difficult to bear out. On the other hand, the biblical eschatology is so obviously and extensively concerned with reflecting on how God meets the people who live in the present in a movement which comes from the future as well as from the past that no art theology can ignore the problem of the proto-eschatological meaning of art.[143] In addition, there are good reasons why many artists perceive their acts of creation and the general autonomy of art in relation to a future-oriented prophetic charisma.

However, it seems problematic to exclusively construe the theology of art around this topic, as it thereby tends to instrumentalize art for the sake of the Church's interests. Consequently, art objects become some sort of guide to a future that ultimately only the theologian can interpret. Küng's position, in particular, where the future is determined christologically and eschatologically, is affected by this criticism.

It appears that an eschatological and not yet developed proto-eschatological aspect will provide an important systematic tool for interpretation of theology's encounter with works of art. However, if one develops the correlation to a dominant theoretical model, one tends to distort the inherent value of art.

It is not the case that all art necessarily says something about hope and the future. All liberation is not necessarily liberation to a "novum" in a different future; it may also involve reconciliation with the past.

The Social Anthropological Model

The perspective on art in social anthropology will be discussed extensively in the next chapter. Here it is sufficient to indicate the common features of the approaches outlined in the next chapter. Art in this model is conceived of as a human, individual and sociocultural function that arises in the interaction between context and artist. Cultural integration is given a special prominence and social anthropology is mainly concerned about the function and reception of art in different populations and consequently there is an increased focus on reception aesthetics.

In one version of the theology of art, this model may reflect on the artworks' potential to embody contextually unique beliefs. In, for example, Clifford Geertz's theory about art and religion as different cultural subsystems, there is a distinct approach that is just waiting to be applied within a differentiated theological interpretation of the visual works of art of different cultures.

The main objection against this model is that this theology of art runs the risk of romanticizing the artistic and religious expression of other cultures. One can even ask to which extent the Christian creation myth could function as a hidden confessional prerequisite for an interpretation of non-Christian, non-European works of art.

Further objections will be discussed in the next chapter, but it does seem obvious that the dynamics of the intercultural art making across different cultural contexts and traditions constitute a potent field of study with great challenges for art theology. As the separation of religion and art, the functions of faith and creativity, cult and image has not progressed as far in all continents, the need for perspectives from Theology and Religious Studies on emerging world art seems even more urgent. Art theology is thus challenged to intensify interdisciplinary communication with both the established Western art history and the emerging anthropology of art.

Summary

• Images are spaces for theological discoveries. Visual arts' challenge to theology can be described in four different aspects.

• Theology is challenged to accept the autonomy of the image as a special medium for God and worship.

• Art's wrestling with spirituality is of such a magnitude both qualitatively and quantitatively that the problem of spirituality goes right to the heart of all art and especially of modern art. The pictorial world goes through a comprehensive transformation process which also challenges the conceptions of God to undergo a similar and equally comprehensive metamorphosis.

• Georg Picht describes how modern art reveals premodern mythical views that help religious movements to a ritual breakthrough. Art objects and myths are historical powers in which universal content is manifested and which neither aesthetics nor religious studies can subdue. Picht interprets art in light of its conflict with faith, reason, and society. Theology needs to ponder over art's ability to embody holiness, power, and mythical reality. Perhaps it is art that now controls the gospel's ability to reveal the myth and not a rationalist Church and theology.

- According to the German philosopher Wolfgang Welsch, a central characteristic of the development of modern society is processes of aestheticization. Deep aestheticizing refers to a material change in the production process, while shallow aestheticizing turns the world into an arena of experience. In shallow aestheticizing, hedonism becomes an ethical ideology and advocates pleasure without responsibility for its consequences. In parallel to the aestheticizing of our exterior there is a corresponding aestheticizing of our inner world and of our apprehension of reality. The concept of aesthetics is, according to Welsch, semantically polysemous and its many different semantic fields overlap each other. The artistic aspect of aesthetics should not be delimited to art, in order to avoid isolating art, turning it into a ghetto, trapped by its own autonomy.

- The theology of art has lived a shadowy existence at the periphery of theology. After theoaesthetics, a number of different of approaches in theology and the history of religion have sought to develop an alternative concept of God with a clear art and religion profile. These approaches base the reflections on the relationship between art and faith in specific analyses of individual artworks.

- For Mircea Eliade, the sacred reveals itself in different shapes in different historical contexts. Cultural history and ontology conflate in Eliade's theory. He relates art and religion primarily through his symbol theory. Eliade notices a certain "symmetry" in the development of art and philosophical theology. In the insight that God is dead, both art and philosophical theology conclude that religious experience no longer can be expressed in a traditional religious language. Eliade seeks a comprehensive and universal view of the connection between art and religion, but his approach is too extensive. However, a positive feature of his approach is the focus on the multivalence of symbols, which entails a positive judgment of art's ability to make the variety of life manageable. Gerardus van der Leeuw, in accordance with Eliade, highlights the sacred as the basic category of art. For Leeuw, God is revealed through the mystery of faith.

- For Paul Tillich, expressiveness (Ausdruckskraft) is the defining property of art. The autonomy of art and the theonomy of culture presuppose each other. Historically, Tillich develops a schema for the relationship between five religious types that corresponds to five stylistic elements of art history. Tillich interprets the relationship between art and religion using the concepts of symbol and expression in accordance with his definition of God as the ultimate reality. Tillich's conception of symbol means that the ideational content of religion is superior to the expressive power of art. Through the contention about theonomy, the theologian reserves the right to interpret everything culturally in light of divine revelation. Tillich meritoriously challenges us to understand the implications of the question of whether both the image-making in art and the cultural expressions of religion are independent dynamic interpretations of existence and the mystery of the Creator.

- The idea of an essential unity between beauty and holiness offers another approach to the relationship between art and religion. James Alfred Martin takes the approach that the value of beauty controls the application of general conceptions of art and the view of holiness, in the same vein, controls the application of the concept of religion. Martin recommends a critical position and argues for the deconstruction of the subject paired with a dialogical principle. However, the conceptual fixation on beauty and holiness will tend to yield a logocentric conclusion to the dialogue, putting at risk Martin's demand for openness. Harries develops an eschatological view on art's objective. The new heavens and the beauty of the new earth in the coming age are already reflected in the beauty of the world and in works of art. The concept of God controls the concept of art, and the discourses of art analysis and theology are uncritically combined and conflated. Matthias Zeindler seeks to highlight the beauty in God's salvation, creation and in God's nature. For him, beauty has preserved its position as a form in which the truth may be expressed.

- For Earle J. Coleman, religion is related to spirituality and art to creativity. In Coleman's religious aesthetics the relation between art and religion is neither a relation of identity nor one of fundamental difference; rather, it should be understood as complementarity and convergence. Despite this apparent equal status, art is ultimately defined as part religion and a means to the ultimate end of religious fulfilment.

- Mark C. Taylor abandons theology's ties with philosophical aesthetics and makes visual arts the key dialogue partner for theology.

Taylor's analyses are related to the concept of "disfiguring," and he identifies three different strategies of disfiguring in modern art. Taylor argues convincingly that there is a remarkable agreement between art history and the history of theology in the twentieth century on common issues. The concept of "A/theoaesthetics" represents Taylor's rejection of the role of theoaesthetics as the metaphysical basis of the theology of art. The dream of the utopia of hope and the possibility of salvation, he claims, without convincing argumentation, should be abandoned by the theologian, paving the way for a better justified "ethic of resistance." It seems pertinent to ask whether Taylor in fact drains art of its moral power and ethical potential. The disparity between the doctrine of creation and the doctrine of salvation is dislocated to a vague idea of the eternal and obscure alterity of God and of being.

- Günter Rombold focuses on art's transcendental quality. For Rombold, all experience has a sensuous and a spiritual dimension, including the production and reception of works of art. A work of art is, according to Rombold, a sketch of the world. While Tillich and Rahner equal religion with transcendental experience, Rombold gives art the same definition. Like Rombold, the Catholic theologian Friedhelm Mennekes seeks to base the intersection of faith and visual arts on the search for the meaning of existence. The benefit of using the concept of transcendence in the theology of art is that one may approach a substantial share of the objects of modern art with an open mind. The catch, however, is that this approach makes almost everything subject to (even confessional) theological interpretation with regards to the search for existential meaning.

- Rainer Volp argues for a semiotically oriented view of the theology of art. Volp regards the metamorphosis of the visual realm in modern art an important challenge to religion, and, in with Schleiermacher, he sees art as a language of religion.

- Wolfgang Erich Müller and Jürgen Heumann reject the concept of truth as an absolute criterion for the interpretation of the relationship between religion and art. They use the state of secularization as a point of departure and observe the demise of religious interpretations as the favoured explanation of all aspects of life. Art and religion are regarded as separate symbolic forms of culture, which both express views of life from a multitude of different perspectives. George Pattison also approaches art as a form of interpreting life and reality which builds on its own specific premises. Soteriology is the theological discipline most appropriate for a theology of art that aims to reflect on the function of art objects and vision in processes of redemption. The theology of art does not belong with natural theology but with a "theology of redemption."

- John Dillenberger seeks to widen the horizon of theological discourse by including other mental modalities. Dillenberger builds on the experience that looking at art will cause a well of experiences that widen people's mental capacities and hence art widens the horizon of the theologian who is overly concerned with text and language, enabling him/her to embrace other forms of expression.

- Based in the Dostoyevsky quotation "beauty will save the world," Orthodox theologians develop an ontological and symbolic theology of the icon. After the iconoclasms of late antiquity, theologians, with reference to the mystery of incarnation, regarded it as perfectly feasible also to give God's revelation a physical manifestation in images. *Logos* and *eikon* acquired equal magnitude in Eastern Christianity, while in Western Christianity, on the other hand, the image remained subordinate to the word and primarily served as a catechetical tool, a pedagogical method for presenting biblical interpretations and theology, an attitude that was adopted by the Lutheran tradition without questioning.

  The theology of icons is characterized by a dogmatic symbolism, where the pictorial elements are conceived of as physical signs of spiritual representations of the message dogmatically formulated by theologians. Art and the image have no inherent power or autonomy. The image is subject to dogmatic heteronomy. The Orthodox image programme also has a political dimension which is evident in the symbols of the former Soviet society. Just as in liturgy, the state representatives were carried in visual processions for public display. The Soviet leaders adopted this thousand-year-old Eastern Church tradition where one visualized the spiritual reality by depiction, and they used ritualization and visualization to express their conviction of the new social order.

- Pavel Florensky creates the first holistic theology of the icon. The icon is, for Florensky, a revelation of an archetype. The icon has the capacity to create a new reality; it makes visible the archetype and opens the unworldly for perception. The technique for making the icon painting embodies a concrete metaphysics. The image is God's tool for becoming visible and open to experience in creation. Florensky contrasts the medieval absence of perspectival development and the "reversed perspective" of the icon painting with the reductionist and atheist Western illusionary art.

- Paul Evdokimov's basic thesis is that the Holy Spirit of God is revealed in beauty. For him all forms of beauty are some form of incarnation of God. The aim of culture is to become a doxology, a song of praise, within the cosmic liturgy. Evdokimov develops a symbolic understanding of images. For him the symbol itself contains the presence of what is symbolized. Evdokimov categorically rejects modern art as a whole, claiming it is dominated by occult forces and incapable of leading the viewer to God.

- The iconologies of Florensky and of Evdokimov, despite their strong emphasis on the spiritual aspect of the visual media, are subject to severe criticism, partly because of their uncritical claim that the ancient Hellenist philosophical ontology is a necessary fundament for Christian soteriology, and partly because of their

generalization of their own anti-modernist viewpoints. This reduces autonomous art to heteronomous, dogmatic visualizations.

- The theological approaches to art can be summarized in four different models. A definition of art which is grounded in a reflection on the nature of art leads to an ontologically defined theology of art. In the historical model the relation between art and religion is determined by a comparison of different historical epochs and concomitant symbolic systems. In an art theological perspective the correlation model develops a perspective for interpretation that focuses on the temporal dimension in the relationship between art and religion. Art provides forms of expression for what is culturally salient in the situation, and the task of the theologian is to relate these expressions to the Christian tradition. The social anthropological model sees art as a human, individual and sociocultural function that arises in the interaction of artist and context.

There are strengths and weaknesses in all four models. The theology of art should not commit exclusively to any one of these models, but pursue a synthesis of different aspects of the models and attempt to unite these in a soteriological perspective. This will be developed further in the final chapter of the book.

CHAPTER 4

World Art

Protected by the Mask

In June 1907 Pablo Picasso visited the Musée de Sculpture Comparée in the Palais de Trocadéro in Paris, and by accident he ended up in the sadly neglected and derelict ethnological department. In spite of the rather unpleasant surroundings, he was drawn in by the objects from indigenous cultures. Later on he would describe his feelings with words like "shock," "revelation," "strain," "coercion," "trauma and revival," taking place all at the same time.

The artist was exposed to the peculiarity and spiritual power of the masks at a critical point in his life. Even before this event took place, Picasso had embarked on the work with the painting of the prostitutes in a state of mortal dread and fear of venereal disease, and the encounter with the ethnographic artefacts installed in him a sense of intrinsic power given to him by external forces. His own chaotic emotional state found an expression in the encounter with the magic of the indigenous objects.[1]

Although Picasso later claimed that the African art did not have any influence on the making of the painting, investigations have shown that the final expression of the painting clearly has been influenced by the exposure to the masks at the museum. The artist's own view of the relation between the familiar and the strange was generally very ambivalent.[2] On the one hand, he spoke with contempt of the people that had created the artefacts: "Art Nègre? Never heard about it."[3] On the other hand, he spoke of the masks with much feeling: "For me the [tribal works] were not just sculptures... They were magical objects... intercessors...against everything – against unknown, threatening spirits... They were weapons – to keep people from being ruled by spirits, to help free themselves... If we *give a form* to these spirits, we become free."[4]

Without any knowledge about the cultural context of these masks, Picasso recognized what was also the worldview of the people that had made and used these masks. The meaning of the object is not only in the object itself but in a context of religious significance. More than ninety years later, in the era of multicultural pluralism, we may ask ourselves to what extent the special expressive force of the mask and its visible religious significance challenge a European viewer.[5]

"Les Démoiselles d'Avignon" is a turning point in European art history[6] as the painting obviously manifests the appearance of the Strange in the Same. Indeed, already in 1520 Albrecht Dürer had become fascinated with the craftsmanship and design of Mexican metal works.[7] But in Picasso's painting, after a time

Image 23. Pablo Picasso, *Les Démoiselles d'Avignon.* 1907, oil on canvas, 243.9 × 233.7, The Museum of Modern Art, New York, © Succession Pablo Picasso/DACS, London 2006.

when artists' interest in the exotic had waned, the European experiences a close encounter with the unknown strange, when the exposed women appear in the protective masks which prevents them from being "ruled by" others.

From 1907 onwards there is a soaring African influence in Picasso's art. He does not remain alone, as the so-called primitivism gains influence and soon becomes a dominant feature, first of cubism and later within several other European art movements. Since then the struggle with the strange in modern art has continuously grown in intensity.[8]

Neither the academic art research, nor the image and art interested part of religious studies, as we have seen above, have paid sufficient attention to the non-European art production or the shifting from a Eurocentric to a culturally situated conception of art. One possible explanation for this is that it is a consequence of Europe being a colonial power for 500 years. The historiographers of modern art have certainly paid attention to the modernists' intense struggle with phenomena outside their own cultural sphere. However, their analysis within the frame of the influence of "primitivism"[9] on modern art has often been dominated by a hierarchical view of the universal superiority of the Eurocentric art concept.

Generally one may conclude that both artists and art scholars share the same ambivalence that Picasso experienced. On the one hand, art became open to the exotic culture,[10] while on the other hand, the foreign art objects were reduced to tools for technical transference of, projection of, and contrast to the own culture. The strange element in art did become visible, but at the same time it became a mirror reflection of the own culture. The works of art were treated without any interest for their creators and contexts; they were detached from their ecological, cultural, and religious context. The cubism of Picasso visually forestalled the theoretical reduction of phenomena to structures and internal relations of Lévi-Strauss and structuralism.[11]

The artists of modernism certainly struggled intensively with the artistic idiom of the foreign peoples whose works they often came across in a decontextualized setting at ethnographic museums or their own voyages of discovery. Apprehension of the foreign was however at this time still very much controlled by the values of the colonial masters and the domestic arts' struggle to liberate themselves from the straitjacket of naturalism, and there was no space for a more profound meeting with the strange culture.[12]

On the one hand, the artists of early modernism in some ways transferred the violence of colonial history to the visual medium in order to acquire, out of self-interest, the unknown techniques and conventions without paying much attention to the artists and their world. On the other hand, they opened up the gates to the other, wide world.[13]

In step with the accelerating development of cultural pluralism and the increasing social inequality, late modern visual arts are getting

Image 24. Karl Schmidt-Rottluff, *Mädchen aus Kowno.* 1918, woodcut, 50 × 39, Wallraff-Richartz-Museum, Cologne, © DACS, London 2006.

rid of the heritage of colonialism. Today the terms "ethno-art," "third-world art" and "world art"[14] cover artists from the economically repressed regions and artists who approach the culturally destitute from the perspective of the former rulers. Artists contribute to their people's search for identity, and they also search for new forms of encounters with artists and viewers from other regions. Rulers and ruled slowly, creatively and painfully leave behind the roles that history has imposed on them.

It is only at the end of the twentieth century that the artists from the third world claim their right opposite the Western public to take part in the reception processes on an equal footing with their first-world colleagues. Western intellectuals' critical investigation of European colonial history and the role of art interact with the growing number of artists among indigenous peoples and in the world's marginal economic zones. Intellectuals and artists progressively contribute to the increasing internationalization and cultural diversity of art. "World art" is taking shape.

The development of world art is further stimulated by the on-going globalization process which in a world-wide communication web creates new conditions for production and reception within visual arts. Hence world art no longer conforms to the relatively stable constraints pertaining to space and place, history and tradition that visual arts had to abide by in earlier times. Globally it becomes very mobile and receives influences from many sources, at the same time as it is constantly looking for new ways of taking root in specific places and traditions, with or without the awareness that even places and traditions are subject to the global dynamic. Artworks often come into existence as amalgamates of seemingly disparate elements, as "collage," "montage" or "bricolage."[15]

The theological correspondent to the global internationalization of art is a significant geographical and cultural expansion of the discourse concerning God, to which the ecumenical movement (1920s onwards) and third-world theology, feminist theology and ecological theology (1960s onwards) have contributed.

In the new awareness of the constraints of time and place on expression, there is no one Church that can claim exclusive, universal validity for its traditions, although this naturally still happens. The interpretation of Christianity is no longer reserved to confessional Western elites; the circle of communication partners is expanded to include worshippers of the non-male sex, non-Western origin, and non-human life. Voices that formerly were silenced and faces that were made invisible now enrich the interpretation of God's actions based on specific experiences from the "underside" of history and power.

The theological method is transformed from a universalistic (kerygmatic or rationalist) propositional paradigm to a contextual paradigm. The preaching and the claim of divinely revealed postulated universal truths by officers true to the system is replaced by conversations that seek the truth and liberating actions by worshippers with different experiences in a multitude of specific sociocultural contexts.

Neither the question of God nor the question of art can any longer be treated as an exclusive, Western affair or with a general precedence of the perspective of Western Christianity interpretation or art apprehension. Both the understanding of art and religion are faced with an increasingly pressing intercultural challenge which demands awareness both of the special characteristics of

Image 1. Asger Jorn, *Im Anfang war das Bild/Au commencement était l'image/I begyndelsen var billedet.* 1965, oil on canvas, 200 × 300, © DACS, London 2006.

Image 5. Joseph Anton Koch, *Das Opfer Noahs*. 1803, oil on canvas, 86 × 116, Frankfurt am Main, Städel Museum.

Image 14. Joseph Anton Koch, *Der Schmadribachfall.* 1821–22, oil on canvas, 131.8 × 110, Munich, Neue Pinakothek. Photo: © Jochim Blauel – ARTOTHEK.

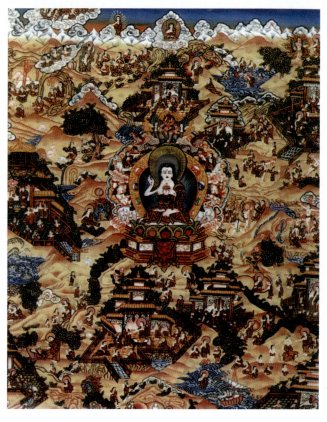

Image 25. Lawrence Sinha, Nepal, *The Life of Jesus.* Watercolour, powder colour and 22 carat gold on Nepalese cotton based on the art of ancient Nepalese painted scrolls (Thanka), © Asian Christian Art Association, Yogyakarta, Indonesia.

Image 31. Bror Hjorth, *Triptych in the Jukkasjärvi Church.* 1958, painted reliefs of teakwood, 193 x 175, (2x) 242 × 271. Photo: author, © DACS, London 2006.

Image 32. Matthias Grünewald, *Isenheimer Altar, Erste Schauseite, Totale: Die hll. Antonius und Sebastian, Kreuzigung Christi, Grablegung Christi.* 1512–16, 269 × 307, Colmar, Unterlinden-Museum. Photo: © Joseph S. Martin - ARTOTHEK.

Image 33. Bodil Kaalund, *Grønlands pietà.* 1990, oil on canvas, 70 × 140 (70 × 70).

Image 34. August Macke, *Zoologischer Garten I.* 1912, oil on canvas, 58.5 × 98, Munich, Städtische Galerie im Lenbachhaus. Photo: © Joachim Blauel - ARTOTHEK.

Image 37. José Sabogal, *Iglesia en las Montanas.* 1955, Ransom Center Art Collection, The University of Texas at Austin, ©/BONO 2007.

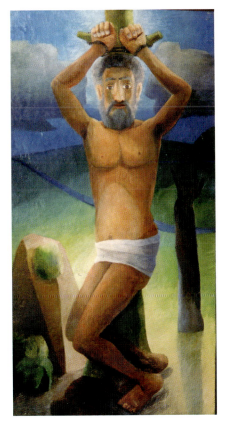

Image 40. Alejandro Alayza, *San Sebastin.* 1980, oil on canvas, 160 × 90. Photo: author.

Image 52. Illustrations in the manuscript "Homilies of St. Gregory of Nazianzus", 867-86. *The Raising of Lazarus* and *Entry into Jerusalem.* Bibliothèque nationale de France.

Image 56. Auguste Rodin, *Danseuse cambodgienne de face.* 1906, plumbago pen, water colour, gouache and pencil on paper, 34.8 × 26.7. Photo: Bruno Jarret, © Musée Rodin, Paris.

Image 53. Arnulf Rainer, *Kreuz mit blauem Anschlag.* 1988, oil on wood with a frame of aluminium, 164 × 104, St Eberhard Church, Stuttgart.

Image 57. Jean Fouquet, *The Right Hand of God: Protecting the Faithful against the Demons*. C. 1452, miniature, 16.5 x 12, The Metropolitan Museum of Art, New York, Robert Lehman Collection, 1975 (1975.1.2490). Photo: © 1984 The Metropolitan Museum of Art.

the Familiar and the Strange as well as of what can unite the two. This challenge becomes particularly visible in works of art which according to the marginal perspectives express local, specifically religious, cultural and universal-human and ecologically relevant perspectives.

See Lawrence Sinha's *The Life of Jesus*, in the colour plates section, Image 25.

In light of the challenge of the emerging world art to the modern conception of art, it seems important that the theology that wished to develop its understanding of Christianity in dialogue with the dynamic contemporary art also abandons its universalistic and essentialist foundation to a more contextually aware view of its objective and method. In the meeting with the object of world art, its creators and their historical and sociocultural contexts, new conditions arise for how theology can express and process the question of the image of God and God's work in a world constantly changing both on a local and global level. The context- and colonialism-aware gaze on art also challenges theology to look at God's work with fresh eyes. How do the works of world art visualize the power of faith? Which understanding of religion do they rely on? Which God and which creation do they express?

In its attempt to explore the encounter with world art, theology has quite a few things to learn from cultural and social anthropology; both strengths and weaknesses. In close connection to colonization history, anthropology and its predecessor ethnography have developed extensive knowledge about the Strange.

While anthropology initially also showed interest in the *made objects* of the other peoples, it has been neglected in recent theoretical developments in the discipline, and the main orientation is towards the study of social patterns of behaviours and to "reading" the "structure" of the culture, similar to Western text-based or concept-based categories. It is only during the past two decades that we see an increased interest in the significance of artefacts in culture and the emergence of a discussion of how one can develop an "anthropology of art."

Art and Culture

For the English artist and anthropologist Susan Hiller both the artist and the cultural researcher, albeit in different ways, are representatives of the hierarchical European worldview which put Europeans at the top. "While anthropology tries to turn the peoples who are its subject-matter into objects, and these objects into 'theory,' art tries to turn the objects made by those peoples into subject matter, and, eventually, into 'style.' Both practices maintain, intact, the basic European picture of the world as a hierarchy with 'ourselves' at the top."[16] Hiller interprets the relationship between anthropology and art as both full of conflict and as complementary. The anthropologist's inclination to make human subjects and other subjects into objects, on the one hand, stands in glaring contrast to the artist's proneness to interpret the foreign objects as subjective expressions. On the other hand, the dispositions of art and anthropology complement each other by Eurocentrically and ethnocentrically maintaining the one's control over the other, our distance to and superiority over the strangers.

In Western art history, we recognize the conflict between objectifying and subjectifying understandings of the classical problem of enlightenment pertaining to the autonomy of art. In the history of philosophical aesthetics there are, as we saw in the previous chapter, two paradigmatically conflicting interpretations of autonomy. The emphasis was either on the autonomy of art or the autonomy of humankind.[17]

The same problem is also reflected in the different views of art in academic anthropology. In this context, most people claim – instead of the presumably universal "human being" of aesthetics – the autonomy of culture, while visual art mainly has a sociocultural function.

Others again separate the non-Western art realm and the Western art sphere using geographical or historical criteria, and hence they depart from approaches which regard art either as function or interaction between artist and context.

Some people search for uniform, autonomous art concepts suitable for studies of non-Western art phenomena, and finally, more recent approaches focus on the conflict-ridden cross-cultural issue.

World art objects, especially those that have been created in an ethno-political dynamic context, are characterized by equivocalness. In part the artworks mirror the conflict that Hiller refers to, in that they, on the one hand, will create a semiotically explicit, ethnic identity and, on the other hand, subjectify the sign system of the older tradition on a modernized global horizon. In part many works of art attempt to visualize and sustain the tension between tradition's making of practical and meaningful artefacts and the "grand art" of modernity, precisely in order to seek and find new individual and cultural modes of expression.

For art anthropology and the theology of art this ambiguity requires a theory that neither reduces art to an autonomous cultural function nor to an autonomous subjective function. Rather, one needs to bear in mind both the personal creative force of the artist and the social function of the work of art, including the individual, historical and cultural dimensions. The artist takes part in her/his historical and sociocultural context at the same time as s/he through the artwork preserves or changes this context, or perhaps even creates a new context.

Bearing in mind this challenge we will proceed to provide a clear review of art conceptions in anthropology by outlining three models, of which the third is the recently emerging cross-cultural art anthropology.[18]

Three Models

How have anthropologists approached art in the twentieth century? We can distinguish three different approximations to defining the relation between art and culture.

Art as a Tool of the Other Culture – the Functionalist Model

In one group we find theories that make a distinction between Western and non-Western objects in an ethnological and anthropological perspective. Among these theories we can identify three approaches: (a) those that define the non-Western art either using criteria like mastering of techniques and volume of production or with the use of a concept of strangeness or otherness; (b) those who regard art exclusively as a sociocultural function; and (c) those that operate with an essentialist conception of art.

The German ethnologist Herta Haselberger in her ample attempt at "art ethnology" regards art as an "artistic practice in people with a low degree of mastering of nature."[19] However, the empirical gradation of "lower" and "higher" degrees of mastering of nature is just as problematic as her view of technology and art as forms of "mastering" nature.

Ingrid Kreide-Damani avoids Haselberger's hierarchical definition and the more neutral delimitation of the culture of "small-scale" peoples[20] using the concept "the art of the strangers" (Fremden-Kunst). In her programmatic art ethnology she focuses on the importance of studying art objects in their original context. Kreide-Damani also makes a clear distinction between "the art of the own culture" and "the art of the other culture."

Furthermore, she questions the use of analysing the art of strangers based on the Western assumption that art is autonomous and she claims that all art is determined by various external factors, namely political, religious, social or individual functions and interests.[21] A fundamental component of her art ethnology is the notion of "function" as the "mediator between art and context."[22] This view is, on the one hand, characterized by a deep awareness about the importance of context and the risk of projecting a Western view of art onto the foreign artefacts; however, there is also a risk that her approach reduces the objects to versatile "containers" for all sorts of cultural functions.

Nancy D. Munn is another representative of a functionalist approach. Munn, a distinguished explorer of the aboriginal peoples of Australia and New Guinea, regards art primarily as a means for structuring and categorizing experiences. For her, works of art are "culturally standardized systems of visual representation, like other sorts of cultural codes, functions as mechanisms for ordering experience and segmenting into manageable categories."[23] The task of the art anthropologist is thus to study the visual representations and their underlying codes, and the purpose of art

is, according to Munn, mainly to create order. In a detailed investigation of the iconography of an Australian ethnic group she shows how the apprehension of the cosmic order is expressed in the spatial representation of visual art and how art contributes to preserving and communicating this cosmic order.[24]

Herschel B. Chipp approaches the scrutiny of Maori art relying on the classical Western distinction between form and content. According to Chipp, art production is primarily driven by two motivations: aesthetic gratification and symbolizing religious meaning.[25] Chipp also highlights art's influence on the spiritual life of the individual.[26] The religious meaning is, however, not necessarily explicitly rendered; it

Image 26. Gottfried Lindauer, *Tomika Te Mutu, Chief of the Ngaiterangi Tribe, Bay of Plenty, New Zealand.* C. 1880, oil on canvas, 50.8 × 40.6, National Library of Australia, Canberra, with kind permission from the museum.
At http://nla.gov.au/nla.pic-an2282975.

can be hidden so that only consecrated persons recognize it. As with Munn, Chipp regards "culture" as the main "actor" whose structures and shapes are subject to the anthropologist's scrutiny. Art – and hence also religion – appears as an expression for and a form of culture and consequently it is subordinate to culture, although Chipp recognizes the potential for studying both art's influence on religion and religion's influence on art.[27]

Unlike the researchers mentioned thus far, James W. Fernandez and Anthony Forge look for art's specific contribution to culture. Although they do not adopt the modern, Western idea of art's autonomous nature, they install in art a functional intrinsic value.

Fernandez, in his studies of the Fang aesthetics, in part uses the analogy between social and spatial organization and in part the positive conception of the role of oppositions. Art is, for Fernandez, not necessarily secondary to culture; he can also reverse the relationship and ask to what extent the social structure reflects aesthetic principles.[28]

What characterizes Fang aesthetics is, according to Fernandez, not its tendency to attenuate contrasts in order to create identity; rather, it refers to retaining a balanced state of opposition between the focal idea of Fang culture that duality and opposition make up the vital force, while uniformity and sameness equals death.[29] Aesthetics and artistic creation contribute in their special ways to maintaining these vital and crucial tensions and contrasts.

Hence, also in Fernandez, it is the cultural approach that determines his analysis of art, by which the expression of art in accordance with a general, fundamental anthropological code is always assumed to comply with other cultural expressions in a positive and harmonious manner.

In his famous thesis from 1965, Anthony Forge investigates the relationship between art and environment among two tribal peoples in New Guinea. Forge's position is the complete opposite of the idea of the primacy of culture, and he wants to regard art as a "system *sui generis*" in which the art objects may demand to be treated "in their own right to relate to each other" and not only as manifestations of cultural facts or as mythology or religion.[30]

Forge studies in detail different aspects of peoples' "visual communication system," and he does not regard these as illustrations to myths but rather as more direct "expressions" of the culture that fostered these expressions. Forge explains the difference between the art of the two tribal groups with reference to the variation in ecological context and the nature which is the "raw material" of symbolism.[31] The artworks and the architecture carry "messages" and statements about the nature and culture of the people. These messages are according to Forge existentially essential for the peoples and they cannot be created in any other media than the visual medium.[32]

Although Forge assigns to art – here conceived of as a system of visual communication – a greater intrinsic value than other approaches, a certain basic code is still retained which assumes that art "expresses" what is given in "culture."[33] An interesting aspect of Forge's approach is that it throws overboard the idealist ballast of its predecessors. The prevailing view was that the content of the culture was the ideational cage and that its artistic forms of expression therefore really were materialized ideas and beliefs. Forge seeks instead to identify direct and ecologically formed connections between art, nature and culture.

Characteristic of all these approaches in *the functionalist model* is that they prioritize the

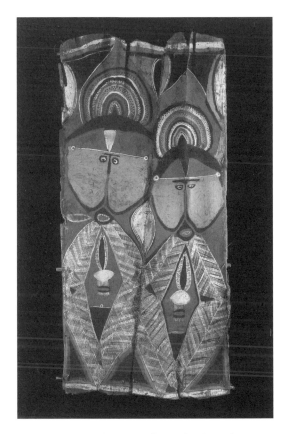

Image 27. Part of a *Painted Facade of a Cult House, Abelam, South of Maprik.* Painted barkcloth, photo: Peter Horner, 1986, Vb 13932, © Archive of Museum der Kulturen, Basle.

cultural analysis in the analysis of the artworks. It is assumed that the art objects positively express the characteristics of the investigated population's culture and that art production contributes to the continuity of the culture by establishing order, preserving dialectics or creating unity in relation to their relation to nature. None of the above approaches acknowledges the possibility that the artistic creation has an independent and critical-corrective role in the cultural process. The functionalist approaches have a heteronymous view of art as the tool and function of culture in the strange sphere, clearly distinct from the Western cultural sphere.

Art in the Tension between Culture and Life Processes – the Universalizing Model

In the second group we find theories that search for an anthropological concept of art which is valid for artistic creation in general, and there are two major approaches in this group. Lévi-Strauss and Bateson locate artistic creation in the bipolar tension between science and myth/magic, consciousness and unconsciousness, or goal orientation versus action orientation, while Boas and Geertz develop their concept of art on a wider horizon. However, they all connect the art concept to their respective theories of culture, although Geertz develops his theory contextually.

Art in-between Bricolage and Engineering

In the book *The Savage Mind*, Claude Lévi-Strauss places artistic creation in the "primitive" culture in-between, on the one side, magic and myth and, on the other, science. Magic, in contrast to science, maintains complete determinism while science distinguishes different levels of determinism.[34] Magic constitutes an autonomous system which is not dependent on science.

Lévi-Strauss interprets mythical thinking as an intellectual "bricolage," that is as some kind of functional amalgam of a limited number of freely chosen instruments and elements.[35] While the scientific engineer seeks to transgress the conditions of civilization, the "bricoleur" always stays within the limits of civilization.[36] While science distinguishes between the event and the structure, the bricolage constructs "structured units" from leftovers after events.[37] The mythical thinking remains, according to Lévi-Strauss, trapped in the events and their meanings, but it can even emancipate by counteracting the perilous idea of science that everything can become meaningless.[38]

Art is, according to Lévi-Strauss, halfway between these two scalar endpoints. The artist makes an object that can become an object of knowledge. For Lévi-Strauss magic/myth, on the one hand, and science, on the other, are opposite to each other with regard to their understanding of the relation between event and structure, while art can glide between the two poles.[39]

The scientist interprets events based on the knowledge of structures while the mythical bricoleur creates structures on the basis of events. The artist can unite the two through his/her ability to reduce and "miniaturize." The creation of myth is, according to Lévi-Strauss, in a reverse analogy to the creation of art objects: "Art thus proceeds from a set (object + event) to the *discovery* of its structure. Myth starts from a structure by means of which it constructs a set (object + event)."[40] Art is, in other words, capable of transforming events into structures.

Lévi-Strauss describes the difference between the "academic professional" and the "primitive" art by investigating the meaning of contingency in three different contexts. While academic art mainly relates to a model, primitive art communicates both to the material and to future users.[41] Lévi-Strauss regards primitive art as the complete opposite to academic art.

Because of Lévi-Strauss' placement of art in-between myth and science – and despite his invalid distinction between academic/professional and primitive art – it is possible to make some observations about what is common for ancient and more recent indigenous art and Western modern art – namely the critical independency in relation to the abstraction and taxonomy of science.[42] Artistic creation displays a different practical connection to reality than the empiric-rational scientist's inclination to distanced knowledge for manipulation.

Methodologically, however, one must ask whether Lévi-Strauss' bipolar localization of art involves too much of a generalization about the conception of art, science and religion. Is it possible that his elegant dualism between event and structure actually obscures the many interesting nuances, differences and overlaps between the artist's, the scientist's and the bricoleur's handling of reality? Even the scientist's imagination of, and "faith" in theoretical constructions involve a substantial amount of mythical thinking.

Moreover, does not Lévi-Strauss' model lead to a heteronymous reductionism which entails that the analysis of art is under the complete control of his interpretation of myth and science? It does not even ask for the independent position of artistic creation in relation to both myth and science, and thus it remains a captive of an early version of art anthropology, namely the subordination of artistic creation under the cultural process.

It is beyond questioning that Lévi-Strauss succeeded in creating a formula for the inherent properties of art in the transformation of event to structure, but it is only when the scientist or the "savage" in their respective ideational systems can perceive the structure and the event as art that it really becomes art. The conception of art remains heteronymous, externally controlled, either by the savage, the scientist, or by the structuralist.

The Epistemological Critique of Art in Spiritual Life Patterns

With the development of his comprehensive theory of the "ecology of spirit," the anthropologist, biologist, and epistemologist Gregory Bateson also presents a proposal for a theory of the non-verbal art in culture. Bateson investigates art both epistemologically and with reference to field studies in Bali. Bateson, just like Forge, also abandons the idealistic approach that seeks the message and content of art by translating it to mythology, and instead he focuses on the "codes" and "style" of the artworks. The codes and the style are carriers of meaning; they reveal patterns that can be interpreted.[43]

For the human ecologist Bateson, and in agreement with the author Aldous Huxley, artistic creation is basically the human search for the "grace" that animals still possess but humans have lost. The issue of grace is, for Bateson, related to the integration of different parts of "mind."[44] The pattern of the artwork has an internal structure and at the same time it is part of a bigger, patterned universe.[45]

Bateson accentuates the quantitative and qualitative limitations of conscious thinking and how it is impossible for any system to be completely conscious.[46] In Bateson's worldview the mind is an integrated network of different type levels, and consciousness can only include a part of the totality of this comprehensive life pattern.[47] In this approach art has a "corrective nature" in relation to the goal rationality that incorporates everything into the sensible sphere of consciousness.

Bateson asserts that "...mere purposive rationality unaided by such phenomena as art, religion, dreams, and the like, is necessarily pathologic and destructive of life."[48] For Bateson, life consists of closely interrelated circuits or cycles of coincidental events, out of which consciousness can only recognize a very limited proportion. Art, in this context, is assigned a positive and important function to preserve a deeper insight through correcting a far too rational understanding of life.[49]

Artistic creation, including both the production and reception of art, is for Bateson a necessary cultural and human function with the purpose of correcting and widening the narrow understanding of goal rationality. As an integration of conscious and unconscious elements in the cycle of life, it expands and deepens insights about connections and meanings in the pattern that unites.

Although Bateson's statements about the grace, style and inherent qualities of art are not particularly coherent, his approach brings about a considerable qualitative enrichment of the art perspective of anthropology. Artistic creation is indeed also placed here within the frame of the broad human-ecological theory of culture and nature, but the question of what specifically characterizes art within this framework is given ample attention.

Bateson's essay avoids – perhaps precisely because of the sketchy form in combination with his all-embracing, wide-open ecological theory – a functionalistic reduction of artistic creation, even though his approach, in the generalizing manner of Lévi-Strauss, incorporates artistic creation in a theoretically given polarity between spiritual-rational and conscious-unconscious. Positive and negative aspects of Bateson's overall theoretical framework have been discussed in other contexts. In relation to art, his multifaceted approach is highly significant. It enables us in one gaze simultaneously to capture art's function as a corrective, its ability to carry meaning in its style and codes, and its simultaneous intrinsic value and connection to cyclical, universal mental patterns of life.

The General Universality and Particularity of Artistic Creation

The gate opener of the anthropology of art was unquestionably the German-born Franz Boas (1858–1947), the most prominent founder of North American cultural anthropology. Boas carried on the doctrines of the equality of all humans and of artistic creation as an elementary human necessity, sentiments that were revolutionary in his time. The study of indigenous cultures should, according to the introduction to his seminal work *Primitive Art* from 1927,[50] be guided by two principles: "...the one, the fundamental sameness of mental processes in all races and in all cultural forms of the present day; the other, the consideration of every cultural phenomenon as the result of historical happenings."[51] Boas' position ran counter to the prevailing evolutionist view of the development from lower to higher forms of culture. It was in direct opposition to the popular view of the qualitative hierarchy of the human races. His view of art was special in that it did not merely reduce art objects to knowledge instruments for the researcher's identification of underlying meaning; rather it approached artworks as independent expressions of a creation process in a cultural and historical setting.

Boas' art view was embedded in a profiled humanist tolerance of otherness highly untypical of his time and in an anti-racist and anti-evolutionary view of art's existential intrinsic value and capacity for gratifying the basic human need to design the object beautifully and to strive for a fulfilment of technical potential and craftsmanship, of which the aesthetic reflection over artistic creation can only be given a secondary role.[52]

Boas' cultural-relativistic approach succeeded in making the inherent properties of the artefacts of ethnic groups the focal area of study of art anthropology. In his historical particularism, the artworks did not have a universal function as evidence for assumedly universal theories that in reality were Eurocentric particular theories about the general cultural development of humankind. Instead, questions about where and why these objects had come into being in their special context and history were used to study the art.

For Boas art of the strangers differed from his own Western, modern art not through given, different mental conditions but through "the quality of the experience." Characteristic of modern art, in contrast to primitive art, was the "manifold character of its manifestations." In the strange culture, however, he saw how "beauty and kindness" very often coincided.[53]

Boas assumed that "...each culture can be understood only as an historical growth determined by the social and geographical environment in which each people is placed and by the way in which it develops the cultural material that comes into its possession from the outside or through its own creativeness."[54] Hence creativity is assigned a great value in itself.

Kreide-Damani points out that Boas, despite all his merits outlined here, "fell victim" of his scientific precision learnt from the natural sciences.[55] By describing and explaining accurately technical and stylistic principles of development, Boas wanted to connect to contemporary art history and show the order of the developmental phases and art styles. The application of the art historical method, made rigid because of the technical definition of style, on non-Western artefacts did, however, make Boas' own theoretical ambition to justly analyse the artefacts in their own culturally and historically determined contexts considerably more difficult.

The political upheavals of the twentieth century, before and during the World Wars, did not exactly favour Boas' approach, and the continuity of the theoretical development was severed. The challenge to unite the awareness about the cultural and historical contexts as well as the intrinsic value and power of artistic creation is still a strong driving force for art anthropology.

Does Boas' art view still have the power to emancipate art anthropology?

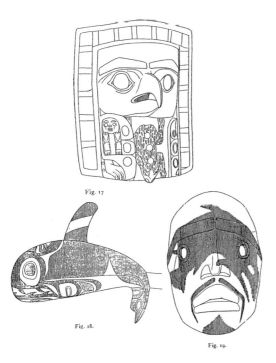

Fig. 17

Fig. 18.

Fig. 19.

Image 28. Illustration in Franz Boas, *The Decorative Art of the Indians of the North Pacific Coast* (Bulletin of the American Museum of Natural History, 1897). Reprinted in Jonaitis (1995: 67).

Because it accentuates the particularity and diversity of cultural history it can obviously inspire to create "space for a multitude of voices" in a multi-cultural world.[56]

Furthermore, Boas' explicit rejection of the possibility to unravel universal laws that govern culture is still valuable for current critical approaches to cultural studies.[57] In addition, it is a challenge for philosophical aesthetics that Boas gave a clear priority to the practical dimension of artistic creation. The Western aesthetic art philosophy does not in any way prove that our own culture is qualitatively superior or richer than the cultures of peoples that do not have a verbal and rationalized art discourse. Through its fundamental apprehension that artefacts have prominence in the analysis of artistic creation in context, Boas' approach definitively gains an astonishing currency.

Art as a Cultural System

The North American anthropologist of culture and religion, Clifford Geertz, follows in the footsteps of Boas in his renowned work about "art as a cultural system."[58] Geertz is aware of the challenge of speaking in general language and theories about art, and initially Geertz criticizes the commonly held view among his colleagues of art as a craft and a technique that one "spiritualizes" in relation to the real content of culture.[59] Geertz wants, rather, to develop art reflection within a wider framework of other human expressions, purposes and patterns of experience. For Geertz, the field of aesthetics is too restricted to cater for a full definition of art. Art must be studied in the context of its relations to other forms of social activity. In agreement with Boas, Geertz clearly accentuates the local character of every process in which works of art are given cultural significance.[60]

Geertz's approach is, in several respects, critical to an anthropological spiritualizing interpretation of the other art as craft and to the aesthetic-discursive generalization of art.[61] Geertz also develops his programme in a critical distance to the so-called "functionalistic approach."[62] While this approach, as we saw above, instrumentalizes the relation between art and collective life, Geertz argues for a semiotic interpretative approach. Following a detailed discussion of art historian Michael Baxandell's analysis of the renaissance painting, Geertz analyses the disposition to perceive meaning in images as the product of a collective experience: "It is out of participation in the general system of symbolic forms we call culture that participation in the particular we call art, which is in fact but a sector of it, is possible. A theory of art is thus at the same time a theory of culture, not an autonomous enterprise. And if it is a semiotic theory of art it must trace the life of signs in society, not in an invented world of dualities, transformations, parallels, and equivalences."[63] Hence, according to Geertz, the task of hermeneutic art anthropology is to study the symbolic expressions within the cultural subsystem of art in different cultures. The theory of art should not be generalized and without concern for context; on the contrary, it should be able to recognize the totality of the culture within which the creation of art takes place. With support from cultural semiotic hermeneutics, Geertz can study in art the specific "signs of life" that characterizes a society.

Against an idealistic, functionalistic, or structuralist conception of art, Geertz develops a pragmatic model of art with a cultural-semiotic grounding. Geertz's pragmatic model of art, as Geertz's pragmatic model of religion,[64]

is concerned with the interaction partly between the specific practical, local and historical expressions of art and partly the major worldviews of the collective group. The semiotic analysis should, according to Geertz, not only shed light on the structure of the communication but also the modes of thought of the group subject to study.[65]

Although the quote above rejects the autonomy of the theory of art, I interpret this primarily as criticism of the superiority of aesthetics over a de-contextualized definition of art and not as questioning the intrinsic value of artistic creation. However, there is need for further clarification of the position on art's specific contribution to culture in Geertz's theory.

Together with current cultural anthropological and developments in cultural anthropological theory in the 1970s, Geertz's approach gives priority to praxis before formation (*poiesis*).[66] The works of art in this context are not privileged spaces for representation but entrances to cultural understanding. In this perspective, culture is no longer perceived as homogenous but as something that is in a state of distressing transformation. Artistic creation is embedded in collective contexts and conventions. In order even to be able to recognize innovative elements, one needs to have knowledge of the canon which the novel departs from.

However, the merit of Geertz's view is primarily the fact that it repudiates the view of cultural continuity that perceives research on culture as a progressive process, by which one acquires knowledge about increasingly more significant aspects of culture, and asks the question of "how the Strange is different."[67] It is this question about art in the process of the cultural *encounter* that is the focus of attention among the third group of anthropologists.

The "Third Text" of the Encounter and the Margin – the Cross-cultural Model

Compared to the two previous models, the third model has a slightly different approach to the problem and also widens the definition of the subject. The questions raised by the former approaches pertaining to what is characteristic of strangeness and the relation between the general creation of art and culture is in this new approach, incorporated into the question concerning *art in the encounter of cultures*. In this group we find, amongst others, art-historical expositions of the relation between what is presumably "authentic" and what is developed by Western modernists, scholarly mappings of third-world art, the criticism of ethno-art, the outline of a new paradigm for a cross-cultural anthropology of art and analyses of art in light of an inter-cultural and creative concept of subjectivity.

If art is regarded as a space for a (post)colonial encounter between the own and the strange cultures two perspectives are needed: firstly, the perception of the other culture in relation to the own culture and secondly, the self-perception of the former colonized foreign culture. Together with a third approach to art these two analytical directions constitute a cross-cultural issue.

As examples, I present three extensive studies of the images of the indigenous peoples and cultures in different contexts that represent the former approach. Art historian W. Jackson Rushing's study of modern art in New York avant-gardism showed how the encounter between artists and the art objects of the indigenous Indian population (though not necessarily their actual lives) was a crucial factor in the groundbreaking renewal of visual art.[68]

Art historian Jill Lloyd has made an extensive study of German expressionists' complex and intensive quest for the genuine in the encounter with the strange, which mainly took place through encounters with artefacts in ethnographic museums. Her detailed monograph shows how contact with the strange world both enabled modernists to break free from the straitjacket of their own culture and also lead to an instrumentalization, de-contextualization, and de-personification of the visual innovations and traditions of the strange, native artists.[69]

The Americanist Hans-Peter Rodenberg has investigated the historical formation and transformation of the image of the North-American Indian in paintings of the colonists. His study shows how the immigrants for the most part created an image of a made-up, "imagined" Indian without any interest of the self-identity and self-perception of the Indian culture in the encounter with the new inhabitants.[70] The construction of the image of the Indian, driven by colonial expansion interests and still present in segments of the commercial film industry, did in turn earn a significant self-driven social function which Rodenberg interprets as *Vergesellschaftung* (social commodification) of the strange other.[71] In the cultural conflict, the indigenous population and the image of the Indian have unilaterally been subjected to the social dynamic of the colonial power. The image of the other has become a social entity with its own purpose.

The other approach, where the interpretation is focused on the self-perception of the indigenous artist, is represented by artists, art historians and scholars who make visible the ethnically conscious art's pursuit for a passage

Image 29. *Portrait of Harry J. Wedge.* 1994, photograph by Greg Weight, gelatin silver, 20.1 × 25.3, National Library of Australia, Canberra, with kind permission from the photographer and museum. At http://nla.gov.au/nla.pic-an12129806.

through the eye of the needle, between tradition and modernity, between on the one hand, the reproduction of ethnic traditions that have stagnated and that are turned into commodities and, on the other hand, an adjustable conformation to the coeval postmodern art realm. In the marginal of the colonized local and the dominant global art a new post-colonial and trans-cultural form of art emerges, some sort of "third text."[72]

Characteristic of this new and dynamic discourse concerning a "third text" is that both ethnically identified artists and art critics from different disciplines, by problematizing and by actively using their own subjective dexterities, analyse the development of art in the distressing encounter between different cultural systems in an increasingly uniform, modernized and globalized world.

Mindful of this new situation, the English-Australian anthropologist Howard Morphy localizes the new anthropology of art in the space in-between the indigenous peoples and the developed world.[73] Morphy describes the task of the anthropology of art as seeking to understand the global processes that connect the traditional ways of life of small-scale communities together with the huge global institutions. With this basis, art anthropology must also shed new light on the Western apprehension of the artefact in general and the art object in particular.

Morphy points out how the selling of art objects changes the conditions for the use of art in native contexts in a major way, at the same time as it means a great potential for integration into the global economic system. What are the consequences when the foreign works of art move from the ethnographic museum and into the art gallery?

Methodologically, Morphy recommends a comparative approach to the cross-cultural art anthropologist. Although previously the method has often led to a de-contextualization of the local dimension, Morphy still argues for a comparative study with the purpose of highlighting the complexity of the conceptions of indigenous peoples in relation to the particular contexts in which these conceptions emerge. Beyond this, the primary challenge of the anthropology of art is to critically discuss the Western conception of art and to visualize "its contextualizing nature."[74]

The anthropologists George E. Marcus and Fred R. Myers characterize the new cross-cultural anthropology of art using a term related to movement – *traffic*. Marcus and Myers see the emergence of a new paradigm. While the older paradigm aimed at the mediation of non-Western objects to a Western audience, Marcus and Myers claim that "critical ethnography" also includes the Western realm of art, something which necessitates a "re-negotiation" of the former relation between art and anthropology.[75] One of the motivating factors for a new paradigm

of art anthropology is the historical turn or "taxonomic shift"[76] in the transformation of cultural artefacts to works of art.

Marcus and Myers clearly demonstrate anthropologists' and art critics' dissimilar approaches to writing about art. The former, in contrast to the latter, do not make any normative statements about art production.[77] Further, Marcus and Myers describe in detail how art has influenced anthropology and even how anthropology has inspired artistic creation. The conceptions of art that Boas, Lévi-Strauss, and Geertz represented did, for example, show clear connections to their respective contemporary developments within art. But even the discourse within anthropology about the primitive has up till the present had a considerable impact on modern art.

Marcus and Myers meritoriously also focus on the ambivalence of postmodern art life in which art reception is controlled by market fluctuations, which both creates an "ethnographic avant-garde" and constrains art reception, because of the competitive market influence, in a feudalistic and elitist manner. The value of the artworks is tied to a global monetary economy, whose problematic effects one rarely ponders over.[78]

The tasks of future critical art ethnography are described by Marcus and Myers using the three main terms "appropriation," "boundary," and "circulation."[79] In their model, art anthropology is concerned with how the art world develops its ideologies, discursive strategies, and micro-technologies in order to assimilate cultural differences. Secondly, it investigates the function of boundaries in relation to the ambivalence of appropriation, and how art maintains its identity by drawing boundaries against other cultural sectors. Thirdly and finally, the new critical ethnography investigates how the objects travel in this interaction between appropriation and boundary-making.

"The social life of things"[80] is studied by following the traffic of objects through different contexts. Hence Marcus and Myers assume that even the process of appropriation contain a dialogical element. They believe that whoever appropriates a work of art carries with them the entire local context of the artwork;[81] however, I believe this assertion is in need of slight modification.

Furthermore, another feature of the cross-cultural discourse in the new art anthropological paradigm is that the normative intention of the participants is to not only regard art as a tool either for the creative autonomy of artists, the experience of the recipients or the extension of European history in a pluralistic world, but also to approach art as a space for independent and specific expressions of and critically revitalizing contributions to both local and global cultural developments. Consequently, the cross-cultural discourse of art anthropology not only reveals its own exoticizing views of the Strange/r but also very much the limitations of its own art conception.

For ethnically aware artists it is all about "reinventing subjectivity within conflicting cultural orders," in the pregnant formulation of artist and critic Jean Fisher.[82] The discursive and visual space, inhabited by all sorts of stereotypical compulsive ideas about the others, and hitherto dominated by Western artists and scholars, must be expanded and liberated, making it possible for even the strange others to be seen and to make themselves heard.

The need for liberation of the visual space becomes especially evident in Sally Price's investigation of the ideas of "the primitive" among educated and benevolent scholars, curators, and art dealers foreign to ethnographic studies.[83] Price makes plain how the so-called "internationalization of primitive art" also has brought the art-making of the strange others to the abyss, namely "the *dehumanization* of Primitive Art and its makers."[84]

Provokingly, Price shows how both strategies for exhibition and interpretation, which originally were meant to further the development of indigenous art in a far from innocent manner, have contributed to making this art less human by objectifying the artworks to objects of manipulation on a cultural arena. Price convincingly demonstrates the strong and dominant influence that the stereotypes of the savage still inhabit, for example, in relation to the indigenous peoples' unrestrained sexuality and presumed closeness to the existential powers of life and death.

Price's exposition of the "primitive" art in the "civilized" places shows with all possible clarity how the Western art conception urgently needs to become aware of and to liberate itself from the conventions that have tied it to a distorted image of itself in the mirror of the other. Unfortunately this process, by which the strong colonial actors visually have projected their self-conception onto the others, has such a long history that many of the artworks of contemporary indigenous art have internalized a range of these historically constructed stereotypes.

The "internationalization" of art thus challenges us to confront the colonial constriction of art and art history, at the same time as the challenge also pertains to the building of a new space for the culturally aware art. "A new internationalism must be a project that both creates and dismantles cultural hegemonies..." says the Indian art historian Geeta Kapur, and in relation to the colonial power's infringement on the indigenous culture she completely rejects the idea of a consensus between the two for her irreconcilable hegemonies.[85] However, the question remains whether she simply argues for the replacement of one dominating power with another.

Equally problematic is the position of radical contextualism, of which the Norwegian anthropologist Signe Howell is an exponent. After an astute analysis of art's significant culture-transcending ability and her convincing argumentation for giving the appropriate credit to the interpretation of the cultural context of art-making, she claims that the analysis of a work of art is *only* possible within *its* cultural context, and thus only possible for someone within the same context as the art in question.[86] A generalization of the implications of the internally driven analysis is completely impossible, according to Howell.[87]

However, in my view this radicalization of contextual awareness runs the risk of putting the entire cross-cultural art-analysis project into disrepute. If the only concern of the context-relativistic position is to defend the indigenous artist's self-image and preference for interpretation, I see no problem in supporting this position in order to counter-effect the exploitation of the "local knowledge" of art making. However, if it claims some kind of universal epistemological validity, objections arise.

Where does one draw the line for belonging to a specific context? For example, can and should a Sami man say something about the art of a Sami woman, given that they share the ethnic context but have different gender contexts? Can and should a non-Sami northerner analyse the work of a Sami artist, despite the fact that they both in different ways have been influenced by traditional and modern ways of living? Is it possible to recognize with non-Sami eyes that the Sami artwork is entirely infused with stereotypical images of humanity that the Nordic colonial history has projected onto the previous generations of the artist? Or, in a different context, is it possible for an African Yoruba woodcarver who immigrated to Italy in his youth and now lives a life marked by double identities to understand anything of the Renaissance ceiling paintings in the Sistine Chapel?

Howell's conclusions seem unreasonable, not only for stipulating a too sharp delineation of cultures or because of its negative view of the cultural meeting and the potential of visual and verbal dialogues in general, but first and foremost because it can be used to legitimize ethnocentrically pure "clans" of artists where the liberal arts are coerced by ideological and ethno-political power interests.

It seems like Howell tends to endorse the concept of context such that the "context" ontologically has the function of something eternal and constant, a view close to what we find in former idealistic ideas about essence and nature.

If the context awareness is reduced theoretically to the epistemological principle "like attracts like" – an ancient principle and dominating view in antiquity that only the same can know the same – then there is a risk that our conception of art is reduced to a reflection of Eurocentrism, albeit on a smaller scale and with a different regional coverage. Anthropology hardly becomes post-colonial because of the application of such a supposedly radical and universal contextualist epistemology.

Another critical point of discussion in the cross-cultural art-anthropological discourse is related to the appraisal of the integration of so-called ethnic art into the globalized art scene. Based on a critical investigation of contemporary ethnic art in England, the Pakistan-born London-based artist Rashed Araeen voices a sharp criticism of this appraisal as a new form of colonialism. Araeen claims that the white monolithic Western civilization at the top of its power pyramid has not at all given up power, but it surrounds itself with multi-coloured cultural attributes of all types. "The great monolith is now covered with patchworks of every conceivable form and colour, shape and material, high technology intermingling with the material from so-called 'primitive' cultures, forming a great spectacle which is as fascinating to watch as *The Triumph of the West*."[88] With the postmodern focus on differences, cultural diversity and internationalization, Araeen sees the same order and same hierarchy of Eurocentric valuations and attitudes as before.[89]

The famous American-Indian artist Jimmie Durham[90] develops this criticism further and refers to the philosopher Michael Taussig and his analysis of how we create roles that the "other" can fill so that we can recognize the alterity that we want right there. Taussig investigates the connection between mimesis and alterity, between the conceptions of representation and difference, and the interweaving of these elements in modern colonial history. He justly points out that the social anthropological re-contextualization of objects is problematic as context itself is dissolving. "The border has dissolved and expanded to cover the lands it once separated such that all the land is borderland, wherein the image-sphere of alterities, no less than the physiognomic aspects of visual worlds, disrupt

the speaking body of the northern scribe into words hanging in grotesque automutilation over a postmodern landscape where Self and Other paw at the ghostly imagings of each other's powers."[91] Difference itself has been levelled out and it has become a universal new uniform ideology. The awareness of difference, whose purpose was to protect cultural autonomy, becomes the tool for a new, different cultural heteronomy. In another context, Durham has also directed sharp criticism against the notion of authenticity as a tool for the power-oriented boundary-making between different "pure" authentic identities. Such boundaries do not fit in well with the pluralistic life world of indigenous peoples fragmented by colonial history.[92]

Initially, we used as a point of departure Susan Hiller's observation that both the artist and the anthropologist in their different ways may contribute to maintaining the hierarchy of the Western worldview, with ourselves on top of the pyramid of power. The proposals of the third model for a cross-cultural anthropology have shown that there has been a growing awareness about this risky pursuit. The encounter between performing artists in different regions of the world and anthropologists, who will not flinch from a critical comment on both the indigenous and the own art life, provides a great potential for a future critical and post-colonial constructive discourse concerning world art. The ability for self-criticism that Araeen, Durham, and Taussig display in the critique of the abyss of difference modernism gives special grounds for hope.

With regards to the third model, the important insight becomes valid that the anthropology of art within its academic mother discipline has never developed an independent theory and method, but it has always reflected the main ideas and ideology of the discipline.[93] In light of this observation, the attempts of the cross-cultural model reflect the development of cultural anthropology through social anthropology and the latter's critical confrontation with the older ethnography.

As a consequence of the discourse concerning the third text of world art outlined here the anthropology of art is challenged not only to critically scrutinize Western art life, but also to reconsider its own relations to the theorizing of anthropological research. What can an anthropological reflection over world art contribute?[94]

A continued development of the discourse concerning the third text of world art, between the anti-modernist traditionalism and late modern neo-colonialism, could become possible in an intensified cross-disciplinary and cross-cultural dialogue. On the academic scene, cultural anthropology's relationship to art studies and art history still has not received much attention, and on the culture reflection scene, one should develop the encounter between performing artists and scholars of cultural studies that has commenced within the third model. The question concerning to what extent a reflection on religion can become of value for the future construction of a critical discourse about world art has hardly been touched by anyone as yet, although it seems to become increasingly relevant.

In this book we have a special focus on the relationship between visual art and theology, and therefore in the final chapter we will address the issue of how one can develop a theological reflection on visual art which is well-informed about the perspectives of image reflection, aesthetics, art theory and the anthropology of art.

Summary

- Ever since Picasso's *Les Démoiselles d'Avignon*, 1907, artists of modernism have struggled intensively with the artistic idiom of the foreign peoples whose works they often came across in a decontextualized setting at ethnographic museums or in their own voyages of discovery. The apprehension of the foreign was, however, at this time still very much controlled by the values of the colonial masters and the domestic arts' struggle to liberate themselves from the straitjacket of naturalism, and there was no space for a more profound meeting with the strange culture. On the one hand, the artists of early modernism in some ways transferred the violence of colonial history to the visual medium in order, out of self-interest, to acquire the unknown techniques and conventions without paying much attention to the artists and their world. On the other hand, they opened up the gates to the other, wide world.

- In step with the accelerating development of cultural pluralism and increasing social inequality, late modern visual arts are getting rid of the heritage of colonialism. Artists contribute to their people's search for identity, and they also search for new forms of encounters with artists and viewers from other regions. Rulers and ruled slowly, creatively and painfully leave behind the roles that history has imposed on them. Western intellectuals' critical investigation of European colonial history and the role of art interact with the growing number of artists among indigenous peoples and in the world's marginal economic zones. Intellectuals and artists progressively

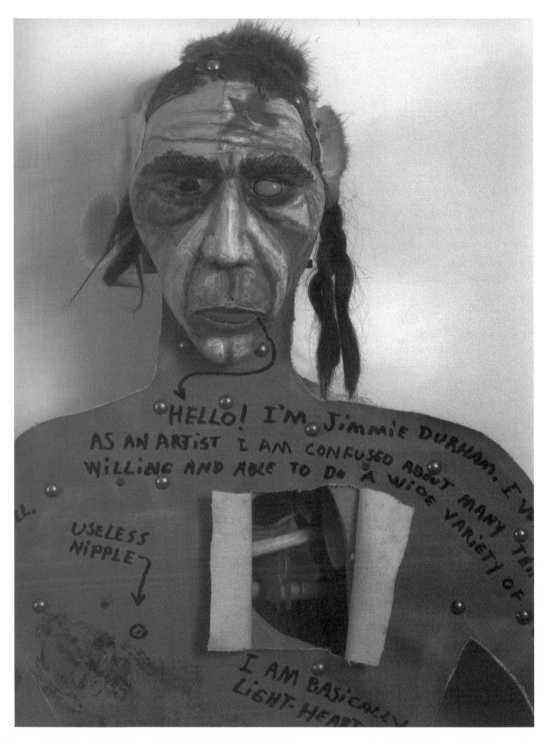

Image 30. Jimmie Durham, *Self-Portrait* (detail). 1987, canvas, wood, paint, feather, shell, turquoise, metal, with kind permission from the artist, 172.8 x 86.4 × 28.8.

contribute to the increasing inter-nationalization and cultural diversity of art. "World art" is taking shape.

- Neither the question of God nor the question of art can any longer be treated as an exclusive, Western affair or with a general precedence of the perspective of the Western Christianity interpretation or art apprehension. Both the understanding of art and religion are faced with an increasingly pressing intercultural challenge which demands awareness both of the special characteristics of the Familiar and the Strange as well as of what can unite the two.

- We can distinguish three different crude models for the relationship between art and culture within anthropology.

- In the first functionalist model we find theories that make a distinction between Western and non-Western objects in an ethnological and anthropological perspective. Among these theories we can identify three approaches: (a) those that define the non-Western art either using criteria like mastering of techniques and volume of production or with the use of a concept of strangeness or otherness; (b) those who regard art exclusively as a sociocultural function; and (c) those that operate with an essentialist conception of art.

- In the second group we find theories that search for an anthropological concept of art which is valid for artistic creation in general, and there are two major approaches in this group. Lévi-Strauss and Bateson locate artistic creation in the bipolar tension between science and myth/magic, consciousness and unconsciousness, or goal orientation versus action orientation, while Boas and Geertz develop their concept of art on a wider horizon. However, they all connect the art concept to their respective theories of culture, although Geertz develops his theory contextually.

- Compared to the two previous models, the third model has a slightly different approach to the problem and also widens the definition of the subject. The questions raised by the former approaches, pertaining to what is characteristic of strangeness and the relation between the general creation of art and culture, are incorporated in this new approach into the question concerning *art in the encounter of cultures*. In this group we find, amongst others, art-historical expositions of the relation between what is presumably "authentic" and what is developed by Western modernists, scholarly mappings of third-world art, the criticism of ethno-art, the outline of a new paradigm for a cross-cultural anthropology of art and analyses of art in light of an inter-cultural and creative concept of subjectivity.

CHAPTER 5

Aesthetics of Liberation – towards a Contextual Theology of Art

"Art is what keeps the image of God alive when it has ceased to exist as an image of God," reads the title of an essay about the history of art following from art's separation from cults in the dawn of time.[1] The historical validation of this assertion is found in the loss of the cultic practices and worldview. It may also serve as a reminder of Hegel's thesis about the death of pre-modern religious art. Nonetheless, in this chapter I question the thesis of the loss of the image of God as a necessary requirement for art.

The process of secularization has admittedly freed religious forms of expression from the dominance of established institutions. However, at the onset of a new millennium, there are no indications that secularization has reduced our capability for reinterpreting our lives with the use of religious tradition, language games, and images when the myths of success, prosperity, and beauty without suffering fail us. Quite the contrary, this process seems to further emphasize the importance of investigating which images of god or which graven images control our lives. Both art and religion are capable of countering the effect of economic disciplining and of widening the life space of modern man. Art and religion are capable of – albeit not automatically – developing liberating forces. Does art mean to give life to the images of God when the image is threatened by idols?

This concluding chapter offers a theological perspective on visual arts based on God's loving gaze[2] on and commitment to those in need of redemption, in his/her love for the poor and the vision of the liberation of creation. In relation to liberation theology, I seek the importance of visual arts and image-making in salvation history.[3] The aim is not to introduce a general confessional art programme. On the contrary, the idea of art's autonomy is the basis of the current approach, and this view even involves a critical corrective of certain forms of the Christian so-called faithfulness in the confession (Bekenntnistreue). What is the impact of "l'art pour l'art" (art for the sake of art) on the religious hope about liberation of the poor and the entire creation? How can one develop a (visual) theology of art within the larger context of theology's contextual paradigm?[4]

The term "theology of art" here simply refers to a discursive reflection over God in visual art. The theology of art investigates the relation between visual arts and God within the larger context of religion. The term "theology" should not be misinterpreted in the sense that "god" (theos) is insolubly connected to the term "logos," with the entailment that the art concept comes into conflict with rationality, as if religious reflection should be considered as more rational than art. The contextual art theologian does not transpose his or her theology onto the images; rather, s/he seeks to discover and understand the "theo-iconic," God's revelation in images, in the making of pictures, in pictures as objects and in their reception. The second part of the term, "-logy," methodologically denotes how the discursive reflection approaches both art and God. Simply put, art theology involves discoveries and interpretations of God and images of the divine in art. Art is keeping the image of God alive.

The implication of the definition of the theology of art as "contextual" for this proposed programme declines an uncritical and universalizing view of art and a "God that exists" for the purpose of a theological reflection over the unique, temporally and spatially situated forms of expression, in relation to the subjective, sociocultural and ecological differences of these forms of expression.[5] Contextual art theology is in line with the new paradigm of the humanities and social sciences, which departs from the empirical, hermeneutic, and rationalist games of objectivism. The theology of art aims to contribute to a more extensive and diversified contextualism, by uniting the contextual awareness of art studies, aesthetics, and world art with the perspective of contextual theology.

In the following I will outline seven major components of contextual art theology. Each section is based on a picture analysis which illustrates one important aspect of the approach.

The Life-creating Rhythm of the Spirit – the Autonomy of the Image in Bror Hjorth's Jukkasjärvi Triptych

Fides ex visu – Faith Comes from Seeing

In the introductory chapter, I argued that theology must learn to understand the uniqueness and autonomy of the visual medium. The image has a unique power vested in its capability of producing inner images with external measures and thus influencing our imaginative abilities and our capability to act in the tension between our internal landscapes and external surroundings.

Creating images is similar to magic. Like the magician, the artist possesses special skills that make him/her capable of influencing and changing our perception of reality. Presumably it was this staged and experience-transforming quality of visual arts that aroused suspicion among the ancient philosophers and caused them to degrade visual arts to charlatanry.

The antagonist attitude toward images in Western culture has not depleted the ability to sustain images of divinity through image-making and worshippers' mental images; however, institutional theology has contributed to giving visual expressions an inferior role compared to the spoken and written word, in spite of art's role in the making of sacred sites and places.

However, a postulated equality between word and images is hardly a desirable solution. Before even beginning to relate the two, one should have a clear understanding of the special qualities and potentials of the visual medium. Contextual art theology will enrich theology with insights of visual arts' remarkable aptitude for expressing experiences of God.

Without an iconographical perspective and a visual dimension, theology necessarily remains biased and confined to a narrow approach to texts and rationality that mutilates the perceptual richness of the human body. Therefore, the contextual art theology does not only aim for an adding of tools for expressing experiences with God, but also for laying the ground for a richer and more complex view of the corporeality of both God and humans.

99

The human body also has the sensuous ability to create internal and external images, to navigate and interpret reality using its spatial intuition. God, who has become human, is no longer a God that only speaks, but an embodied God with eyes, hands, feelings, and a sense of taste and smell. God the Creator is not only an acoustic God that preaches and is being sensed with the ear – a major principle of the Reformation: *fides ex auditu* (faith comes from hearing, cf. Rom. 10:17) – but a visual God that one can see, feel, touch, taste, and smell: *fides ex visu* (faith comes from seeing). God is not only a God of the tongue, but a God with a complete body. While the medieval scholastic theology and rationalist theology of the Enlightenment have tried to lay down God's rationality verbally, the challenge of the future is how to lay down God's intuition visually.

One way of viewing and meeting with this earthly God is found in Bror Hjorth's altarpiece in the church in Jukkasjärvi by the Torne River in Norrland (Northern Sweden). (See the colour plates section, Image 31.)

How Do Line, Colour, and Volume Attribute Meaning to Each Other and to Creation?

In 1952, Erland Waldenström, CEO of the Swedish Mining Company LKAB, commissioned an altarpiece from Bror Hjorth, which he planned to donate to the Jukkasjärvi congregation. An enthused Hjorth visited the region for several months, and during this intense period he got to know and came close to the landscape, the people, and the tales of Jukkasjärvi. Inspired by his friend, the writer Stina Aronsson, he chose to depict the early history of the revivalist Laestadian movement. Back in his atelier in Uppsala, the artist made

watercolour sketches and small-scale sculptures of the altarpiece. Today one of these sketches is found in the altar area in the Karesuando Church in the famous biologist and theologian Lars Levi Læstadius' own congregation. Hjorth personally carved the original reliefs from pieces of teak and painted them. In 1958, at the 350th anniversary of the church, the three-part altarpiece – following heated discussions in the congregation, the diocesan chapter, and in Swedish national newspapers – was finally inaugurated in the refurbished church.[6]

The special features of the church and the altar walls were of utmost importance for Hjorth in the creation of the triptych, whose shape and placement carefully interacts with the vaulted ceiling, the lines of the wood, and the position of the beams, which frame and support the image of Christ in the middle. Today the paint on the beams' iron nails has worn off. Hjorth attributed such an important role for the overall impression of the work to these iron nails that he chose to expose the black iron and procured two more nails that were placed on two new crossbeams placed above and under the image of Jesus. "The rhythm of these black iron nails against the bright wall mimics a cadenza and a final chord."[7]

How can seven black iron nails create a ringing final harmony for an artistic depiction of God's salvation history in Lapland? The purpose of my picture analysis in this section is to help the reader discover how an external, material object can influence our human perception and create impressions that inspire discursive meanings based on verbal thinking.

Hjorth's painting is characterized by a complete integration of spatial and discursive aspects of meaning. It can be interpreted narratively as a descriptive portrayal of the nature of Laestadianism and its early history. It can also be interpreted visually as a grand expression for a modernist Nordic and primitivist departure from the problem of form in relation to colour, surface, line, and volume. Additionally, the painting can be interpreted in an art historical perspective in relation to the invention of a previously unknown visual idea, where the Christ figure melds together with a cross that stylistically resembles the shape of an Egyptian throne.[8] There are a number of other possible interpretations.

My point is that these layers, the plastic and the iconic, the material and the conceptual, as well as the verbalized thought level, meld together in the image space and narrative movement in a way that does not discontinue the medium of the image or the word. Nor are image and word dissolved in each other; rather, they are interwoven, with all their unique characteristics kept intact. They support each other with their unique modes of expressions.

In this respect, even the iron nails can take on a decisive meaning in relation to the entire form play of the triptych as they create an open space between the taut forms in the three panels. They even have a function in relation to the theological meaning of the altarpiece. We can almost see and hear the heavy blows of the hammer, hammering the iron nails into the image, into the church, and into the flesh of the Incarnated. The toothed, dark texture of the iron nails and their sharp, square shape make a stunning contrast to the soft, white wood of the walls. The figure of Christ appears to be lifted by the iron and moves towards the viewer.

The position of the nails relative to each other may appear to be uncomplicated, but is in fact rather complex. If you draw different lines between the nails, and continue these lines towards the images, you get an amazing result.

Although the nails are not part of the actual altarpiece, they connect the different components of the piece. The nails visualize the rhythm that the artist has created in the superb interaction of colour and form, and they create a completely independent rhythm between the image and us. Is this how the Spirit creates life?

A striking feature of Bror Hjorth's artistic expression is his sophisticated ability to unite painting and sculpture with a unique form and colour technique. He creates a deeply integrated unity of image components that on the surface are disparate and complex. The colour scale in the Jukkasjärvi triptych is based on primary colours. It is a relief carving, and the relief adds shades and volumes that change along with daylight's play through the church windows.

Artificial light emphasizes the grey and blue colour shades and the colder nuances that somehow relate to the cold winter light of Lapland. Especially when the sun is low in the afternoon, sunlight accentuates the red and yellow colour shades and the warmer colour shades that are related to the warm midsummer light. Sometimes the cold light of the left piece floods into the right piece, and sometimes the bright light of summer from the right warms up the winter night in the left piece.

The seasonal variations and the breadth of the colour scale can even be found in the tripartite division of the artwork. While the events on the left – the image of the law, absolution, and awakening – take place on a freezing winter's night where the cold and the night underline the severity and gravity of absolution, the events on the right – the image of the gospel, of liberation and of joy – unfold on Midsummer's Night, when the low setting sun creates a halo around the Sami Virgin Mary, and the "eternal" light makes the flowers in the meadow burst with life. The events in the middle panel, however, unfold in-between the winter (the Law) and the summer (the Gospel) landscape of Lapland in a warm, Mediterranean early summer landscape with olive trees and cypresses (which in ancient time were symbols of the flaming sword of the Spirit). The three drops of blood from Jesus that fall to the ground are transformed into three red poppies that encircle a blossoming daffodil, which Hjorth himself has characterized as a symbol of resurrection.[9]

The northern light in the dark winter's night illuminates Jesus' crown of thorns, and the lakes of Palestine stretch all the way up to northern Lapland. The people of the Bible and the people of the North are one unity. Jesus, the figure with the most distinct Semitic-Jewish features,[10] is preached by Læstadius in the left piece and is seen in the inner vision of the figures on the right piece. The Son, who sits at "the right hand of God, the Father Almighty" is on his right-hand side surrounded by people who seek redemption, and to his left people are already on their way to redemption. That even Laestadians are not free of sin is hinted at by the contours of a tree, known to the local people as "the spruce of booze," placed between the preacher Johan Raattamaa and the Sami girl, leaping out of joy.

Several other encounters take place in the altarpiece – in addition to the meeting between the separate worlds of image and narrative, the common history of humans and the environment is depicted. The expression of the landscape, the light, the seasons, and the weather meets the expression of culture, human, and the Creator incarnate. What Paul describes as the history of creation's and thereby also human's need for liberation is visualized in the Jukkasjärvi Church: "...in hope that the creation itself will be liberated from its bondage to decay and brought into the glorious freedom of the children of God. We know that the whole creation has been groaning as in the pains of childbirth right up to the present time" (Rom. 8:21f). We see this in the left piece while in the right piece we get an impression of the freedom that is the goal of life.

As Hjorth often – in connection to so-called primitive art and to the tradition in Swedish "folklore" art – uses a figurative and often narrative technique, a natural approach is first to look at the verbal meaning of the components of the altarpiece and then try to understand the technical tools the artist has used.

However, this approach would not do justice to the work, as the narrative content never has superiority over the meaning of Hjorth's visual and artistic expression. The visual, artistic techniques should never be regarded as opposite or inferior to the creation of verbal meanings. The point is that the plastic and iconic dimensions of the image co-exist, side by side, within each other and for each other. Thus we try the opposite approach and move from the material and plastic meanings of the image to the discursive meanings.

The shape of the three components of the triptych corresponds to the shape of the church's walls and ceiling. The body of the church and the body of the altarpiece harmonize. If we start by viewing the three pieces and the wall as one continuous image, we can see a complex network of lines; the interfaces interwoven in an almost chaotic manner. There is an incredible opulence of form in the image: circles, triangles, vaulted semicircles, ovals, squares, cubes, and crosses. A number of other shapes are also found – adjacent and intersecting. An artist who does not possess Hjorth's ability to focus – the ability to simplify and interpret the most complicated matters – operating on a similar degree of complexity, would probably end up creating a visual chaos. Nevertheless, Hjorth manages the arduous task of creating a continuous whole with a serene profundity from this diversity.

In the same way as life on Earth is characterized by ecological and cultural diversity, Hjorth's image has a distinct richness of human, natural, and spiritual shapes. The biological variation in his image is in close agreement with Læstadius' interests and scientific work as a botanist, for which he later received recognition as a pioneer in the field of ecology, internationally on the same level as Linné and Humboldt.[11] To the right of the kneeling Læstadius in the meadow we see the poppy named after him, the *Papaver laestadianum*.

How does the artist create the connection between diversity and unity? One method is found in Hjorth's lines. Another can be seen in the internal arrangement of shapes and a third can be sought in the combination of colour, textures and lines, which creates a sense of volume.

The lines in Hjorth's images partly create contours, partly volumes, and partly autonomous surfaces that stretch through different parts of the image. "The line is what actually gives meaning to the volumes and the colours."[12]

The shape of the mountain in the left panel, for example, is made using only four lines, of which only one line gives the contour of the peak, while the other three plastically build up the volume of the mountain. The contour line meets the line of the Mount of Olives, and even corresponds to the parallel structures of the aurora. In the right panel, the contour line

is found as the contour of the peak of Mount Nankitunturis.

From Léger, Hjorth has learned to appreciate the autonomous role of lines, although in this work the role of lines is downplayed to accentuate the lines' capacity for creating volume. In spite of the fact that Hjorth employs an array of lines, these lines never actually interfere with each other. The balance between the spatial lines – for example in the clothes of the figures, the mountains, and the sky – and between the lines that swarm with small details – is carefully considered. The simple bodies of the people are surrounded by a biological and cultural diversity of life forms.

Both nature and culture harmonize in a shared pulse which flows through the entire semicircle of the image (including the wall), the lower parts depicting the congregation and the ground. The movement starts in the left piece of the relief, runs through the resurrection scene on the right and then takes a turn back to the centre, before it proceeds towards the ceiling and finally down toward the altar and into the open space of the church. The eyes of the viewers – who let their gaze wander through the rich world of images – follow a circular spiral path and follow the theme of the image as the various events unfolds – from sin and evil to awakening and redemption.

Even the correspondence between the different components contributes to creating a unity of the many different sub-parts. The plastic surfaces in Mary's pleated skirt play with Læstadius' slicked down hair and the headdress of the Sami thief. The short lines on Jesus' chest correspond to the woman's dress in the reconciling embrace rite (*liikutuksia*) down in the right corner. The shape of the cross monument behind the cypresses is also found in the fence surrounding Jukkasjärvi Church. The rounded stars on the winter sky allude to the rim of the poppies. The daffodil petals intuitively lead our gaze toward the arms of the leaping girls – stretched towards the sky. The resurrection and redemption of Jesus Christ, of growth and of humankind is portrayed in the corresponding shapes of the image – far beyond verbal description.

Hjorth's work is distinguished by an impressively large number of shape correspondences that always are thoroughly prepared, both plastically and in terms of content. I leave it to the reader and the viewer to venture on the journey into this alluring pictorial landscape. Whoever has vision will see and interpret.

A third quality of the artwork is found in the colour. Hjorth is usually regarded as a sculptor rather than a painter, although he always sought a synthesis of the two art forms. In the Jukkasjärvi Triptych he uses both the expressive qualities of drawing, wooden sculptures, and painting. What is the role of colour in relation to line and volume?

At first sight, the choice of colours seems uncomplicated. The basic colours are repeated in different tones and colouring is used to create surfaces. The colouring may at first seem childishly naïve and fairly picturesque; however, on closer inspection and in relation to the lines, it becomes clear that the artist consciously contrasts the simple surface effect produced by the colouring against the sense of volume and contours created by the line. "The secret of volume" (U. Linde) appears in colour and lines. The piece of cloth across Jesus' lap, for example, has a curved shape (similar to the church ceiling) that is not caused by the plasticity of the line or the colour in isolation. Both the line and the colour, in combination

with the sculptural volume, give the shape a distinct character. Here Hjorth refers both to the colouring technique of folklore art and to the woodcarvings of Axel Peterson which he admired greatly.[13] The synthesis of the two, however, bears Hjorth's unique signature.

Even though Hjorth employs relatively simple colour tones, the observations that were made in relation to shape are valid here too. A diversity of colour tones is interwoven into a whole, placid, and diverse unity extending in a complex movement across the entire image. While Léger attributed the viscous colour line a very special function in his visual universe, the internal correspondence of the colour surfaces of Bror Hjorth are always secondary to the main idea of the image.

The deep-blue colour tone – a focal element in textile craft (*duodji*) in Sápmi (the land of the Sami) – is repeated in the clothes, in a lighter hue in the sky and in Jesus' clothes, and with a greyish shade in the snow-covered mountains bathed in the dim light of the winter night and on the ground. The yellow surfaces are found in the aurora, the summer sun, the thorn crown, the reindeer, the drink, and in the Sami clothes. One should not look for symbolic meaning in the colours, as for example in Kandinsky's use of the colour blue to represent the Spiritual. In Hjorth's visual universe, the colours and the tones are elements that connect the different components of the entire image creation. Just as the sun shines on everyone, all colours that refract light and air are a gift to everyone.

Even though the three images have different colour tones – winter, summer, and spring – the colour tones are still so close that the eye will appreciate the similarities before recognizing the differences. Diversity does not create division but rather wholeness, peace, and harmony.

The Rhythm of Christ in Norrland and Sápmi

Bror Hjorth's work of art can be approached purely as an artistically motivated and excellent expression of some form of Nordic modernism, uniquely related to French cubism (Picasso) and symbolism (Gauguin, Léger), to Swedish folklore art (the "Döderhultarn"[14] and others) and folk music, and to older French historical and landscape painting (Delacroix, Poussin). One may simply regard the Jukkasjärvi Triptych as one of the most important Swedish works of modern visual arts from before the transition from the modern to the postmodern era.

It is even possible to regard the altarpiece as a simple narrative representation of the early history of the Læstadius movement, as a decoration of a liturgical church space.

However, both approaches fail to spot the essential and for me most interesting aspects of the work: in every tiny little detail of the rhythmic composition of the artwork, Hjorth melds together form and content in a manner that makes it meaningless to distinguish the two. The painting challenges us as such to aim at the closest possible treatment of the material and spiritual, plastic and iconic, spatial and discursive meanings of art theology.

Even though Hjorth himself explicitly would denounce Christianity as an institution,[15] that is to say, he denounced the patriarchal, authoritarian Church of Sweden of his time; he struggled incessantly throughout his life to portray Jesus. Even Socrates, St Francis, and Albert Schweitzer have inspired the artist. One does no justice to Hjorth if one places his work within a liberal theological tradition where the Jesus figure is mainly the ethically perfected model of the human. Hjorth creates " 'a man of pain' of our time, a Christ that literally embodies human frailty and shares the suffering on our terms."[16]

Even though Hjorth's humanist, social democratic project tends to reduce "the Son of Man" by accentuating the human rather than the divine nature of the incarnated God, there are several signs of susceptibility to divine and spiritual elements in Hjorth's work. It is characteristic of these expressions that they are neither uniformly connected to the man Jesus nor to the stories of the Bible. For example, in Jukkasjärvi the growth of the flowers and the daffodils symbolize a message about the genesis similar to Grundtvig's creation theology approach:

> The world now born again/ renews joy
> On Earth now wanders/ the Resurrected Lord
> East and West and South and North
> Fire and Water, Air and Soil
> Sing the hymn of Easter
>
> ...
>
> From the bottomless depths/Creation flows
> Life gives life and harvest gives crop; crop gives new harvest
> Death was deprived of all its power
> Corpus Christi, laid in the grave,
> Resurrects and transforms[17]

The Jukkasjärvi vicar Fredrik Pappila, who was a great support to Hjorth when critics tried to stop the installation of the altarpiece, rightly pointed out that the altarpiece is a brilliant portrayal of the dual nature of Christ – of his human and divine nature.[18] Pappila aptly summarizes the profound duality which characterizes the Christ figure and the cruciform throne: "The Christ figure, with swollen knees – witnessing the agony of Gethsemane, is carried by the suffering of the cross, and at the same time he carries the suffering of the cross."[19]

The mystery of God's Trinity may also help us analyse the image. Even though Hjorth has not mentioned the Trinity explicitly, we may view his work in the light of the Trinity and the Holy Spirit. The inscription on the stone monument under the leaping girl may give us a hint:

> And Læstadius preached: The Holy Spirit performs a great miracle, appearing like a gale from the heavens and wipes away all sins as were they clouds, leaving nothing but a sweet grace in our hearts. The first person to experience this heavenly gale was a Lapp woman. The event took place on 5 December 1845. She was so happy that she took a huge, joyous leap out.[20]

In view of the ecstatic leap of the redeemed girl, is it possible to interpret the entire form- and colour-creating movement and rhythm of the image as an expression of the life-giving work of the Holy Spirit? To me as a viewer, this creates a trembling feeling of a liberated state somewhere in-between a powerful movement and a comforting serenity. Has the Holy Spirit of God revealed its creative life rhythm between the image and me? Does the altarpiece remind us of life in the universe, created by the Holy Spirit? Trinitarianly one should be able to extend the analysis by emphasizing the relationship between the incarnated Son, born of the Father, and the Spirit of God, which emanates from the Father and imbues the people and the nature of Lapland.

From a salvation history perspective, the Jukkasjärvi Triptych represents a tripartite layer of geographically determined events. First, it portrays a regionally and locally determined event, namely that of Læstadius' revival sermon, the work of the Spirit and their ramification in terms of conversion and redemption of sinners. In the same vein as Læstadius theologically criticized self-righteousness, virtue, and the rationalism of natural sciences and instead emphasized the

importance of "atonement with God, with the source of life,"[21] Hjorth's altarpiece places the sensual experience of meetings with God before the rational understanding of the Mystery.

This specific sub-Arctic mission history from the mid-nineteenth century is connected to another local story, from Palestine at the beginning of the first millennium. The different segments of the biblical Passion story are interwoven in the timeline, enabling us to see events both in Gethsemane and Calvary.

Hjorth never uses a biblical or naturalist representation; he is always hermeneutically analytical and expressive. He visualizes his theological – or "theo-iconic" – interpretation of the events of Easter and of the Revival, and interweaves the two into one entity. Thus Bror Hjorth turns out to be a first-rate contextual theologian. He unquestionably fulfils all requirements of a contemporary theology that is aware of the importance of inculturation and contextualization for the interpretation of God and life, long before the theory of contextualism was part of our vocabulary.[22]

Hjorth grasps the soul of Laestadianism in an intuitive manner. He became, as he expressed it, a Laestadian himself when he worked with the altarpiece. The image is a manifestation of an analysis of the meeting with the revived living God in an ecological and cultural Lapland waiting for redemption. It catches a glimpse of what happens in God's sub-Arctic, Sami-Swedish realm, and in this sense it becomes part of God's salvation work.

Although I am aware of the fact that Bror Hjorth never personally engaged in the community of the devout, and certainly did not sympathize with the institution of the church, I would not hesitate to characterize him as one of the leading Nordic contextual liberation theologians of visual arts. The criterion for this designation is uncomplicated.

In his work, Hjorth shows great consideration for the most important aspect of Christian faith: people's experiences with a God who reveals him/herself and acts on terms that are temporally and spatially determined, and s/he is submitted to those terms without relinquishing the divine status. Hjorth is, in other words, an incarnation theologian even though he always puts the human, earthly, historical, and the visual aspect first. He takes himself as a human seriously.

Another way in which Hjorth distinguishes himself is through an artistic search for the power of liberation. This is related to the classic question of social justice within Swedish social movements, but above all it seems to relate to finding and liberating the creative powers of art and image-making. It is not to Hjorth's disadvantage that he, without denying his origins in the rural forest area of Uppland, never attempted to develop the creative power of art in favour of the Establishment. In spite of his academic success, Hjorth was always aware of the ability of ordinary people to creatively handle their problems. His opinions about the works of Döderhultarn and the misinterpretation of Döderhultarn in Swedish art history, speak for themselves.

Even though Hjorth, in accordance with the modern primitivist search for an exotic, primordial natural state, was concerned with recreating a stylistically stripped primitive art, we should raise the same criticism toward Hjorth as we do toward Picasso and other modernists.

Are Hjorth and modern primitivism really interested in the exotic pre-modern art expression in its original context, or is this element of the exotic more of a tool shed for the transfer of techniques and a projection mirror for a utopian quest out of the tyranny of contemporary society? The fact that Hjorth embarked on his artist life in a rural, forestry village, characterized by folk art and handicrafts, certainly speaks to Hjorth's advantage, and also in his academic career he worked to keep the connection between these two worlds.

While the theologians in Latin America introduced the expression "option for the poor," one may in relation to Hjorth's work talk about the option for liberation of the individual, the people, and nature. Although the figures of the altarpiece are characterized by stylistic continuity, they all have individual features and relate to real people in Hjorth's immediate surroundings. Hjorth himself is seen to the left as a preaching Læstadius.

The Peruvian Catholic theologian Gustavo Gutiérrez developed another aspect of liberation theology – the belief in one shared history in a creation whose conflicts, on the background of this shared history, for the best interest of all people must be handled in a peaceful manner. This quality is found also in Hjorth's visual universe. Together with the space of the church it represents a diverse, comprehensive history, and in all its variety it includes us perceptually in a harmonic life rhythm in God's creation, billowing back and forth towards perfection.

In the formulation of a contextual art theology, the image-making of Bror Hjorth may teach us to respect the unique value of the visual media. Distinctive of the contextual art theology is the recognition of the independent expressive force of the image and the autonomy of visual arts. The *theo-logy* – the discursive, linguistic reflection over God and portrayals of God – should not control and subdue the theo-iconic – the visual, spatial, intuitive representation of God and the expression of experiences of God. Rather, theology and the theo-iconic should complement one another in mutual respect of each other's unique values by contributing to an outlook on life based on the unique qualities and dexterities of the visual and linguistic medium. God does not only act through words but also through images.

God Becomes Visible in Suffering – Pictorial Empathy in Bodil Kaalund's "Grønlands pietà"

God's Suffering in Images

A second characteristic of a contextual theology of art is based on God's suffering and crucifixion, and the visual medium's ability sensuously to give rise to empathy.

The cross has indeed become a symbol for the Christian Church. However, historically it is rather the fish, the shepherd, and the lamb[23] that were the first Christian visual symbols for identification and recognition in the Christian persecutions during the Pax Romana of the second century. In the early days, images were not used to decorate churches but sepulchres and sometimes baptism chapels.[24] The emergence of the cross symbol, however, is closely related to how the Empire's power and political interests were assimilated by Christian communities and integrated into the Christian worldview. In his famous vision of the cross, Emperor Constantine saw the cross as a symbol of victory. After Constantine's conversion to Christianity, the cross became a symbol of Christ's victory over death, but also of the Emperor's victory over an empire in decay. Pieces from what legend described as wood from the True Cross were spread across Europe with evangelization, and the legend of the journey of these relics from Jerusalem played an important role in support of Christianity's claim to be a universally legitimate religion.

In the early Patristic ages the cross was not used as a symbol of identity, and the metaphors were based on the analogy between the Tree of Life and the stem of the cross: Christ, as the second Adam and the new human, reopens the gates of the Garden of Eden and the Tree of Life through his death on the stem of the cross.[25] The wood of the cross is a symbol of God's recreation of the entire life rather than a military victory in armed battle.

Nevertheless, the iconography of the cross in the maze of church history and art history[26] is not the real topic here; rather, it is the significance of the crucifixion for interpretations of God and for the theology of art. Luther formulated aptly and concisely the core principle of the reformational theology of the cross in his Heidelberg disputation:

> That person does not deserve to be called a theologian who looks upon the invisible things of God as though they were clearly perceptible in those things which have actually happened. He deserves to be called a theologian, however, who comprehends the visible and manifest things of God seen through suffering and the cross. A theologian of glory calls evil good and good evil. A theologian of the cross calls the things what it actually is.[27]

The reformer contrasted his image of God to the prevailing ideas among the church elite that the primary task of the faithful is to praise, worship and obey the glorious God that the Church's priests presented.

Contrary to the historical reduction of early scholastic theology, according to which the educated clergy rationally interpreted the essence and the will of God as they were revealed in nature, the Reformation movement emphasized Christians' embrace of the gift of the active, liberating God in faith. The experiences of the man of pain and his liberating actions with the creation through law and gospel made it possible even for the ones who did not hold the same privileges as theologians to be responsible before the face of God (coram Deo). It was not theological knowledge or social obedience to power but faith alone, that is, trust in God's loving care, that could create justification.

We see the effects of this new-old insight on ecclesiastical and societal developments in the sixteenth and seventeenth century in master Grünewald's famous altarpiece at Isenheim. (See the colour plates section, Image 32.) The suffering among the sick and dying people in the poor-house in Isenheim, who presumably suffered from illnesses following from corn poisoning, is represented in the painting in the distinct contours and accentuated wounds on Christ's body.

Medical studies of the painting show that the painter must have studied the symptoms of the illness in painstaking detail, and transferred these symptoms to the painting. Grünewald introduces a new historical art movement with an increased interest for realistic representations. His artistic expression is strongly influenced by and reflects basic characteristics of the reformationist view of God, namely the search for meeting the physical God as saviour. The drama and the symbols meet. God's struggle against the dark forces is rendered with intimacy in a down-to-earth manner in an everyday context.

The Burial of Greenland…and of the Creator?

A similar theme is found in the Danish painter Bodil Kaalund (born 1930). In the triptych "Greenland's Pietà," (see the colour plates section, Image 33) which was not made for a particular church, we get an excruciating insight into the suffering history of the people of Greenland.

The altarpiece consists of five pieces. Just as in medieval altarpieces, the side panels can be shut, and a new, two-part painting is displayed when the panels are shut. The front shows a Greenlandic landscape where we see mountains, valleys, clouds, and the moon. On the horizon is the mountain Sugar Loaf close to the Kangerlussuatsiaq (the Eternity Fjord) on the west coast of Greenland.

The soft light accentuates the impressive volume of the mountain range. From the damp air, a yellow-greyish light spreads like a veil from the top to the bottom of the painting. The faint nuances in the blue-grey darkness with faint shades of green bring out the plasticity of the rocks. Arctic darkness dominates in the painting.

The hollows on Sugar Loaf mountain can be seen as eye holes in a skull – a blank stare, beguiling us into the painting. Is the Land itself, Greenland, dead? A dim reddish-brown colour adds a secretive feel to the painting. As if the colour carries a message about something that penetrated into the dramatic light/darkness contrast of the land.

When the altarpiece is open, our attention is immediately drawn to the same, but now much more intense and in copious shades, red colour tone. In the centre panel, the blood from the dead figure permeates the entire painting. The greyish blue in the face and on the chest, without any hints of green, suggests that there is no life left in the body. Another bald-headed figure embraces him or her from behind. He or she is perhaps attempting to lift the dead person out of his providence. By the feet we see a third figure whose hand is resting on the dead figure's hip. Close to the dead figure we vaguely identify a fourth body, recognizing the belly button and the chest. This body appears to be on its way down into the abyss; perhaps it belongs to a previously deceased person.

The contours are fine, sometimes only suggested. Still, the bodies' volume materialises plastically and in an intense, fixed co-existence with the land and the air of the natural space. The entire surface of the centre panel is dominated by the blood from the dead person, pouring and then coalescing. In a bottom-up movement the hues become brighter and the dark red dissolves in lighter tones. The bodies appear both as plastic and flat. They are transparent, and we dimly see the horizon as if were the figure transparent. The suffering of the bodies is carried by the land. Sorrow and pain fills the painting, the green land has turned red, being drained of life.

Anyone who has participated in the slaughtering of whales or seals during the hunt on a shore in the Arctic in the winter will easily recognize the colour tones and the somewhat unbearable, at least for urban Central European people, closeness to the meat. In the centre panel, Kaalund unites in part visual impressions from the human-ecological tradition where animals, slaughter, and ritual sharing of the game is an essential part of life in arctic culture, and in part the tragic truth that too many Greenlanders have taken their own lives as a consequence of the little less than 200-year long encounter with the colonial history of modern society, either in Greenland or in Diaspora, as nearly invisible outcasts in Denmark. Using the Pietà tradition of classical art, Kaalund gives a theological interpretation of the event on the beach. Christ, who in the classical tradition is taken down from the cross and embraced by Mary, is here represented by the Greenlander who is taken care of by his companions. The painting is inspired by the message to the artist that another young promising Greenlander (among many) had committed suicide, and Kaalund has also subtitled it "Homage to a suicide victim."

The title of the painting, just as the name Sugar Loaf, clearly expresses that the suffering of the individual person should not be interpreted individually; we are dealing with the Pietà of the entire population and of the entire country. As viewers we are drawn into this suffering, we become part of this passion, and when we rest our gaze in the centre of the painting, our eyes carry the dead body.

The two side panels are different in terms of artistic expression. In the centre panel the colour play is central to the composition, while in the side panels the colour is secondary to form. The contours and the contrasts are more powerful. The mother and the child at the left and the hand with the gulls create space and depth in the tripartite picture. The transparency in the centre panel contrasts the plasticity of the bodily shapes in the side panels.

In the left panel we encounter another classic motif: the Mother and the Son. While the Sami Mary in Hjorth's triptych is illuminated by the midnight sun, the halo in Kaalund's triptych is created with a thin shawl illumined by a yellow-brown glow. The child, representing Jesus, is covered in the traditional white Greenlandic costume that keeps the cold out and serves as camouflage during the long hunt for sea mammals. The eyes of the mother and the child are the eyes of the living, looking down on the closed eyes of the deceased.

Between the bodies of the Inuit child and its mother we see another dark brown face of the same size as the child's. This child is also bathed in a bright halo. Perhaps it is the famous spiritual double from Greenlandic mythology? Is it the hand of the mother or the dark child that rests on the thigh? At the front yet another figure appears – a child. We see its bonnet from behind the back and the child's hand pats the foot.

To the right we see a hand that stretches from the top and down into the main frame. It holds in a firm grip three blood-stained three-toed gulls, *dateraqs* in Inuit. The bird symbolizes the soul in the iconography of antique and arctic religion. Just like life has escaped the dead body, the gulls have also lost their lives to the hand of the hunter. The souls of Greenland are kept captive. They are held in a firm grip. Their health and fortune are in the hands of others. Greenland did gain partly political independence in 1979, but they still have a long way to go to develop cultural autonomy in a frightfully oppressing modern world system.

Kaalund's characteristic artistic expression binds together the many different human-ecological, cultural, theological layers into one balanced unity. With an exceptional feel for colours, layer added onto layer, and by the harmonized earth colour tones and lines that adds depth, she creates a space which in its plasticity and expression is reminiscent of or even physically becomes a piece of Greenlandic nature and cultural history. In a stage play, which was staged in Greenland in connection to the celebration of Bodil Kaalund in 1999, "Greenland's Pietà" was carried onto the stage and became one of the actors in the play. The play, inspired by R. M. Rilke's "The Duino Elegies," portrayed the history of the people in the encounter with modernity and modern art.

Theologically I consider Kaalund's altarpiece to be a poignant expression of a contextual interpretation of God's liberation movement in a Greenland brutally affected by colonization. The souls are still kept captive,

even if many formerly muted people have begun to let their voices be heard and even if the visual arts in Greenland are undergoing a revival.

The painting provokes the question of God's place and presence. "My God, my God, why have You abandoned me?" Has God abandoned Greenland? Or is the Greenland Pietà the passion history of God? Does Christ suffer in and with his people? Is the Inuit child Jesus only biding his time in Mary's arms, waiting for his moment to come? The triptych opens a visual space between birth and death – but when and where does the resurrection take place? When shall the dead come back to life and when will the prisoners on Earth's largest island be redeemed – both body and soul?

The nuances of red in the visual space of the bodies and the surroundings are so rich that it becomes difficult for the eye to cut loose from the visually entrancing event, despite all the grief involved. The centre panel consists of so many corresponding colour and form layers that the complexity between front, middle, and background layers creates an inferno of visual sensations. Just like Bror Hjorth, Bodil Kaalund also manages to create a complete, rhythmic unity with great complexity, although unlike Hjorth, she does this only with the help of the painting itself.

"Greenland's Pietà" gives us a remarkable, painful experience of the suffering of Greenland, the Inuits, and Christ. The image touches us. And despite all the tragic and the grief, it still holds elements of hope.

The figures in the painting touch each other's bodies with their hands. They cuddle, guard, feel, sense, travel, carry, and care. The little hand in the leftmost corner probingly reaches out to Jesus' foot. With the exception of the hunter's hand, Kaalund's delicate shaping of the hands, both with regards to surface, form, colour and movement, is an expression of a warm, positive and powerful view of people who are able to feel loss and pain and who can carry and overcome grief.

By looking at and contemplating over this painting we become participants in the grief, the love, and the hope. Kaalund's altarpiece is an emphatic, profound partaking in the suffering of this foreign country, and it enables the viewer to take part in the Greenlandic people's struggle for a new future. The painting is a brilliant example of how visual art can communicate empathy visually and in this way mentally enables us to experience physical contact, understanding, and solidarity with the grief of people whom we do not know.

The sufferer does not remain lonely. He is carried by the other person. His gaze detects the traces of the suffering that now has ceased, and in the future this will be a redeeming reminiscence. Greenland's death struggle has ended. The anguish fades and it will be transformed into a redeeming power. The hands are beginning to move. The mother and the son are probing the event sedulously. The altarpiece is shut. Night falls. The faint moonlight gives clarity. The longer our eyes search for the light, the clearer the dark mountains become. Guided by the colour nuances our eyes meander up and down the mountains, slide in-between the valleys. The power that the dead Sugar Loaf mountain has over the country is beginning to wane. It becomes a monument of an era that is soon to end. Will a new dawn emerge?

A second characteristic of contextual art theology is the demand that the passion history of God and the inculturation of the crucifixion constitute one incontestable element in the Christian worldview and thus also in Christian art theology. In the trinitarian theology of Early Christianity, the Passion of the Son meant that the corporal, mental and spiritual wounds are deeply embedded into the very nature of the Triune.

According to the Early Church theologian Gregory of Nazianzus, God "experiences" through suffering what it means to be a created being.[28] The suffering Son is not absorbed in the Father but his experience of suffering leads Gregory to clearly express his view on the corporality of the resurrected Son, which persists even after the Son has returned to his Father. The theologian makes plain in relation to Isaiah 63:2f how the angels at the Son's ascension no longer recognize the physical Son and how they are disgusted by his bloody wounds.[29] Contrary to the condescending attitude of the angels, Gregory claims that suffering has adorned Christ's body.

The Christian God is thus a God that does not passively stand on the outside of or above the suffering of humans and the creation; s/he takes part in this suffering. Only the God who knows suffering can deliver us from evil.

For art theology the task is thus to specially interpret the art expressions that contain the enculturation of a living, corporal God who voluntarily decides to take part in the suffering of human beings, the people, the land, and the creation. The ability of the visual media to emphatically express events and feelings in a way that touches both body and mind is very often overlooked in theologians' art reflection. However, love of the poor is, according to the early Christian tradition, the primary sign of people's love of their neighbour, God, and themselves.[30] Art theology reflects on how this compassion in the love of the poor is expressed in pictures.

Vision Becomes Reality – the Pictorial Realization of Utopia in August Macke's "Zoologischer Garten"

Paradise in-between Animals and People in the City

A third triptych exemplifies a third characteristic of art theology: the vision of a reconciled liberation.

In 1912 August Macke (1887–1914) painted "Zoologischer Garten."[31] (See the colour plates section, Image 34.) The composition of the painting is subject to a rigorous structure. The back of the man at the front of the painting delineates the right image space from the centre space, and the contour of the parrot frames the left image space. The centre of the image revolves around the tree, with the trunk and the branches making up a roof covering the entire scene. The structure of the component parts is created by the painter at the same time as the internal shape of each entity seems to contribute to the composition.

The relative proportion of the three parts of the painting gives associations to the sacred form of the altarpiece. The park can either be seen as a diptych (the trunk functioning as a border) or as a triptych.[32] Just as Hjorth and Kaalund, Macke's artistic expression relies on the use of colours. Macke visualizes the plastic qualities of colours. The colour correspondences bind the different parts rhythmically together. While the yellow-brown hue of the deer to the right draws attention to the animal in contrast to the tree, and connects it to the rock with its lighter yellow tone, the red and yellow of the path extend into the deer at the left, making his head transparent.

While the artist anonymizes the male figures, the animals are given highly individual, almost personal traits. The eye of the man to the right is taking on a shape resembling the eye of the deer. One may assume that the artist has been influenced by his friend Franz Marc, who aspired at making the painter see and sense the world like a deer would perceive it.[33]

The humans and the animals take part in several different spatial relations: They resemble each other; they turn away from each other; and they are parallel. The painter fills the space between humans and animals with aesthetic and ethical eigenvalue. The painting exudes peace, quiet wit, and a social atmosphere. The painting is a representation of a utopian view of life's social peace. The artist's world is a space where the eyes sparkle and the observer is seen. The flow of time that the contemplator follows when she lets the eye wander through the picture space is created with intent through the colour-based composition of the play of surfaces.

The painter says the following about his relation to nature: "There still exists a realism which is fundamentally different from naturalism. Many painters experience a vitality that bursts towards them and then breaks out. An independent work, as a reaction to the effect that this fantastic life has on us… We instinctively create order while we create from chaos."[34]

Altarpiece or Vision?

Macke's zoo should not automatically be interpreted based on verbal meaning. In his relatively short artistic career, Macke is too intensely dedicated to problems related to the making of images. On the one hand, we should hardly interpret the painting as an "altarpiece for the pantheistic nature religion"[35] or as a "pantheistic symbiosis."[36] But on the other hand, we cannot overlook the fact that Macke and his friends in the modern avant-garde movement "Der blaue Reiter" acted as pioneers for a new universal spirit similar to the Holy Spirit, and they promoted their visual arts as an expression of a new metaphysic.

I interpret analogically the artistic realism which Macke creates in the tripartite altarpiece composition.[37] Just as the church altarpiece, in a world burdened by evil and violence, makes visible the existence of God's kingdom to those who have the eyes to see and the courage to believe, Macke's zoological garden creates a picture space which makes possible a peaceful and mutual community among the living.

The zoo does not depict nature naturalistically, even though the painting is figurative. Rather it shows how the painter sees the world, which is reflected in the painting's perspective and the many spaces present in the painting. Macke's visual themes reveal themselves to the onlooker through surfaces and colours. Our gaze starts to resemble that of the deer.

It is not the purpose and figures of the painting that shows the liberation of the reconciled life to us; rather, it is how the animals and we look at the paradisiacal garden. Through the painting, the artist creates a vision beyond our eyes. The quiet aimless gaze wandering through the painting, whose corresponding colour shades rhythmically initiate us in the secret of the light flow, deeply affects those contemplators who take the time to feel the space of eternity. Profoundly Macke defines time as surface.[38] Time arises and flows as the eyes sweep the room, thereby creating surfaces.

The creative power that Macke ascribed to the painting is rare among artists today. For Macke, the vision of a reconciled creation became real when the painting was created and the viewer appropriated the image. Just as God,

according to the Hebrew genesis, saw on the seventh day that his creation and the world were good, we can approach Macke's pictorial world hoping to meet a liberated reality plastically, physically, visually, and sensuously. Regarding Macke's intention as a (post-modern) distancing between image and reality is not doing justice to Macke. The zoo is not a picture of a vision. In the zoo, humans and animals are reconciled and liberated from evil. Vision becomes reality in the image.

Was it perhaps this artistic capability of bringing out and making visible that triggered the suspicion of the antique philosophers, the same attitude that is seen in the iconomachy of the Western world and theologians' ignorance of God's revelation in images?

A third characteristic of the contextual art theology is found in the awareness of visual arts' capacity for visualizing and realizing visions. Visual art embodies the anticipatory power of showing what no one has seen, of visualizing what we can see only with our inner vision. This makes visual art an important, specific tool that can help the expansion of the Kingdom of God in the (entire) creation. Visual art, by its inherent power and emphatic capacity, has an eschatological power to represent the visions of God and the faithful. The image is not only in the beginning; it forebodes redemption and the arrival of the new creation. The spirit breathes life into "the coming world's life" even in images.

"And the Word Became Art…" – the Transcultural Power of Visual Art and Christianity's Indigenization in Peru

In the previous chapter about the challenges of world art, we put a special emphasis on the interpretation of the "third way," which focuses on the meaning of visual art for cultural meetings. However, in this section the discussion is not based on one single work of art but on a country.

My exploration is based on a shorter research stay in Lima, Arequipa, and Puno and on selected works from Peru's modern and pre-modern art history. We meet a visual reality where syntheses have evolved over centuries of cultural meetings and conflicts. These have, in part, taken place between the native peoples of Peru, between indigenous people and the Conquistadors, the European conquerors, and between traditional folk art on the one hand, and the European modernist avant-garde art and the exoticizing world art market on the other hand. We have a special focus on how the relationship between art and religion is expressed in the chosen artefacts.

The Diversity of Colours

Economically Peru is one of the poorest countries in the world, although culturally and ecologically it belongs to the planet's richest and most versatile regions. The country south of the Equator has an enormous span in elevation between the coastal beaches in the lowland, the tropical forests of the Amazon jungle and the mountain plateaus in the Andes. In a relatively small area we find a number of climatic zones and affiliated ecosystems.[39] Peru offers a geographical and ecological colour diversity of unique complexity.[40] This colour treasure is particularly abundant in the cultural realm, and this is directly connected to the country's rich plant and mineral resources, which are invaluable sources for colour production.[41]

The country's diversity is reflected even in its cultural and historical abundance. A great number of cultures, with partly corresponding and partly diverging subsistence conditions,

developed in ancient times through mutual intercultural exchanges, demarcation conflicts and conflicts of power over access to the limited arable land, especially in the Andes.

The masks that even today are used at the carnival in Cuzco, the capital of the Quechua people in the northern parts of the Andean plain, Altiplano, still bear the stamp of syncretism between the colourful aesthetic of the tropical people, with sounds and shapes inspired by birds of the rain forest, and the art and faith of the Andean people.

On the one hand, Peruvian history is characterized by an enduring syncretism and an advanced intercultural exchange which even includes transculturation processes[42] where mode of expression, subsistence, way of thinking and religion have criss-crossed through the climatic and cultural zones. On the other hand, the country is characterized by intercultural violence that developed long before Peru was transformed by the arrival of the Spanish Conquistadors in the sixteenth century.[43]

The exotic, fabled Inca culture evolved from the Inca's massive colonization of other smaller and less aggressive ethnic groups in pre-Columbian time. Earlier on the so-called Wari culture showed expansionist, military, and urban characteristics. Thus, the predominant macho culture of the patriarchal Latin American continent is deeply rooted in the history of the continent several thousand years back, and part of the explanation for the rapid expansion of the Spanish can be found in the regional colonization processes between 700 and 1400 CE.[44]

The ancient Andean cultures had a unique skill for developing special cultivation techniques adapted to the limited access to arable land and the harsh climatic conditions. In addition they had a special architectural talent for creating concentrated dwelling forms that satisfied religious, political, social and economic needs. There was, as in most pre-modern cultures, an unbreakable connection between religion, art and human-ecological structure.[45]

In September 1532 Francisco Pizarro founded the first Spanish city in Peru, and in November the same year the Inca emperor Atahuallpa was captured. It was the end of the Inca Empire. Now the world lay open for the European-controlled transformation of the manifold cultures of the earth into one homogenous global system. The centre of power was displaced from the Andean agricultural Cuzco to coastal Lima, a town of seafarers and merchants. The architecture of the monumental cathedrals is an expression for the Spaniards' strategic goal to make Lima a second Rome. The immigrants from Spain held the highest positions in the new society, followed by the mestizo, and at the very bottom the indigenous people of Peru. This socioethnic hierarchy persists even today. During the nineteenth century armed conflicts with Spain eventually led to independence for Peru. During the nineteenth and even the twentieth century the country was at war with Ecuador and Chile.

Following a destructive economic crisis in the 1980s, Peru's quasi-democratic dictator, Alberto Fujimori, with the support of the World Bank and with brutal neo-liberal measures succeeded in creating a slow economic upturn increasing the country's GNP.[46] The economic restructuring took place at the cost of cultural homogenization, and neo-liberalism seemed to be the only liberating religion and the leadership cult demanded from the subjects that they denounced their (in Peru historically very vital) folk and church piety. The class distinctions added even more

potency to mammon's neo-liberalism. At the same time it gave rise to a submissive middle class mainly employed in the service sector. After the mass media revealed massive fraud at the 2000 presidential election and ruthless violence against people of differing opinions, the president and the leader of the security police had to flee the country. Democracy still has an uncertain future in Peru.

The Catholic Church's interpretation of God is the result of an extended and mature inculturation and integration process with pre-modern religions and ways of living. Liberation theology found its first academic formulation in a poor congregation in Lima, whose priest Gustavo Gutiérrez used the term theology of liberation in the – now classic – book from 1972, "Theología de la Liberación." [47]

As an applied pastoral strategy, liberation theology introduced alternative social survival networks in Peru, in Central and South

Image 35. *Mask from the Cuzco Region.* Peru, 1999. Photo: author.

America, and in almost every corner of the world. In these networks, congregations, orders, and ecclesiastical institutions represented a well-functioning alternative social organization based on values such as justice, solidarity, and human equality at the underside of history.

The political conflict in present-day Peru is between a neo-liberal dictatorial ideology and a Catholic religion deeply rooted in the population where the liberation theological vision of the Kingdom of God is realized in humanitarian actions. A third power, which potentially could balance the conflict between State and Church in a well-functioning civil society with new social organizations, is unfortunately still weak. The prolonged and agonizing, now ended, conflict between the army and the armed Maoist-utopian guerrilla movement, the Shining Path, prevents many people from taking part in new political movements, although there is a significant and hopeful increase of such movements.

In 1999 the Roman-Catholic leadership in Rome promoted an archbishop, who was a member of the militant conservative Christian world movement Opus Dei and the regime's spiritual advisor, to the cardinal chair in Lima, a choice made on political grounds rather than being theologically justified. However, the Peruvian Christian Church remains a Church among, with, and of the poor. In light of the Vatican's overarching strategy – for John Paul II as well as for Benedict XVI – to eliminate the representation of this branch of Christianity from the church leadership, the development of the Christian congregations in Peru today seems even more of a challenge for the church leadership and the entire ecumenical Christianity.

Christ's body on Earth is becoming even more "indigenous," that is, a part of native cultures, and in relation to the practical aspects of Christianity in Latin America there is a trend within liberation theology towards a colourful, diversified, gender and context-aware, emancipatory worldview. Liberation theology becomes a multifaceted, liberating culture theology. No matter how many times it is pronounced dead by know-all meddlers in power positions, it will re-appear again and again, spreading to new cultural contexts.

Image 36. Anonymous artist from the Cuzco School, *Virgen niña hilando a la usanza quechua.* 18th century, Colección particular, Lima.

Since 2006, however, Pope Benedict XVI – in accordance with his vision of a homogenous unity of the Church – intensifies his work to weaken and finally destroy the process of Christianity´s indigenization in Peru and elsewhere.

The Peruvian Art Encounter between Cultures

What does visual art in very wide-ranging Peru say about God's work?

One central trait of Peruvian art history after the sixteenth century is the country's position between two worlds. In the encounter with the conquerors of the New World, native artists quickly and profoundly adapted the perceptual and artistic techniques of European visual arts. The works of the famous Cuzco school show how the local painters, taught by the immigrants, brilliantly mastered the style of the Spanish painting at the same time as they "wove" into the picture symbols of, stories from, and references to their own culture.

The conqueror would find this art familiar, without recognizing its deeper dimensions, based in the foreign culture, which the native artist had added to the picture (the most he could hope for was sensing it). The conquered could express him/herself using the visual symbols of the conqueror and at the same time making a connection to the native culture's worldview on a new horizon.[48]

This encounter brought about a vital, so-called "colonial art" which gave the indigenous people pride on a personal, collective, and regional level. Colonial art even created a common visual sign system and form of expression that both the immigrants and the native population could use.[49] The visual imagery offered a visual space for the intercultural meeting, which from a European perspective remained a one-way exchange.

While the indigenous artist and viewer used the double competence both for expression and interpretation, the immigrant and the conqueror remained confined to that part of the pictorial world that he could identify. Consequently, the indigenous artist had acquired a new symbolic and perceptual system, while the conqueror had only expanded his system without gaining knowledge about the foreign system. Peru's modern art history is marked by the struggle between this simultaneous duality/one-sidedness in an asymmetric relation between the conqueror and the conquered; between the Western stranger (in the perspective of the natives), who gradually became part of the native culture, and the foreign natives (in the perspective of the Europeans) who always remained subordinate strangers.

Peruvian art history shows how the Conquest did not take over the manufacturing processes of cultural art despite the fact that they conquered and mastered the ideological, religious and economic dimensions of culture.[50] The colonization process only partly meant the victory of the strong over the weak.

Within music and visual arts, especially within textile art,[51] we see how manufacturing processes have changed only to a limited extent, and how these techniques, within the frame of a symbolic system which primarily has a decorative function, have succeeded in conveying religious and cultural elements pertaining to the native worldview. The natives were indeed deprived of their objects, but the technical, individual, and social conditions for the making of the objects remained intact. The conquerors sufficed at mastering the objects without taking control of the manufacturing process.

The cultural memory of painters, musicians, and dancers remained fairly intact and in every new historical period they were a creative potential for resistance against and associations with the new immigrated, foreign element. Woodwork still has an identity-preserving and assimilating function; although today it is mainly produced for commercial purposes. Luis Millones and Mary Louise Pratt summarize the artists' competence in the term "double consciousness."[52]

As we saw in the previous chapter, twentieth-century art history in modern Western society fed on the encounter with "the Strange." Primitivism and the pursuit of "authenticity," along with an intense quest for "the Spiritual," are fundamental pillars of modern art. In Peru, closeness to the original culture and everyday life in a culture with a well-developed syncretism creates other conditions. In this context there is no need to do like Picasso and seek the other in museums, but every person finds it in his or her biography and immediate surroundings.

In the 1920s and 30s the cultural encounter between the two worlds led to a marked "indigenization" of visual arts. While the artists in Latin America during the 1920s individually rather than collectively acquired the western art expression through an adaptation of the different styles of modernism; they developed an independent so-called "indigenism," which should not be misconceived as an emulation of the western primitivism.

Indigenism aimed at a new perspective on images, reviving and revaluing indigenous cultures and traditions, using local themes and stories, which often were an expression of social protest during the struggle for liberation from Europeans and in the Peru's struggle for becoming an independent nation.[53] Once again the national elite used the foreign semiotic system to further their own interests. There was a growing interest in the other, entailing an increased risk of objectifying the strange element.

A striking parallel in contemporary society to the process that took place in Peru in the 1920s is how semiotic symbols of the indigenous Sami population are used aggressively in advertisement campaigns to represent something typically Scandinavian, as, for example, in the Swedish telecom company Telia's advertisement in the SAS (Scandinavian Airlines System) in-flight magazine.[54]

The Latin American indigenism melded together ethnic, feminist, and social aspects in a social realist expression. Thus the rulers could at least begin to see the people they ruled.

In Peru, José Sabogal founded an indigenism that tried to create unity among the different peoples through folk art. (See the colour plates section, Image 37.)

Even if the Latin American indigenists, in contrast to the western primitivists, were more familiar with the nature of the foreign culture, they remained captives of the objectification of the foreign element, just like their western contemporaries. The indigenous culture is transformed into a screen for the projection of protests against the establishment and a projection of the utopian idea of a different society based on a presumably better and purer foundation. Inca culture became Inca-ism. Any sign of internal conflict was beyond the horizon. Even today the semiotics of Inca-ism is exploited for national and private interests.

Contemporary artists in Peru share the challenge to handle two different worlds with other world art artists in other places.[55] The synthesis that continually arises between tradition and modernity, between ethnically local and decontextualized global elements, between native and strange elements is a challenge. By the end of the twentieth century, the life experience of mestizos has vitalized Peruvian visual arts. "The notion of *mestizaje* has become central to art's resistance to colonialism."[56]

We see the same dynamic effect here as we saw with Læstadius. He also used his double ethnicity to develop a critical perspective on the modernity of his contemporary society. Even the founder of liberation theology Gustavo Gutiérrez has the same double ethnicity through his mother's indigenous family, although it is not reflected interculturally in his theology.

Peru's 500-year long process, consisting of a meeting between two worlds, continues in our time when tourism offers new sources of income for indigenous people through craft and music. Profit seekers are admittedly trying to homogenize handicraft and tailor the design to the exoticizing eyes of prospective buyers. Nevertheless, for many native artists, the emerging globalized art market means the opportunity to express, convey, and renew the unique characteristics of their own culture. While Aboriginal artists in Australia attempt to and partly succeed in keeping control over the distribution of their own art, Andean peoples have largely lost control of the crafts distribution to other agents; however, the final chapter in the story of Peruvian handicraft has not been written yet.

The Art of the People Shall Survive

Another characteristic of Peruvian art is the contact between folk art and academic art.

The painter Alejandro Alayza (born 1946) combines in his painting "Crucifixion" elements from native crafts (in the expression of the three crucifixes) with a progressive

Image 39. *Ceramic Vessel, Moche Culture.* Peru, c. 450 CE. Photo: Staatliches Museum für Völkerkunde, Munich (S. Autrum-Mulzer), with kind permission from the museum.

Image 38. *Drawing* by a member of the parish of Santiago de Pupuja. In Schulte and Orzechowski (1993: 248).

120

modernist, expressive colour combination where the lucid, deep colour tones harmonize with the warmer earth colours in a dramatic-plastic scenic space. The colour nuances and flow of light ascribe equal value to the figures, the mountains, the houses, the trees and the soil. The Earth and the mountains – in line with the Andean faith in *Pacha Mama*, Mother Earth, get an independent aesthetic and ethical value. (See the colour plates section, Image 40.)

The narrative of the Creator who is raised towards the sky on a cross merges with the expression of the plastically formed life-space that is created by colour and light. The saint on the cross is carried by the God of light and colour space in the painting. The two female figures at the front, dressed in deep-blue robes, guide our eyes into the painting, and later they will perhaps take care of the body of the saint. A ladder, which is a significant object in Andean folk religion, is raised against the cross. The path between God and wo/man is open. Although Alayza'a production must be regarded as part of the academic art tradition, it clearly has kept the connections to the individual context of the artist – through references to biography, Peru's multi-ethnical and transcultural identity and the special environmental spaces of Peru.

The "retablo" is a forceful expression for folk art's central position in Peru. The retablo is a

Image 41. *Retablo,* painted wood. Peru, 1999, 17.2 × 10 × 5. Photo: author.

Image 42. *Hair Slide.* Peru, 1999. Photo: author.

Image 43. *Textile* (with a pattern from a reference book on Inca culture). Anonymous artisan, 1999. Photo: author.

tiny wood-carved and colourful miniature altarpiece, which now is made in a number of craft collectives for contemplation and/or retail. Don Joaquín Lopéz created a synthesis of traditional and modern handicraft from tiny chests with carved figures from Andean pre-modern religion and Christian religion. The chests were developed into small altarpieces, which soon became popular among locals and among tourists.

In 1975, Don Joaquín Lopéz was awarded Peru's National Art Award. This led to massive protests with racist undertones, and critics warned that folk handicraft would come to be considered as fine art.[57]

The demarcation between handicraft and fine art should be as pure and clear-cut as the divide between European blood and indigenous Andean blood. But the retablo gained in popularity, and in the Ayacucho region it underwent several developments. A local market arose which today has developed into an international market. There are new generations of manufacturers, and the retablo spreads as a symbol of the creative forces in folk art and religion.

Recently textile art has grown and spread throughout the country. Applications with themes from agricultural living appeal to both children and adults and not only to a restricted audience with a special interest for fine art.[58] And we have seen from other regions, for example, in Sápmi, how textile art supports women's freedom of action and expression. Because of its diverse and wide application, the manufacturing of textile images has a special and more direct significance for the cultural sphere, as it can be used for clothes, fabrics, and as a decorative element in a variety of contexts.

Collapsing the difference between folk art and academic art was also, as we saw above, an important drive for Bror Hjorth, who remained loyal to his childhood teacher, the woodcarver Elias, throughout his entire career. The challenge from the third and the fourth world to the artists of the first world is to acknowledge the creative energy involved in the manufacturing process and to somehow display this energy in the transformation of exhibition art. The craftsmen and women in Peru balance on the border of subsistence, but they are driven by the creative power for the sake of survival.[59] What can academic art learn from these artists?

And God Became Art

A third distinctive feature of Peruvian art is its profound spiritual basis. Visual arts is characterized by a transcultural and transhistorical stream of signs. These signs refer to different religious belief systems, in part historically to pre-modern Columbian, medieval and modern cultures, and partly geographically to Andean, lowland, and rain forest cultures. The secularization process is indeed taking place even in contemporary Peru, but it begins at a completely different stage than in Europe. While the European modernization process developed slowly in the span of two centuries, Peru has only taken part in this development the past few decades. The cultural change in the meeting with the modern has admittedly taken place both in Europe and Latin America, but it is radically different in those regions that have been included in the global economy only recently.

Bearing in mind that the Catholic understanding of Christianity has dominated Peru ever since the Spaniards arrived, it is not surprising that art styles of late medieval Christianity and modern Southern Europe are frequently used. It is obvious that the Christian imagery has melded together with a number of other religious conceptual systems in a profound way.

Peru's religion can be regarded as a syncretistic religion. Christian-Catholic ideas are integrated into the worldviews of the native peoples, and the native religious belief systems have in turn brought about a new understanding of Christian ideas. This amalgamation has formed over a fairly extensive period of time, and today it is difficult to discern what is of Christian or non-Christian origin, as the historical synthesis has involved a mutual give and take.

Naturally, even the religious transculturation process has been dominated by the political and economic asymmetry between the rulers and the ruled. However, just as with textile art, we still see how the native capability for acquiring the new religion has not destroyed but merely fragmentized the older indigenous religion. Through the synthesis of the old and the new the old survives in a different and revived form.

The transcontextualization of indigenous religious traditions, as well as the trans-contextualization of artistic production, has enabled indigenous peoples to keep their pride and their multifaceted view of the world. For an outsider it is very difficult to fully realize the depth in this different worldview, as western religious scholars are trained mainly to examine cultures and religions dichotomously, that is, through delineating identities. However, in a Peruvian context this approach will only lead to affirmation of quantitative diversity, losing out on the most interesting aspects; namely, the transculturation and transcontextualization of religious traditions and worldviews. Some artworks from the Andean countryside can illustrate this.

Santiago de Pupuja is a small town high up in the Andes northwest of Puno on the Altiplano plain. Over a period of twenty years, the visual artistic expression of the Catholic congregation in this town has undergone an impressive and unique development.

Image 44. *Drawing* by a member of the parish of Santiago de Pupuja. In Schulte and Orzechowski (1997: 84).

Within the frame of the Western Catholic, catechetic visual theology – which in contrast to the liturgical iconography of the Eastern image theology focuses on the educational function of religious images, the two mission sisters Cristy Orzechowski and Berna Schulte have stimulated the members of their congregation to express their faith visually.[60]

Artistic education, catechesis, Bible education and even social events have been related to the production, exhibition, and distribution of various artworks. The entire process is accounted for in four volumes, containing a massive picture material, entitled "…y el Verbo se hizo Arte" (…and the Word Became Art).[61]

In the middle of the ruthless violence of the civil war, where the town was misused by both sides as a remotely situated battle stage, the inhabitants of Santiago de Pupuja manifest their vision of a peaceful kingdom of God and their community with the crucified and resurrected Creator and the Holy Spirit in the Andes with pride and firm devotion.

The artistic production commenced in the 1980s in connection with the making of catechetic teaching material and from then on it has only gathered pace. The Christians in the congregation, most of them of the Aymara people, choose symbols from Christian iconography that appeal to them. They use and transform these symbols in their art, which finds its expression in textile art, paintings, and drawings. The meeting with Christianity adds a narrative element to the native tradition and many artworks depict biblical stories. The symbols come into being as the creative process takes shape.

An interesting aspect to the creative process is that the Aymara artist often finds it challenging to form lines, while planes and multidimensional spaces are mastered superbly. This makes us wonder whether the creative technique of the Aymaras on a profound level is connected to a worldview characterized by dynamic relations. Is the defining line conceived of as an incision rather than the contour of a figure or an object? How do visual-technical forms of expression relate to worldview and perspectives on life in general?

The central deity in the Andean religion is Pacha Mama, Mother Earth, who embraces her

Image 45. Pabla Parqui P., *Without Title*, painting. In Schulte and Orzechowski (1997: 226).

Image 46. *Drawing* by a member of the parish of Santiago de Pupuja. In Schulte and Orzechowski (1993: 259).

124

children. Without the cultivation of seeds in the soil, no culture can survive in the borderland between the burning sunlight in the thin air during the day and the biting frost during the night. For centuries the Andean peoples at the Altiplano have developed a unique cultivation technique, involving for example the use of irrigation canals to stabilize the microclimate surrounding the cultivated fields. The preparation and use of the poor soil are among the most fundamental components in the human ecological subsistence structure, and thus it is not surprising that the Earth is regarded as a life-giving deity among Andean peoples. The fact that Mother Earth also can be understood as the Mother of God's Son is not a limitation of Andean faith; rather, it adds an extra dimension to the religion. The old and the new religion converge and become even stronger.

Another expression of the convergence between the Andean cosmic religion and the Christian creation myth is found in Sánchez's painting, which the editor of "…y el Verbo se hizo Arte" placed in the section "The Spirit of the Andean World."

The mountaintops, the sun, and the river with their eyes, faces, and hands have human features. According to Andean religion, divine guardian spirits, *apus* and *auquis*, reside in the mountains, and their internal hierarchical position is determined by the altitude of the peaks.[62] Earth, light, and water represent independent, life-giving elements. Fire is at the centre of the picture, and the dancing couple represents in a dual, two-sexed worldview the perfection which, according to Andean religion, always reveals itself in couple relationships. The pigeon, a symbol of the Spirit of God, the fox, the sheep, and the llama inhabit the upper part of the painting, while the burial mound with the cross is a reminder of the path of Christ's suffering.

The musical instruments signify the Andean peoples' connection to the Earth, and this connection is manifested in the most significant cultural expression, namely dance. The feet touching the ground I find to be the real core of the universe of Andean religion and human ecology. When the sole of the foot is carried by Mother Earth and floats above the Earth in the dance, God carries the body, society, images, and thoughts rhythmically through thin air over the wide plane. The collective dance during the special festival season is beyond doubt the most important

Image 47. Valentin Quispe Sánchez, *Without Title*, painting. In Schulte and Orzechowski (1997: 178).

Image 48. *Altar Cloth.* By an Aymara artist in Juli, Peru, c. 1980 (?), chapel in the guest-house of the Maryknoll Order in Puno, Peru. Photo: author.

stole is in stark contrast to the polished dark wood of the face. The new religion's clerical attire enfolds the body of the tall Aymara man in the shape of a cross. The sun disc with the cross sign creates a dark halo around his proud face. His neatly trimmed hair frames the cheeks and is reminiscent of the hairstyle of the Inca emperors. The accentuated round mouth area between the nose and the chin corresponds to the circular shape of the halo. The headband with triangles expresses the connection to the people.

In the crucifix, light and dark meet, and the new Christianity meets the cosmic religion. God has died as one of the people here in Juli. In a strange way, the aura points both toward life and death: as if the spirit still warms the body and the blood is still viscous. Proud, and with an inner, radiant, plastic power the Spirit carries the life of the facial features and the body. Just now did God die as Aymara, and he

Image 49. *Crucifix in Hardwood* (detail). Produced by a local artist in the 1970s, chapel of the vicarage in Juli, Peru. Photo: author.

rite in Andean culture. Additionally, the foot is also found in images from pre-Columbian times, where it is used as a symbol of human and how people are tied to the cosmic life process. Even churches are often decorated with motifs from dance festivals.

Inculturation and transculturation processes become obvious in the representation of Christ, the Word that became flesh, image, and art. In the parsonage chapel in the town Juli at the centre of Altiplano we meet the resurrected Christ as a Brother of the Aymara people.

The crucifix was made in the 1970s by a local artist. The painted white vestment with the

Image 50. *Painting* in the Church of Juli, Peru. Photo: author.

is still waiting for his resurrection through the Spirit.

Below the parsonage we find the majestic baroque cathedral, and just opposite from the church, close to the square, is the first building that the Spanish inquisition built in Latin America at the beginning of the seventeenth century. Today the building is closed down and it is no longer in use. "Just as well," is the scant comment from a local passer-by. The recently deceased, but in image and art already resurrected, is awaiting the liberation of the people and the entire cosmos in the place which once was the centre for European colonization of the strange and foreign land. In the 1970s the conquerors' "White Christ" became a dark Aymara in the Andes. The indigenization of Christianity continues.

However, the story about God becoming flesh in the Andes as a brother of the indigenous people began much earlier, and this can be seen in another artefact in Juli.

The baroque painting in the Juli church depicts the events of Christmas in the Nativity. The composition of the painting follows the conventions of its time. The three kings from the East adoring the child have Spanish features. Maria's pale complexion is hardly

Image 51. *The Cathedral of Juli,* Peru. Photo: Alfredo Bianco Geymet.

native of Palestine but belongs to the face of a South European, privileged and refined girl.

However, the cloth that the baby Jesus is swathed in indicates that the artist – long before anyone spoke of "inculturation" – made an independent theological interpretation. The Aymara Indians have a tradition, still alive today, of wrapping up their babies in an intricate, artistic manner using a combination of narrow and broader bands, just as the baby Jesus in the painting. The artist makes us aware of the fact that in Juli Jesus was born an Indian, although he fulfils all requirements with regards to the representation of the conquerors' visual power over the interpretation of the gospel. It is possible that the newly baptized Aymara Christians of the seventeenth century did not identify with the image of Mary and the three kings, but they did know how to receive, wrap up, take care of and look after the God that came to them as a child born in their midst.

As a conclusion, Peruvian art can teach us something about the transcultural power of visual arts. The encounter between the old and the new world, between the cosmic, local religion and Christian religion, between the small-scale, earth-bound culture and the global, large-scale, self-reproducing culture did lead to, in spite of all the violence, the emergence of creative survival art in the country.

Indigenization Challenges Art Theology

Our brief excursion to the colourful visual world of Peru yields three important insights for a contextual art theology.

First of all, the location of visual and world art in-between two worlds is highly influential for how we conceive the creative and reconciling potential of art theology. The art anthropological reflection over the cultural, technical, and socioeconomic preconditions for art production is just as important for art theology as a hermeneutic interpretation of the iconic expression of the artefacts. In a world with asymmetric and unjust relationships between people, ethnic groups and ecologically defined life forms, a central question is how artworks come into existence at the intersection of different identities.

Theologically, it is possible that the doctrine of Christ's two natures in a mutual, communicative union can shed some light on this encounter between two cultures. Perhaps the communication between the human and the divine continues in the cultural encounters among human beings? Can we imagine an analogy between the mystery of the incarnation and cultural syncretism?

Secondly, there is a distinct expression of the contextualization of Christianity in the turbulent intercultural space in Peruvian art. The indigenization was only given an historical interpretation in two directions: (a) from the Eurocentric Central European worldview through conquerors and missionaries to indigenous peoples, and (b) through adaptation, assimilation and transculturation from indigenous religion and art to creative and independent artefacts and belief and life systems that are understood both by the conquerors and the conquered.

However, there is a third direction in this spiral-shaped cultural exchange that we can only see traces of at the moment: (c) the reception of the indigenously reconstructed and newly constructed Christian worldview among the Conquistadors' heirs and descendants who wish to create a postcolonial culture in the context of the former rulers.

How can contextual art theology contribute to visualizing the liberating power of arts, not only among the victims of colonization, but also among those who wish to put an end to the colonial history that they inherited? The importance of postcolonial world art in the third and fourth world is obvious, but what power can it develop today and tomorrow in what used to be the first world?

What happens to the old world's interpretation of Christianity through and, not least, after indigenization? The challenge to a more profound synthesis, where indigenous and European traditions meet in a critical-constructive cultural process, where what is "best" and what is most beneficial for the people of a future common world from and for both cultures, can at this stage only be suggested. Art theology's reflection over artefacts can demonstrate visually the feeling that this synthesis is possible, albeit still only in small-scale artistic experiments.

Thirdly, and with reference to the treatment of the sensuous power of images, the earthbound religion of Peru offers a fundamental and precious insight for art theology, namely, how image-making is bound to physical and material elements. The hand, the eye, and the world of ideas remain steadily and insolubly connected to matter, canvas, colours (often made from minerals and plants), and tools, as well as to the imaginative and expressive powers of the body. The physical dimensions of religion and of art remain harmonious. Could visual arts even be regarded as a dance feast where people, only using their eyes and hands – glide over the planes of the created planet? Can religion and art unite in the feast with the Earth?

And the Icon Became Flesh – the Significance of Apophatic Theology for Picture Analysis

What is the relation between picture analyses and understandings of God? How can we relate picture theory to theology?

Should one even try to relate the two? One possible objection is that visual arts involve human production, while faith is a god-given knowledge of something non-human. Images are of this world and of humans, while God and faith in God is supernatural.

There are many good arguments against this dualistic conception of reality.

Firstly, in art history, both in the Western world and in other cultures, the depiction of the divine, spiritual, invisible and un-created has always been a fundamental dimension of visual arts. Even during the peak of rational science as opposed to what is regarded magical worldviews, artists have intensified their struggle for "the spiritual in art," at the same time as they have joined in on, reinforced and sometimes critically transformed people's general belief in the technological feasibility of most things. There has been no separation between divinity and secularism in modern art; rather, art has in a visionary manner revived the relationship between the two.

Secondly, Christianity's history of ideas shows that the idea of God becoming human, the incarnation, is an essential element of the Christian worldview. If one is concerned about God's actions, here and now, at specific times and in specific places, one cannot maintain a purely metaphysical understanding of the concept of God. "True God *and* true man," the ecumenical creed from 381 CE states as a formula of faith. It is not about the partition of divinity and humanity; at the heart of faith is the communication between the two.

With this background, we may freely search for creative answers to the question of the relationship between God and images. Which theory of image corresponds to the Christian idea of God according to which "God is One" and "God is Greater" than all things at the same time as God meets us like brother or sister, as one of us?

In this section I seek to answer this question through a reconstruction of the epistemology of the apophatic theology in late Antiquity. The view of the relationship between the nature of God and the work of God that was formed in the fourth century will serve as a tool for finding "God in images."

First we will investigate the characteristics of apophatic epistemology. Then we take a look at Byzantine imagery to see how it was able to visualize the invisible without abolishing its invisibility. Related to brief remarks in the third chapter,[63] we review how modernist artists sanction the iconoclast tradition by making pictures that defy the definition of a picture. In conclusion, I offer four reasons for constructively developing a contextual art theology in accordance with a classical apophatic, theological theory.

The Invisible Visualized – an Apophatic Pictorial Interpretation of God the Liberator

The apophatic theology developed in the Greek-speaking part of the Early Church in late antiquity.[64] The demand for an expression of Christian faith as an answer to the rational plausibility requirements of the prevailing intellectual elite mounted as the prosecution of Christians came to a halt around 350 CE. The orientation of the imperial power towards the new "religion" brought about a change in the imperial educated elite, whose demand for philosophical rationality was covered by theologians like Augustine and the three Cappadocian Fathers.

Based on expositions of the texts of John and Paul and philosophical conceptions of antiquity – first in Alexandrian theology and later in Cappadocian theology, primarily in Gregory of Nazianzus – the insight and epistemological principle evolved that neither angels nor humans can have knowledge about the *nature* of God but only about God's *work*, that is, about the liberating revelation of God's liberation economy that is open to humans and other sentient beings. Because God's nature and work ontologically are not separate entities, the creatures experience their Maker as the God that is the liberator of cosmos.

Ludwig Wittgenstein expressed the first thesis of this epistemology in the frequently quoted sentence: "Wovon man nicht sprechen kann, darüber muss man schweigen." (Whereof one cannot speak, thereof one must be silent.)[65] Wittgenstein stops here – before he develops his ideas about language games – while the apophatic theologians of late antiquity conclude that exactly because one is aware of the limitations of reason, one should speak about what one after all is able to say something about, that is, about our experiences with and of the acting God. Kant has developed the same idea for his critical, rational theology – but without having read the Cappadocians – in the principle that theology should contribute negatively to the "detection of the dialectic illusion" and positively to "the ideal of pure reason" which should not be regarded as identical to God's existence.[66]

It was imperative for the Early Church to establish beyond doubt that God the Creator and the Father essentially was one with the

Holy Spirit and the Son. God's only begotten Son is "of the same essence as the Father" (*homoousios*) and the Spirit "the Lord" – these were the most concise formulations of this doctrine at the ecumenical council in Constantinople in 381 CE.

In light of the historical continuity of Christianity, the ecumenical identity of the Eastern and Western church, and contemporary Christian dialogues with postmodern criticism of universalization approaches, it seems useful to revive apophatic theology within the context of an historical trinitarian doctrine. A modified version of apophatism may bridge the gap between ontological atomism and ontological holism within the discourse of postmodern epistemology.[67]

The difference in method between apophatic theology and negative theology is historically important, but sadly not properly acknowledged by many theologians.[68] While theologians of late antiquity formed the basis for the apophatism developed by Dionysius in the fifth century, the transference of this theology from the Greek-speaking Eastern Empire to the Latin-speaking Western Empire meant a reduction in content.

The negative and positive dual epistemology became a one-sided doctrine about the impossibility of having any knowledge about the essence of God (in general). Despite the vital patristic research into the topic, theologians still seem to think that apophatic and negative theology is the same thing, but this is missing the most important point. The cataphatic (positively action oriented) is part of the apophatic (negatively essence oriented) and is the goal of apophasis. It is this emphasis of the theologian's positive ability to express something about God that may make apophatism valuable for

art theology. Can a picture express God without abolishing the parallel greatness and littleness of the mystery of God on earth?

Another misconception is that apophatism is mainly a conception of the mystical experience of God, a contention not supported by historical facts. First of all, the modern concept of "mysticism" in general presupposes the renaissance idea of the autonomy of reason and rationality, an idea that does not exist in this formulation in antiquity. This view would entail that mysticism is the counterpoise of rationality, which is a very modern and not a classical idea.

Secondly, the apophatic theological method developed in a pronounced hostile and antagonistic discourse about the philosophical epistemology in confrontation partly with Neo-Aristotelian and Neo-Platonic positions and partly with the Neo-Arian monotheistic movement of the fourth century.

The Middle Platonic reception of some of the central parts of the Phaedo dialogue by the Late Plato paved the ground for a critical revision of the Aristotelian and Arian conception of the Creator's exemption from movement and passion. The contention of the superiority of the infinitely apathetic God, the Father, over all of creation and the earthly, corporeal and historical Son and his sister Spirit in and with us was successfully challenged and overcome by the Cappadocian Fathers by the use of exegesis, trinitarian theology, sophisticated apophatic epistemology, and analogous-imaginative ethics. In modern words: God's alterity, his monotheistic sublimity, was extended to the alienation of the social God, to the belief in God as a communion that came to us from afar.[69]

In the apophatic theology of the Eastern Early Church the tenet that one can only experience the *essence* of God negatively is related with the other insight that one may and should meet his/her *actions* positively, since essence and creation are one in God, while preserving the awareness of the incomprehensibility of God's essence. The second part of this insight has been obscured in the Western tradition, possibly because of the pneumatological reduction starting from the fifth century. Because one is aware of the negative, one should positively speak about the experience of and with him/her whose essence one can only be silent about, namely the experience of God's liberating work.

Gregory of Nazianzus interpreted God's essence and his work in God's "liberation movement"[70] in the creation as "being peacefully with each other." The divine hypostases, the Spirit, the Son and the Father, were to him, in all their liberation historical difference, united in one supreme unity of movement and will. The Cappadocian conception of God primarily focused on God's movement, the motion within God and the outward motion in a liberating movement with the created beings. According to Gregory[71] God also has an ethical purpose when he allows humans to use the concepts of justice, peace and love in relation to his intangible nature: because humans use these terms to analyse God they can actively aim for justice, peace and love for themselves. Just as God has become human in Christ, humans become divine through Christ, and this supports their practical strife for justice.

From here the analogy between God's kindness and the earthly justice developed – in spite of its basis in Middle Platonic philosophy – not *ontologically* but first and foremost *soteriologically*. One does not speculate about God's existence and essence but interprets the acting God today. The theologians of the Eastern Church, just as the Reformists later on, primarily pursue a salvation-historical line of thinking. They appropriate Platonic ontology for their interpretation of the divine "economy." This economy is analysed in an incarnation theological and synergetic perspective as a salvation history in which God and humankind interact according to the Theandric pattern for the co-existence of God and human, created and non-created in Christ.

Ontologically in patristic philosophy God is neither a "Being as Communion" (J. D. Zizioulas) nor a "model" for society (L. Boff)[72] but a communal "God in Context,"[73] a God who reveals him/herself in the different spaces of nature, culture and society as a compassionate and vital Liberator – in Luther's words: "...the visible and manifest things of God seen through suffering and the cross."[74]

In the Christian worldview, ontology is always inferior to soteriology. What is central is not the philosophical question of God's essence but the hopeful and suffering devotees' question about God's work: which God works for us, where, how, here and now?[75] Thus apophatic theology, even today, offers a fully fledged theory and method for discussing God's essence with a critical awareness of limits. Such awareness furthers an even more constructive and creative discussion about the ongoing liberating works of God. Perhaps apophatic theology can even help us not only to "speak about God" but also to "express the God who acts"? If the answer is yes, an apophatic art theology would be asked to interpret pictures that aim to portray God in relation both to God's invisible nature and to God's visible work: God *the creator* invisibly, but God *the liberator* visibly.

One part of this art theology connects the pictures' intrinsic value and God's greatness, while another part relates human creativity to the liberating power of the Spirit and the Son.

For art theology, first of all there proves to be a strange correspondence between the emphasis of God's supremacy and integrity, on the one hand, and the autonomy and intrinsic value of the work of art, on the other, a value many artists often have interpreted with the use of metaphysical and religious reference frameworks. In accordance with the epistemological method of apophatic theology one may analogously develop an art theological method that maintains the autonomy and intrinsic value of art without detaching art from the contexts of production and reception. However, the analogy between art reception and God experience should not be taken too far, involving an ontological juxtaposition of the integrity of the artwork and God's integrity. Similarly, one may not pantheistically deduce the existence of the Creator in the Creation based on one's experience of nature's sacredness, or physico-theologically from our knowledge of structures in nature. The analogy of art reception and God experience should not be interpreted ontologically but functionally soteriologically. Just as the making of a work of art purifies human vision, God liberates the creation of its agony.

Secondly, one may relate the experiences of an active, liberating God and the traditions of the resurrected Son and the life-giving Spirit, whose "truth liberates," to the dynamic relationship between artistic creation, artefact, and reception. In this sense, contextual art theology becomes apophatic through focusing on the question: how does God liberate in, with and through images?

The proposed programme is contextual in the sense that it takes a different approach than metaphysical-theological art theories which aspire for an ontological equality between religion and art or an ontological equality between God and the true, the good and the beautiful. In line with Friedrich Schleiermacher, I therefore take as a point of departure the Protestant understanding that in the freedom and autonomy of art we find what is also theology's concern, namely the freedom of artistic expression of and reflection over the creatures' liberating experiences with their Creator.

There is no God that we can imagine in general; rather, there is a God in particular whom the art theologian seeks in the specific visual universes. The art theologian does not seek a universal sort of person but unique human beings in the artefacts – people with the ability to communicate with each other and distance themselves from each other; people who are sinners yet justified and divine all at once. Suffering, struggling, hopeful, and liberated natures of all kinds possible in the creation become visible. The art theologian meets in art both the creation that suffers under suppressive regimes and the creation that hopes for its liberation. Both the clear experience of God that is reincarnated in the Son and indwells the world in the Spirit and the obscure experience of God as an "ultimate reality" (P. Tillich) have a place in this proposed aesth/ethics. Clarity and obscurity are not opposites; rather, they presuppose each other.[76]

Visualizing God's Creation in Image and Word – the Critical Potential of Image-making and Art Theology

In the following we will turn our attention to two image conceptions in late antiquity and the late modern image history that will further support the development of an apophatic and contextual art theology.

In the monumental work on "Bild und Kult," the German art historian Hans Belting heavily criticizes both historical and contemporary image theologians. Belting discusses the "power of images" against the "powerlessness of theologians," which theologians try to compensate with their text-based dominance of power. Belting's study purports to tell a "history of the image before the era of art," and he has collected an extensive material of eastern and western artefacts and gives a detailed account of the creation, style and reception of these objects. The noble objective of image history is to liberate religious images from the limitation and repression imposed on them by image theologians and modern art scholars.

Belting aptly criticizes theologians' methodological approach to images: "Their concept of visual images is so general as to exist only on the level of abstraction. They treat the image as a universal, since only this approach can yield a conclusive definition having theological significance."[77] Further, according to Belting, image theology has a practical purpose: "it supplied unifying formulas for an otherwise heterogeneous, undisciplined use of images."[78]

Belting justly emphasizes the meaning of the unique, visible artefacts in their context. It should be clear from the first chapter of this book that image theology with necessity, must always base and centre its interpretation in and around the physical and historical images in their context. Furthermore, it should be clear that this is not based on the hermeneutics of images; ultimately, it is related to incarnation theology. Just as theology within the contextual paradigm connects its interpretation of God to the situated experiences of the earthly-historical God, contextual image theology should preserve the connection to the visible image and thus also keep intact the image of God.

It is disturbing that an historically prominent image scholar like Belting does not recognize the emphasis in late antiquity and during iconoclasm on protecting the images' and image-making's intrinsic value and independent ability to interpret God's work. Just like Belting, the theological defenders of the image aimed at the visual medium's possibility and right to visually produce and initiate different experiences and traditions of encounters with God. Belting's sharp exposition of the entire political power dynamic is not only related to the Church but equally much to the court and even the sociopolitical world of artist organizations. The history of images has always encompassed both conflict and synthesis between a bottom-up/inside-out creativity and a top-down/outside-in representation. Giving theologians the sole blame for a general sociological power dynamic bears witness to an all too narrow understanding and lack of insight into the social system.

One example of the independent force, which is seen in the intrinsic value of images and image theology's ability to support this power, can be found in two pictures shown in the colour plate section (Image 52). The images are reproduced from a Byzantine manuscript with texts by Gregory of Nazianzus which was made for Emperor Basil I (867–886 CE).

In the upper image, we see on the left side how Jesus resurrects the dead Lazarus and on the right side we see his visit to Lazarus' friends Martha and Mary (cf. Jn 11:1–44 and Lk. 10:38ff.). Mary anoints the Lord's feet with "perfume" at the table, and she kisses his feet at the grave.

The lower image shows Jesus' entry into Jerusalem. In the same purple robe he, riding on an ass, together with the disciples approaches the city and its people. In the ninth century, artists added a narrative element to icon paintings. The purpose of the older icons was to accentuate the timelessness of the Godhead and of faith, but now icons were enriched with a narrative intention to represent an historical event – relatively loosely connected to the biblical text.

Naturally, one may regard these pictures as simple illustrations of the scriptural texts, whose primary aim is to give biblical legitimacy to the "theological speech/homilies" of the Cappadocian Father. However, on closer examination, we see in the picture the theological independence of the, to us, unknown artist.

The representation of Jesus' halo and robe follows the conventions, while his feet guide our eyes and thoughts to a highly topical theme, especially in our time: the relation between God's and women's corporeality. While the upper half of the picture depicts the male sphere, we find the women in the lower sphere. At the grave, Martha's eyes seek Jesus, whose illuminated eyes gaze slightly upwards.

In the Gospel of John, one of the points in the narrative of Lazarus is that Lazarus' death will show "the glory of God." The artist shows us that the women not only see God's glory but they also feel it with their hands. The artist binds together the two accounts of Jesus' visit to Martha and Mary in the Luke's Gospel and their plea to Jesus to resurrect the beloved Lazarus in John's Gospel, amongst other using the two women's physical touch of the God person.

It is difficult to decide whether Jesus or Mary is the main figure in the scenes. Perhaps they both are. The visual centre of the picture is naturally in the head and hands of the Jesus figure, while the gaze is drawn downwards to the centre of action and the meeting between the surfaces of the brown and the violet bodies.

Is one to assume that the artist offers us his own specific interpretation of the relationship between divinity and earthly matters, between men and women, the theo-logical narrator and the visually represented dimension in the gospel? The picture questions – just as icon paintings inspired by incarnation theology – the relation between the divine and the human, visible and invisible, and it does so on the terms of the visual media, without interference from general conceptions of theology. In this sense, the picture even speaks to the theologians and it sheds a new light on Gregory's text about God's body in Christ.

Against this background, Belting's opinion that "we are everywhere obstructed by written texts, for Christianity is a religion of the word" rarely seems convincing.[79] Rather, in this manuscript, the Word (the two Bible texts in this context) seems to have inspired the artist to develop a stronger visual theological expression in communication with the texts and their contexts, and thus also in interaction with Gregory of Nazianzus' interpretation of the mystery of God's incarnation.

Belting's cutting observation of how theologians seized power over images is very much to the point.[80] But it would be both historically and systematically wise to distinguish between the power interest of the church and that of theologians. Belting should have been even more differentiated in seeking support for a positive theological argumentation for the inherent value of images, as this view is equally common throughout the history of image theology as are the failed attempts by rulers to transfer the power of images to words.

What contextual theology can learn from Belting's criticism of image theology is that one must constantly maintain self-critical reflection in relation to one's own execution of power. From the criticism against Belting, contextual theology can learn not to accept uncritically a generalizing art historical programme that seeks one universal explanation of the history of the image[81] instead of searching the image of God in the many different visual universes where we meet the liberating, trinitarian God.

The art anthropological approach outlined in the previous chapter seems more apposite for an understanding of religious images, even before art, than does Belting's programme. The most important reason for choosing this approach before Belting's historicizing reproduction of collected empirical observations is that it is more in line with artists' self-comprehension. The pre-modern artist belongs to a community of believers who visually can express their encounter with God in the pictorial medium, both individually and within a social context in many and versatile traditions. Both the artists and the contemplators, especially the illiterate viewers, have at all times constituted a concentration of power too strong for men of the cloth to break, even though this constellation obviously always has been and still is a threat to those who wish to rule over people's eyes, hands, bodies, and thoughts with the power of the word.

Historically it is also clear that the synthesis of image and word, of the God who is "Image"[82] and the God who is "Word"[83] has always been an important topic for image theologians, albeit sadly confined to the narrow corridors of power. Thus we have another reason for claiming that now is the time for a creative, self-critical reconstructing image theology in a contextual and apophatic awareness of the intrinsic value of images and of God.

Down the "via negativa" towards an Apophatic and Cataphatic Theology of Art

A totally different account of relations between the visual arts of late antiquity and contemporary art theology is found among leading German art historians' and art theologians' reflections over the reception of the image ban in modern abstract art.[84] This reflection is based on the assumption that the image ban in the ancient biblical tradition and in Byzantine ideology has been appropriated and transformed in some segments of modern art.

Artists like Barnett Newman make pictures that resist being interpreted as images. In a way that resembles the ban against physically reproducing divinity, the inherent "sacredness" of pictures is being shielded. Visual art is reinterpreted as an "internal iconoclasm" under modern conditions[85] or as a battle against "the content of imagination" which, like the theological image ban, stems from the idea that God's supremacy expresses the "negation with regards to something higher, which otherwise one could not obtain knowledge of."[86]

The Swiss theologian Kurt Lüthi seeks a positive development of this line of thought in his analysis of Arnulf Rainer's oil paintings of the crucifixion within the framework of negative theology.[87] (See the colour plates section, Image 53.) Lüthi pertinently analyses Rainer's pictorial world in relation to his ability to express the invisible in the visible pictorial medium, without giving the invisible physical expression. It is merely suggested, hinted at, and its existence can be felt without becoming tangible and graspable.[88]

Up till now I have analysed both artists in the modern context and the image theologians that follow them in relation to negative theology, and thus I take them to be representatives of a typical Western Church tradition. In connection to what was said above about the historical reduction of the cataphatic (positive) and apophatic (negative) dimensions of apophatic theology, I find the idea of an art theology that only travels down the "via negative," the road of negative God cognition, very problematic.

Firstly, this reduction involves a clear separation of what is human and what is divine, and thus has the risk of seeing theo-ontology as superior to the salvation-historical purpose of the incarnation.

Secondly, this reduction is fundamentally tied to the conception of God's essence and tends to see ontology as superior to soteriology by emptying any visualization of God of aesthetic qualities and the ability to act.

Just like the enlightened, contextual apophatic theology of the Eastern Church, it ought to be the undertaking of art theology to expand the horizon in order to make both the invisibility of God's nature and God's visualized nature in the artistic portrayals radiate brilliantly.

Four Arguments for an Apophatic, Contextual Art Theology

The following four assertions support further development of contextual art theology with the help of apophatic epistemology.

Through correlation to apophatic theology, which had a major influence on ecumenical Christianity and both Eastern and Western theology, art theology gets a continuity that helps transcontextualize a pillar of the methodology of the Christian worldview. The method of late antiquity, melding together the self-reflexive insight about the mystery of God's invisible, and for humans and angels, unattainable essence with the constructive interpretation of the concrete experience of and with God's liberation work in different places and at different times, offers both a contextual basic theory of the perceptual experience of God and a classic theory of the mystery of God's transgression of time and space.[89]

Secondly, the apophatic awareness can contribute to a theological aesthetic; a sensuous interpretation of God's incarnated visual work in an abundance of worldly and historical contexts. Taking into consideration soteriology's superiority over ontology in classical theology, this aesthetic is primarily the aesthetic of liberation, that is, an interpretation of the creatures' sensuous experiences in the meeting with God's liberating actions.

In relation to contextual art theology's specific interpretations of works of art, the aesthetic of liberation focuses on the follow basic questions: How is God represented sensuously-corporeally visually through the image-making and reception processes in the physical works of art? How do these artefacts interpret God? How do we sense and understand God's liberating actions in images? How is art developed as a "place for aesthetic life praxis" where religion vitalizes social, ethical relations?[90]

Thirdly, an apophatically formed art theology offers an analogy to the incarnation mystery in accordance with the classical and contextual paradigms of theology. "Communicatio idiomatum" (the communication of the natures) was the early Christian formula for the incarnation, signifying the communicative union of divinity and humanity as the defining characteristic of a Christian worldview.

A Christian art theology that reflects this mystery only iconographically, that is, in relation to the artefacts selected for interpretation, does only fulfil ecclesiological requirements, not theological requirements. Only an art theology that in theory and method offers an analogy to the "theandric"[91] mystery will be capable of functioning as an interpretative tool in accordance with early church and biblical continuity.

Like the iconoclastic theologians of the eighth century and contemporary art scholars, contextual art theology should pay heed to the special nature of visual art, with its capacity for expressing visually and independently human perspectives on God. In agreement with the image-friendly theologians of the iconoclastic controversy and the autonomy that modern art claims, contextual art theology preserves the freedom of images, albeit in mutual communication with the word and other forms of expression (e.g., music, poetry, drama, and popular culture).

The tradition of incarnation theology presents partly an image programme for Christian pictorial arts and partly a creation-theological, open iconographical programme for seeking novel and surprising revelations of God in a diversity of visual universes. Incarnation theology is about protecting the ongoing, rather than the historical, revelation mystery. The image was not only in the beginning, but the image continues to exist even in the middle of salvation history and towards its conclusion. Art is giving life to the icon after it has ceased to be and is resurrected as God's image.

Fourthly, the sketched apophatic epistemology provides a solid defence of the autonomy of visual arts. Although this idea was not developed in Byzantine theology, it seems to me that such an extension would be in full agreement with the intentions of the Cappadocian Fathers.

By establishing a self-critical, reflexive reservation against human speculations about the essence of God, a conjecture that could easily lead to the development of individual representations of God that are made idolatrously normative for other people, the Eastern theologians of late antiquity managed to keep the integrity of God's mystery and the experience of God in specific contexts. Only by speaking specifically of God, that is, of the work of God, can one maintain devotion to the Creator of "everything visible and invisible."

If God not only reveals himself in text and word but also in image, the same principle applies here: only by seeking out God's work in images, and not embarking on a general conjecture of the nature of God with the risk of mistaking God and image, can image theology sustain the simultaneity of negative and positive interpretation in apophatism.

The dusk embraces the light, and darkness is no longer only dark. God's creatures can only see his/her nature in God's creation. Aesthetics is the mother of theology and ethics. The perception of God in image precedes the discursive reflection over God in picture analysis. The method for picture analysis developed in the first chapter of this book is thus further supported by another theological argumentation. Because God meets us in his/her and our bodies, the interpretation of God in image and word should continually search for their origin. In the beginning was God, and God became image and word, and both became flesh.

"...and the Life of the Coming World" – the Significance of Trinitarian Theology and Pneumatology

Spirit, Who Gives Life...

The early Christian belief in a God that through the Son became flesh, lived, suffered,

Image 54. Julius Schnorr von Carolsfeld, illustration no. 226, *The Outpouring of the Holy Spirit*. Woodcut, in Julius Schnorr von Carolsfeld, *Die Bibel in Bildern*, 1852–1860.

died, and resurrected was never confined to human metaphors. Naturally, the experiences of and with the worldly and historical "Son of Man" brought about a proliferation of metaphors from the human sphere, although visual representations of Jesus were introduced with some caution and relatively late in Christianity. Pictures of Christ did not get a place in the church till after the politicization of faith and of the Church in the late fourth century.[92] But for the early Christians God always was more than man. The communication between the human and the divine, created and non-created is interpreted soteriologically from the fourth to the ninth century, primarily with the use of images and ideas about God's Holy Spirit.

In order to speak, primarily in the tradition following the Gospel of John, about God's ongoing salvation history after the Son has returned to his Father in his "ascension," Gregory of Nazianzus coined the term "inhabitation," to dwell in something.[93] After God has become flesh in the human Jesus, the Creator continues his liberating work with and in Creation through the Holy Spirit. The Son and the Spirit swap place in creation. After the incarnation, becoming flesh, follows the inhabitation, the in-dwelling. God inhabits the world in the Holy Spirit. In the Eastern theology of the fourth century, the image of God and especially the ideas about the Holy Spirit are connected to the understanding of space. The older Hebraic and Christian

139

traditions emphasized the unbreakable connection between the Spirit and life.[94] After the consolidation of Christianity and before its imperialistic politicization (350–391 CE), theologians reflected on the life-giving work of the Spirit, especially in relation to space.[95]

What contemporary art theologians can learn from the apophatic trinitarian worldview of the fourth century is apophatically, both negatively and positively, to analyse expressions of God's nature and liberating work in concrete image worlds.

Secondly, we can learn how to seek visual representations of the Son and the Spirit with salvation-historical and trinitarian awareness. Rather than reductionistically identifying only explicit references to selected biblical narratives about the person Jesus, art theology should expand its horizon and include sign systems that go beyond the human aspect. The Spirit should not be reduced to one single sign: Spirit = pigeon.

Instead one should understand the image symbolism epistemologically apophatically: the sign signifies the signifier, which means that the sign/image is not entirely that which it signifies, but that the signifier takes part in the signified. God meets us in images; s/he acts in, with and as image, albeit not entirely visible.

Thirdly, trinitarian theology offers a religious-philosophical tool for interpreting diversity *and* wholeness, continuity *and* change, and spatial simultaneity and unity in a mutual relation.[96] The key to what appears as pressing challenges in the late modern globalization process may, perhaps unexpectedly, partly be found in late antiquity.

Finally, trinitarian theology offers a social dimension of immense ethical and thus also aesth/ethical significance. Through the emphasis on God's sociality as a community in dynamic motion, it presents a theologically qualified perception of reality from which the Eastern Church tradition develops its aesthetic-based ethic. Orthodox theologians often say that "God's trinity is our social ethic," and by that they mean that the experience of the encounter with the triune Godhead offers a model for and a vision of a better society and a creation liberated from ecological violence.

Similar to the analogy between the image of God and the ethical nature and social vision of justice in all life's good relations one could develop an aesthetic of liberation based on the trinitarian view of God.

Can images shed light on the mystery of how God appears before the faithful as a divine, perfect communion ruled by peace, love and justice? Can the liberation of the social and nature relationships that are destroyed by evil take place in, with and through pictures? Can images be regarded as a tool for God's creative liberation movement in and for the creation?

...Liberates Space...

The Basque sculptor Eduardo Chillida (1924–2002) gives the following response to a question about his view of space:

> Space to me is some kind of medium. We are part of it. Space is the most vibrant force that surrounds us. It is like Spirit... One cannot actually say anything about space. One has to feel this type of space; it must be some kind of reflection of something inside us.[97]

Chillida proceeds to describe the sensation deriving from looking around in an old Roman church in Burgos. After a while he can feel and interpret "the unity between the shape of the windows and the bricks."

> Then my eyes moved outwards, through these opposites (in shape) that I perceived as a unity. There were no longer any windows or bricks.

Image 55. Eduardo Chillida, *Esertoki III*. 1990, iron, © DACS, London 2006.

There was only space. I stood before this open space; I looked at it from the inside and out through the windowpane; and still this space, that I watched, was different from the space that surrounded it. Believe it or not, it had a different intensity and density.[98]

The confined, constructed space that surrounds us and the open space that surrounds the confined space and us are, for the artist, both part of us in a spiritual and physical sense. One can feel it, see it, and sometimes even hear it. Spaces, both the open and confined ones, are alive. They are spaces that breathe time. Our experiences of and sensitivity to space are important to us. Space is like spirit.

Spirit is from an old Greek name called the "life giver." Through and in open spaces the Spirit of God gives life. Is what we find here – the same thing that the theologians of early

Christianity before us found when they accentuated the Spirit's active presence in the world – one of the richest wells of art theology? Is the space in which all pictures emerge the gift of God's life-giving Spirit?

Chillida said that space was *like* Spirit. Space is not the Spirit but a fruit of the life-giving work of the Spirit – in early Christian vernacular. It is the vestibule to "the life of the world to come" referred to in the Nicene Creed of 381 from the first council in Constantinople. And thus the artistic medium opens up for an interpretation of pictures as one of the Spirit's places in the home of the Creator.

In the following we will look at three works of art that have come into existence under very different circumstances. Only one of them refers explicitly to a biblical narrative of God's Holy Spirit. In relation to the other two, the pneuma-topological, spiritual place-related

141

interpretation takes place in my own reception, although I do seek support for my interpretation in the painting and in the artist's context.

In 1990 Eduardo Chillida made "Esertoki III." Corroded iron in two compact blocks welded together; so what?

Our eyes will probably linger for a moment at the spaces in the right part of the piece. The two blocks are angled slightly over the perpendicular; the angle between the horizontal plane and the vertical erect block is versatile in its complexity where the different cross, square and angular shapes are integrated into each other in multiple ways; they complement and mutually confront one another. The pointed shape extends out of the object towards the surrounding space to the right. The space in the angle seizes the object from the outside and in, while its upper right corner probingly stretches out into the open.

The entire object rests heavily on the ground while at the same time slowly and with great concentration pulling itself upwards. The joint between the two blocks is not a border; rather it melds together the two seemingly divergent velocities to a strange plastic force.

A recurring issue in Chillida's production is the exploration of the invisible inner space that is surrounded by the visible shapes. Early on the artist experimented with the clenched hand that conceals the space it grabs and at the same time gives an indication of its inner shape through the lines and surfaces of the hand. There is a reciprocal interaction between the exterior and interior in Chillida.

The hand in *Esertoki III* has opened and shows us its simple and yet complex space within the space that carries the exterior of the eroding blocks. The shape of the cross is varied plastically in the upper part and through the revealing and concealing play of the spaces in the middle. Chillida generally places his cross shapes in open or hidden spaces. The reference to the passion of "the Son of Man" is one of his basic tools. Considering what was said above about the artist's view of the Spirit's manifestation of, in and through space, a trinitarian interpretation of *Esertoki III* does not seem far-fetched.

The object invites us, as on a bench, to take a seat and let our bodies and eyes rest for a while. Corporeality and spirituality do not become converses but melt together in a union that invites our minds to join in. What is pulled down turns and moves upwards. What faces outwards turns inwards. What is pulled up is drawn to the ground. God's creative liberating movement is top down and bottom up, inside out and outside in. Heaven and earth are open to one another and they create life, that is, several spaces between themselves in the artwork.

Gregory the Theologian was convinced that the Spirit worked together with the living and resurrected Son.[99] Chillida's sculpture takes shape in the cross. The cross is straightened out, straightened up, bent, stretched and compacted; it is varied till it begins to live from within again. The explosive force and strength of Chillida's hands condensates the artwork. Our minds are pulled into the centre of the piece: the biggest "gap" of the sculpture, which only consists of air and sphere, the open space in the elongation of the contour of the two blocks just right of the vertical golden section of the middle section.

Paradoxically – or perhaps more accurately – apophatically, it seems as if the most significant space of the object consists of air! Here the Spirit blows wherever she likes. Out and in, back and forth, up and down and back up again. The crosses (in the plural) do not in this context remain motionless, but they start moving slowly. The indicated crosses and the actual cross shapes morph into each other, emphasizing the feeling that the Spirit gives life and space to the cross and the heavy matter.

"Space is the most living entity," Chillida said. "Except for the holy life giver herself," we should add, in communion with the enlightened faithful of early Christianity.

...Moves and Touches...

The movement in, through and of space was also a concern for Auguste Rodin.

In one of the great works in the history of drawing we meet the dancer in an undefined space. (See the colour plates section, Image 56.) The image space comes into existence through her movements. In France 1906 Rodin had seen the Royal Cambodian Ballet and he was tremendously fascinated by the harmonic movements of the ballet dancers. Enthusiastically he compares the group of dancers to the marble that he loved so dearly, and he praised the "suppleness and the exotic element from the Far East" that the ballet communicated. Rodin saw in the dance the element that stays unchanged over time and space; however, he did not postulate generalizations over this topic – he had one absolute requirement for the interpretation of universality: "But this constancy relies on one term: sensitivity for tradition and religious faith."[100]

Although visual art by its very nature must accentuate stillness, what rests in the time of the eye, by balancing four different techniques, Rodin succeeds in an unprecedented manner to capture the spiritual form of the dance movement; "the dance gesture in essence," as Rainer Maria Rilke aptly described Rodin's Cambodian dancer drawings.

The drawing does not have any explicit references to the religious world, and a theological interpretation can only be made tentatively based on a few observations.

Rodin's drawing is of interest to our contextual art theology because it is so intense in its quest for a synthesis of both time and space in the unique and universal gestures of dance. The dancer preserves her Cambodian identity, discreetly represented in her clothes and hair. The dance of the image comes first, by the unique connection to not only the individual and cultural identity of the dancer, but also to the specific moment and place when the artist experienced her, a quality of simultaneous uniqueness and universality that goes right to the heart of contextual theology.

It is not the deduction from the general to the specific but the experience of the specific that is the basis for the artist's conception and interpretation of the universal.

Like the contextual theologian based in God's flesh and dwelling on earth in an historical context, Rodin bases his unique expression of the dance in his very personal experience of it, and thus he communicates to viewers in different cultural spaces a sense of the profundity of the dance and the spiritual movement. The Spirit blows whichever way she likes and she both touches and is touched. The dancer does not move as she pleases but "sensitive to tradition" and "faith." The contemplator must also follow the movement in his/her tradition and faith if s/he wants to take part in life's movement in the Spirit's creative image space. The woman's movement in the dance extends into the movement in the viewer´s eyes and body, and continues into Rodin's hand that in turn leads the movements of our eyes further through the perpetually open space.

...and Creates Land and Cityspace Anew

Finally we will look at a painting whose title certainly is a direct reference to a traditional belief in God's Holy Spirit; however, the artistic expression in its own right supports the Spirit's contemporaneous and co-spatial visible invisibility.

The French painter Jean Fouquet (1415/20–1477/81) made this miniature as an illumination to *The Hours of Étienne Chevalier* around 1452. (See Image 57 in the colour plates section.)

According to the landscape conventions of renaissance painting – where the presumably "reborn" human being with her restricted perspective visually starts to conquer the landscape – Fouquet shows that he has a good command of the rules of landscape painting at the same time as he freely and independently gives the medieval urban landscape an autonomous and unique character. With a characteristic style – which in its formal abstraction reminds me of Lionel Feininger, the excellent modern painter known for his depiction of human-made environments – Fouquet joins the versatile shapes of the red rooftops to one continuous unity with both melody and harmony. The play of the house shapes has an intrinsic value in relation to the meaning of the theological scene and the content of the text. The portrayal of the landscape, the cityscape, the community of the faithful, and the spiritual drama in the heavens remain continuous. In all four significant aspects of the painting the overall theme resonates: "The Right Hand of God Protecting the Faithful against Demons."

The demons are depicted as small devils with pointed, bat-like wings. Even in their flight they bicker and pester each other. "Violence breeds violence breeds..." was the slogan of the peace movement in the 1980s.

The hand of God reaches out from a sky that reminds us more of an ocean whose surface is broken by the upward or downward reaching hand, creating peace-bringing, harmonious ripples on the water. These ripples create a closed, vaulted room that the demons desperately try to escape. The light beam flows vertically down onto the meadow on the riverbank. Here it creates a corresponding white-greyish circular surface that we apprehend as the centre of the spring that slowly spreads its greenery and sprouting plant life on the town's surfaces. The trees have just budded, and one feels the rising temperature. The walls vibrate from the light that slowly grows in intensity. The cathedral with its compact space gives stability and continuity to the city's body.

On the nearest riverbank is a group of worshippers. The clergy are standing with their backs against us, and the painter identified them with robes characteristic of older Byzantine iconographic style. The praying monks with tonsures are not obediently hunched and bent; rather their bodies are open and face upwards, unable to see the drama with their eyes, but contemplatively in touch with the exorcism taking place above.

The city is liberated. The Spirit has defeated evil and gives new life to the town and the land, water to the beasts, and peace to the people. Hildegard von Bingen later characterized the work of the Holy Spirit with expressions like greening, blossoming and enlightening.

The power of the Church in Fouquet's painting is not found in the building but in the fact that the faithful are gathered in a circle before God and the liberating Spirit. Their community is a consequence of and a part of, not a prerequisite for, the liberating work of the Spirit.

We do even see a hint of criticism against the Church in this artistic interpreter of God. The shapes of the priests' mantles indeed follow the traditional iconographical conventions, but why are the edges jagged, similar to the demon's toothed wings?

In Fouquet's time there was conflict between the poor people's theologians, the Franciscans, and the appointed church leaders higher up in the hierarchy. One may possibly detect a critical question in Fouquet's picture, especially in the group of figures at the front, about whether the demons have been banished from the creation for all eternity or whether they possibly from time to time can be seen in unexpected places, for example in the Church.

Even if spring and liberation through the life-giving Spirit now have reached the city and the surrounding land, the cosmic drama has not yet seen its conclusion. The believers still await "the life of the coming world" and the arrival of "new heavens and a new earth."

If the concluding parts of the book have succeeded in showing the potential of a theological picture analysis which is based both in the classical trinitarian pneumatology and in an interpretation of what is unique in the time and space of the visual realm, then the author will count himself blessed.

As made clear in the introduction, the concluding chapter merely offers a sketch, not a fully developed programme. As a sketch, it will hopefully provide the reader with some tools from traditions within picture analysis and theology, and from the author's personal inventory.

Despite the fact that the author, and now also the reader – in full awareness of the iconic differences in picture analysis – have wasted

quite a few words on talking about images, the reader may developed a sense of and even increased insight of the fact that God not only meets the faithful in written signs but that God also liberates creation in, with and through images. And even if the final part of this tenet expresses an insight deriving from faith rather than science, we have hopefully managed to argue rationally for the thesis that image-making in different cultures at different times in no way has abandoned the challenge to express the encounter with God in pictures. "The lack of images distances God"[101] – creative pictures lessen the distance between creatures and God.

The reflection over this continuous, intense, and obvious encounter with "the spiritual aspect of art" and art images has in a destructive manner been ignored in the academic reflection. What you may have gained as you finish this book is the recognition that this should no longer be the case.

Summary

- The process of secularization has admittedly freed religious forms of expression from the dominance of established institutions. However, at the onset of a new millennium, there are no indications that secularization has affected our inclination to reinterpret our lives with the use of religious tradition, language games, and images when the myths of success, prosperity, and beauty without suffering fail us. Quite the contrary, this process seems to further emphasize the importance of investigating which images of God or which graven images control our lives. Both art and religion are capable of countering the effect of economic disciplining and of widening the life space of modern man. Art and religion are capable of – albeit not automatically – developing liberating possibilities.

- The theological approach to visual arts in this chapter is based on God's love for those in need of liberation, for the poor, and in the vision of liberation for the entire creation. In the context of liberation theology, the salvation historical significance of visual arts and image-making is focused on. The idea of the autonomy of art is thus a necessary prerequisite, and also a critical corrective to the Christian faithfulness in confession. What is the impact of art for the sake of art on the religious hope for liberation of the poor and the entire creation? How can one develop a (visual) theology of art within the larger context of the contextual theology paradigm?

- The chapter sketches seven fundamental components of a contextual art theology. Each section is based in a picture analysis that visualizes one important aspect of contextual art theology.

- The theologian must learn to recognize the unicity and autonomy of the visual medium. The contextual art theology will contribute to expanding theology with the insight of image-making's unique ability to express experiences of and with God. Without an iconographical perspective and a visual dimension, theology necessarily remains biased and confined to a narrow approach to texts and rationality that is completely ignorant about the perceptual diversity of the human body. Therefore, contextual art theology not only aims at adding tools for expressing experiences with

God, but also at laying the ground for a richer and more complex view of the corporeality of both God and humans.

- The second characteristic of a contextual theology of art is based on God's suffering and crucifixion, and the ability of visual media sensuously to give rise to empathy. This second feature is also the requirement that the passion history of God and the inculturation of the crucifixion constitute an incontestable element of the Christian worldview and thus also of a Christian theology of art. The ability of the visual media to emphatically express events and feelings in a way that touches both body and mind is very often overlooked in theologians' art reflection. However, compassion for the poor is, according to the early Christian tradition, the primary sign of people's love of their neighbour, God, and themselves. Art theology reflects on how this compassion in the love of the poor is expressed in pictures.

- A third characteristic of the contextual art theology is found in the awareness of visual arts' capacity for visualizing and realizing visions. The visual arts embody an anticipatory power of showing what no one has seen, of visualizing what we can see only with our inner vision. This makes visual arts an important, specific tool that can help the expansion of the Kingdom of God in the (entire) creation. The visual arts, by their inherent power and emphatic capacity, have an eschatological power to represent the visions of God and the faithful. The image is not only in the beginning; it forebodes redemption and the arrival of the new creation.

- Observations of the multicoloured visual universe of Peru yield three important insights for a contextual theology of art. First of all, the location of visual and world art in-between two worlds is highly influential for how we conceive the creative and reconciling potential of art theology. In a world with asymmetric and unjust relationships between people, ethnic groups and ecologically defined life forms, a central question is how artworks come into existence in the intersection between different identities.

  Secondly, there is a distinct expression of the contextualization of Christianity in the turbulent intercultural space in Peruvian art.

  Thirdly, and with reference to the treatment of the sensuous power of images, the earthbound religion of Peru offers a fundamental and precious insight for art theology, namely how image-making is bound to physical and material elements.

- What is the relation between God and images? We may seek the answer through a reconstruction of the epistemology of the apophatic theology in Late Antiquity. The view of the relationship between the nature of God and the work of God that was formed in the fourth century will serve as a tool for finding "God in images." In the Byzantine visual world, the ability to visualize the invisible without abolishing its invisibility was developed. Modernist artists accept the image ban positively by making pictures that desist being perceived as images. The final part offers four reasons for constructively developing a contextual theology of art in compliance with a classical apophatic, theological theory.

- What contemporary art theologians can learn from the apophatic trinitarian worldview of the fourth century is to analyse apophatically, both negatively and positively, expressions of God's nature and liberating work in concrete visual universes.

  Secondly, we can learn how to seek visual representations of the Son and the Spirit with a salvation-historical and trinitarian awareness.

  Thirdly, trinitarian theology offers a religious-philosophical tool for interpreting diversity *and* wholeness, continuity *and* change, and spatial simultaneity and unity in a mutual relation.

  Finally, trinitarian theology offers a social dimension of immense ethical and thus also aesth-/ethical significance. Through the emphasis on God's community in dynamic motion, it presents a theologically qualified perception of reality from which the Eastern Church tradition develops its aesthetic-based ethic.

  A focal question for a contextual theology of art, within the paradigm of classical theology, is how God's Holy Spirit liberates and brings life to the space of creation.

Notes

Preface

1 Tapies (1994: 19).

2 The term "west" in this context should be taken to mean "Western," i.e., it refers to the modern European culture rooted in the ancient Egyptian and Greek cultures. The term "Western Church" refers to the Catholic, Protestant, Anglican and Evangelical Christian traditions, as opposed to the Orthodox tradition of the Eastern Church.

3 For a more elaborate discussion of the "visual culture", see Bergmann (2004). The notion "life interpretation" is a literal translation of the Swedish term *livstolkning* or *livsåskådning*, and it applies to the analysis of ideologies, attitudes, values and worldviews in religious and other ideational systems.

4 Whoever demands an iconology with logic and constant postulates needs to learn more about the nature of images and iconology. Böhme (1999: 12) makes this entirely clear: "Das Ziel der ästhetischen Theorie kann auch nicht die Aufstellung allgemeiner Sätze sein, vielmehr geht es um die Ausarbeitung von Unterscheidungen, durch die ästhetische Erfahrungen sprachfähig werden."

5 Freire (1972: 38ff.). According to Freire (p. 42), freedom is an absolutely necessary requirement in the struggle for the perfection of humankind. In my opinion the aesthetic dimension is an unavoidable and necessary element in this struggle. Cf. even Marcuse and his account of the independent dimension of aesthetics and the critical function of art (1980: 11-17, 70f.), in relation to Marxist social philosophy. According to Marcuse, the individual's lack of freedom is reflected in the autonomy of art. Art makes a critical contribution to the struggle for liberation through its aesthetic form (p. 17). For Marcuse (and Adorno), art is an authentic utopia based on reminiscence (p. 74).

6 Nobel discusses how the training of the hand in woodwork has a special position in the Nordic countries and how an opposition toward an education system dominated by Western culture has emerged. Based on different philosophical traditions and tradition from different continents, this opposition movement emphasizes the importance of the *hand* for learning, for critical thinking, and for creative practice.

7 See Virilio (1999) for a discussion of the impact of time acceleration on our worldview and the breakdown of our reality concept in the telecommunication age.

8 Stock (1990: 175-81).

9 Molander (1995) gives several good arguments for this.

10 Cf. Volp (1980a: 338f.).

11 Bergmann (1994a: 60).

12 In order not to make the text more specialized than is required for the present purposes, I have chosen not to give an exhaustive account and critical discussion of all current theories of images. A comprehensive

account of the image concept in theology can be found in Volp (1980a). For a philosophical and historical account of the concept of image, I refer the reader to the chapter "Bild" in Historisches Wörterbuch der Philosophie (I, 913-21). The reader who, for example, anticipates a semiotic account will be disappointed. In my view, the semiotic approach focuses too strongly on the linguistic sign, and this may divert attention from the unique nature of images. Furthermore, semioticians often tend to ignore the historical dimension of image creation and image analysis. In this context it is also relevant to question why I have not included other French philosophers – in addition to Merleau-Ponty, Foucault, Lacan, and Virilio – especially within post-structuralism. In Martin Jay's comprehensive and recognized study it is shown how the post-structuralists tend to be stuck in an "iconophobian," image hostile tradition. This is given thorough coverage in my essay on the challenge of visual culture to theology (Bergmann 2004).

13 As in Chapter 1, I give a presentation of the essentials. For more comprehensive accounts of art theory, see Henrich and Iser (1993), and for the history of art theory and an overview of the different theoretical approaches, see Belting (1988).

Chapter 1

1 Andersen (1989: 171).

2 Asger Jorn, *Gotik kontra germanisme*, in the Danish newspaper Politiken, 16 November 1965. Quoted from Shield (1995: 44).

3 About Jorn's view of the order and symmetry of nature, see Shield (1995) and (1998: 128-35).

4 In 1961 Jorn founded "Skandinaviska institutet för komparativ vandalism" (Scandinavian Institute of Comparative Vandalism). One major goal was to write the history of Scandinavian folk art over the past 10 000 years, cf. Shield (1998: 1f.).

5 Nørredam (1986: 25).

6 The version of the Bible used in this book is *The New International Version* from 1973, 1978, 1984.

7 Bultmann (1962: 16). See also Kieffer (1987: 22f.), who focuses on John's intent to describe God's creation rather than speculating on the relation between logos, divinity and God.

8 Cf. Sandqvist (1994: 18), who points to the similarity between the stories of creation in Genesis, the prologue to the Gospel of John, and Egyptian religion (according to Henri Frankfort), where the word in the former refers to the "sign of the ideality" while it is significantly identified with the object in the latter.

9 While John develops the concept of logos within a semantically very wide horizon, Paul's concept of "letter" (gramma) refers to an expression of God's will in the written Jewish law. Cf. Rom. 2:29 and 7:6; 2 Cor. 3:4-18. Both John and Paul value the meeting with the life-giving God in the Spirit higher than the meeting with God in the written word.

10 Cf. Volp (1980a: 557f.).

11 Tertullian, *Adv. Marcion* 4.40

12 Wittgenstein (1973), Tractacus 2.12.

13 "Was das Bild darstellt, das ist sein Sinn." Wittgenstein (1973), Tractacus 2.221.

14 In "Philosophical Investigations" Wittgenstein (1971: 63 [77]), compares sharp and blurry pictures and speaks of a necessary "family of meanings" (Familie der Bedeutungen) as an idea in language games. Cf. Welsch (1996: 23f.).

15 Böhme (1999: 9ff.).

16 Förster and Rosen (1993).

17 Goodman (1973: 122).

18 Goodman (1993: 571f.).

19 Eco (1972: 213). Cf. also Eco's definition (1973: 8) of "the open artwork," as "a fundamental polysemous message."

20 Volp (1980a: 557f.).

21 Lacan (1995: 83).

22 Cf. the book title: Rorty (1992), *The Linguistic Turn: Essays in Philosophical Method.*

23 Cf. Wittgenstein, who in the Tractacus uses logical language-philosophical imagery summarized in the thesis: "Der Satz ist ein Bild der Wirklichkeit" (4.01, 4.021, cf. 4.032).

24 Cf. the extensive argumentation and the source texts in Stöhr and Boehm (1995). Analogous to the term "pictorial turn" – see Mitchell (1994: 11-34), who gives Panofsky a focal position – the term "iconic turn" is sometimes also used.

25 Boehm (1995: 19).

26 Lacan (1995: 75ff.).

27 Lacan (1995: 83).

28 Weimarck (1999).

29 Boehm (1995: 35).

30 Boehm (1996: 160-65; 1995: 29-36).

31 Boehm (1996: 162).

32 Sandström (1988: 5).

33 Sandström (1993: 87, 96ff.). Cf. Sandström (1995: 23-26).

34 Sandström (1995: 16).

35 Naturally, the question of the relation between the image and mental imagery to verbal – spoken and written – language is a far more complex issue than what has been suggested here. This issue requires a volume on its own. My point is that one must *first* acknowledge the intrinsic value of image-making before one starts formulating questions about the imagery of language. In general, I regard language philosophers' discussions of the meaning of metaphors as an important widening of the former restricted view of language. However, in my view, the theories of metaphors do not pay adequate attention to the role of mental imagery for language. For an orientation of the theological relevance of metaphor theories see Soskice (1987: ch. 3).

36 See Bergmann (2005a: 297-99), for more on von Uexküll's theory.

37 Sebeok (1994: 113, cf. 121-24).

38 Sebeok (1994: 113f.).

39 Sjölin (1993: 11-101). According to Sjölin (1993: 70), the term plasticity does not aim at the traditional shaping of volume; it characterizes all kinds of pictorial techniques that create the picture's three-dimensional space.

40 Cf. Sandström (1988: 17ff.), who proposes four aspects of picture analysis: a sensuous, a perceptual, an iconic, and an imaginative aspect.

41 Bätschmann (1988: 197f.).

42 Hirn (1964: 73).

43 Cf. Frank (1995).

44 Virgil *Eclogue* 4, from J. B. Greenburg's edition.

45 Paillard (1987: 53).

46 Roters (1995: 99-102).

47 Roters (1995: 101).

48 Cf. Frank (1995: 7f.).

Chapter 2

1 Eco (1973: 15ff.).

2 Dio Chrysostom, *Oration* 12. Blomqvist provides a comprehensive analysis of the speech and a discussion of its influence of the image debate in antiquity.

3 In a polemic and not very well-founded thesis of the theologians' "takeover" (p. 24), Belting (1991: 11–17; German edition) claims that the main drive of theologians from Early Christianity up till today was to deprive material images of their power to retain control of power in the Church. Belting accuses theologians of merely developing a very general concept of image in order to regulate and control image reception. Belting's thesis has been rejected as "ethnocentrism" and his adjudication over theologians goes against the historical diversity of image use in religious communities. Cf. Stock (1998: 11ff.).

4 A comprehensive, detailed and methodologically eminent art historical and

church historical church exposition of Byzantine theology's positive relationship to images is found in Hellemo (1999: 30). Hellemo characterizes the Christian image as a depiction of "inner beauty, understood as innovation on the premises of religion." Hellemo develops his interpretation within the framework of the Western Church's view on the catechetic, illustrative, and decorative function of the image and sadly overlooks from what is the focal purpose of this book, namely the unicity of the visual medium and its autonomy in dialogue/ dia-graphy with theological traditions. Although I completely agree with Hellemo's intention to revalue iconography's importance as a source, I find his theology of the image problematic: "The purpose of the image is to give visual form to the core of belief conceptions and outlooks on life." To separate between image as form and faith as content only to subordinate form on an idealistic basis entails an Aristotelian reductionism which is more a characteristic of the goal rationalistic machine age than antiquity and the Middle Ages. What is the "core" of Christian faith has been less of a concern of systematic theology in the past few decades. However, the question about the contextual correlations of faith and its cultural/historical autonomy and relationality (cf. Bergmann/Bråkenhielm 2000), is a question which should be very relevant even for an interpretation of the history of images in the Church.

5 Bauer (p. 440) provides an overview of the meaning of *eikon* found in the New Testament and other antique souces. The history of the image of Mary provides enticing insights into the creative tradition of late antiquity. Beskow (1991b: 11f.) shows how closely connected, e.g., Christology and Mariology is at this time. An intriguing insight into the antique battle between, on the one hand, the iconoclasm of monotheism and, on the other, the image revelation in cosmotheism is given by Assmann. The issue of the Jewish image ban, which is central to the topic of this book, is left out because of limitations of space.

6 Just as Dio Chrysostom earlier on, cf. note 2.

7 A clear and comprehensive account of the two phases of iconoclasm and research pertaining to iconoclasm is found in Beskow (1991a). Cf. also Rice (1993: 74ff.).

8 Zaloscer (1997: 18).

9 Cf., e.g., the panoramic gaze through which modern humans visually acquire the natural space and "conquer" this space, Weimarck (1992: 78f.). More references in Bergmann (1997c), fn 6 in the German version.

10 Quoted according to Zaloscer (1997: 29).

11 Croce (1969: 22), cf. Raters (1998: 181).

12 However, "iconologia" is an older term that has acquired new meaning in modern times. Schoell-Glass's study shows that Warburg's important project was also motivated by a normative, anti-Semitic intention by seeking answers to the foundation of the hate against Jews.

13 Quoted according to Zaloscer (1997: 34).

14 Dilly (1988: 10).

15 Zaloscer (1997: 125).

16 Dilly (1988: 10).

17 Kemp (985).

18 Cf. Bätschmann (1997), who investigates the influence of traditions for exhibiting art on the transformation of art making.

19 Scheer (1997: 1). Welsch (1996: 136).

20 Gethmann-Siefert (1995: 7ff.).

21 Scheer (1997: 46–52).

22 About Baumgarten, see Scheer (1997: 51–72), Gethmann-Siefert (1995: 41–53), and Schweizer (1973: 9–101).

23 Taylor (1995: 17–47) uses the concept "theo/aesthetics" as a collective term for the theologically based aesthetics of the eighteenth and nineteenth century, against which he, in accordance to Kierkegaard, formulates his own programme of a postmodern "a/theoaesthetics" (pp. 309–19), with a general and vague concept of alterity as the primary category.

24 About Kant, see Scheer (1997: 73–111), Gethmann-Siefert (1995: 69–106), and Vilks (1995: 58–62).

25 About Lyotard, see Scheer (1997: 97).

26 About Hegel, see Scheer (1997: 112–42), and Gethmann-Siefert (1995: 202–32). Cf. also Zaloscer (1997: 25ff.).

27 "...das Schöne bestimmt sich...als das sinnliche Scheinen der Idee." Hegel (1952: 146).

28 A notable reception of Hegel's aesthetic is found in Heidegger.

29 Cf. Gethmann-Siefert (1995: 159–83).

30 Marcuse (1980: 65, 67).

31 Marcuse (1980: 70f.).

32 About Kant's philosophy of religion, see Picht (1990b) and about the relation between Kant's philosophy of religion and the apophatic epistemology of late antiquity, see Bergmann (1995: 374f.).

33 Iser (1993: 33).

34 Kant (1977: A481, 53).

35 Taylor (1995: 46).

36 About the preconditions that made Auschwitz possible and that still are characteristic of modern society, see Bauman.

37 Philosopher and media critic Boris Groys in DIE ZEIT No. 49, 2 Dec. 1999, p. 54.

38 Various argumentations for and against an essentialist definition of visual arts in Bryson, Holly and Moxey (1991).

39 Iser (1993: 34).

40 Cf. the introduction to Bryson, Holly and Moxey (1991).

41 Iser (1993: 35). Art theories can be subcategorized into three groups that conclude the theory in different ways. This either happens by the use of a metaphor, an open concept, or through a specific logocentric explanation.

42 Gethmann-Siefert (1995: 9).

43 Cf. Wallenstein (1996: 149), who observes how conceptual art challenges "the contemplative attitude of the viewer" and interprets this as part of the dissolution of the paradigm of the established aesthetic paradigm.

44 Scheer (1997: 3).

45 Welsch (1996: 9–61).

46 Cf. Chapter 3, "The Spiritual Element of Art."

47 Pattison (1991: 134).

48 Relevant essentialist conceptions of art build on a metaphoric perceptualism or phenomenological assumptions. Anti-essentialist, often semiotic, conceptions always perceive representation as an expression of conventions in relation to the historical context. For a comprehensive exposition of these two opposing views of visual representation and their weak points, see Bryson, Holly and Moxey (1991: 1–12). The proposed contextual attempts to avoid "essentializing" context, by balancing the creating and the receiving subject, the artefact, and their situating in sociocultural, historical contexts in relation to each other.

49 Bergmann (1997a: 14).

50 This should happen in accordance with the new epistemological paradigm of theology. Cf. Bergmann (1997a: ch. 4).

51 Cf. Bätschmann (1997), who investigates the influence of traditions for exhibiting art on the transformation of art making.

Chapter 3

1 Mädler claims that Schleiermacher's aesthetic even today offers unfailing resources for turning the conflict between art and the Church. For a brief presentation of Schleiermacher's aesthetic, see Mädler (1998). A more comprehensive exposition is found in Mädler (1997). Cf. also Bergmann (1997b: 65–70).

2 Cf. Bjerg (1999: 76), who in connection to Mitchell's concept of image creates an interesting scale of how different traditions relate image and work, where the so-called graphic image (the icon) and the so-called verbal image (the metaphor) are given different meanings in the Eastern and Western Church.

3 Stock (1990: 175–81).

4 Schmied (1984: 113). Cf. Volp (1990b: 307–20).

5 Schmied (1980; 1990).

6 Tuchman (1993).

7 Mennekes (2000: 182). I fully concede with his conclusion that this freely developing artistic spirituality is in dire need of "a methodological-theological thinking through." This assertion is also a part of the basis of the present book.

8 Roters (1984: 23f.).

9 Volp (1980b).

10 Cf., e.g., Bergmann (1994a: 72), and Pattison (1991: 132f.), about Kandinsky. Kandinsky (1965: 6; German version), states that the purpose of his famous book *Concerning the Spiritual in Art* is to show that the spiritual element of materiality as well as of abstractness. In his publication funded by the Donner Institute, Ringbohm notably reduced Kandinsky's metaphysic as he based his interpretation of the painter's work in the artist's theosophical library. Ringbohm ignores Kandinsky's Eastern Orthodox background and the fact that Kandinsky never underestimates corporeality. Kandinsky stands closer to his own Orthodox tradition than any art scholar has realized. Neo-Platonic terminology has often been misconstrued in the West; and other artists than Kandinsky have been victims of this dualistic miscomprehension. I would like to propose that the work and writings of Kandinsky are tested based on the hypothesis that art for him seeks to make cosmos, including matter, *divine*. Cf. also Boehm's critical remark against Ringbohm (Boehm 1986: 104).

11 Schwebel (1980).

12 "Religiösität ist heute nur noch in der Kunst möglich," in Beck (1984: 198).

13 Picht (1990a: 7–41).

14 Picht (1990a: 9).

15 Picht (1990a: 9).

16 Picht (1990a: 15).

17 Welsch (1996: 30ff.).

18 Welsch (1996: 41f.).

19 Welsch (1996: 108).

20 Cf. Bergmann (2000a).

21 Cf. Bergmann (2000a).

22 That this neglect has deep historical roots in the history of Christianity is partly demonstrated by the reduction of the image to a pedagogical tool of illustration in Western Christianity during the first millennium and partly by the suspicion against images of the Reformation and what Bjerg (1999: 88), calls a "stunted theology of the image and a poor pedagogy of the image." However, Bjerg (1999: 223–35), argues convincingly for reading Luther's theology – in light of his doctrine of the Eucharist and theology of the cross – as a sublime and positive interpretation of the influence of vision on faith. Despite all the tendencies of the Reformation to repress the image, the iconophile outlook of the Reformation still shines through in Matthias Grünewald's famous altarpieces in Isenheim. Cf Bergmann (1994b).

23 Eliade (1961).

24 According to Martin (1990: 80), the aesthetic sensibility and analysis influence Eliade's theory of religion.

25 Eliade (1985).

26 Eliade's ideas, either in spite of or because of its extensive generalizations, have attracted a number of artists. A.-C. Weimarck (1995: 26f.), assumes, without providing evidence for her argument, that Joseph Beuys is influenced by Eliade.

27 Here I follow Martin's analysis (1990: 80–88), of van der Leeuw.

28 Cf. Heumann/Müller (1996: 72). Tillich's collected art reflections are found in the new edition: Tillich (1987). About Tillich's theology of art, see Martin (1990: 88–96), Heumann and Müller (1996: 72ff.), and Palmer (1984), for a comprehensive account.

29 Cf. Kurtén (1982: 96ff.).

30 Tillich (1985).

31 Tillich (1985: 233).

32 A pertinent criticism of Tillich's symbol theory – not in the context of art philosophy but in the context of the philosophy of religion and language – is found in Jeffner (1972: 55–60).

33 Martin (1990: 3).

34 Gardiner discusses the contribution of Bakhtin studies to "a metaphoric of perception" beyond an eye-centred vision that thwarts the other.

35 Harries (1993: 147).

36 Schwebel (1998: 45).

37 Zeindler (1993: 5).

38 Zeindler (1993: 175).

39 Zeindler (1993: 191).

40 Coleman (1998: ix).

41 Coleman (1998: xiv).

42 Coleman (1998: 1–11).

43 Coleman (1998: 21).

44 Coleman (1998: 155).

45 Coleman (1998: 156).

46 Coleman (1998: 162ff.).

47 Coleman (1998: 188).

48 Coleman (1998: 195).

49 Coleman (1998: 196).

50 Taylor (1992: 142).

51 Taylor (1992: 5).

52 Taylor (1992: 12).

53 Taylor (1992: 317).

54 Taylor (1992: 316).

55 Taylor (1992: 319).

56 Against Bauman (1995: 205ff., 223ff.), who in his cartography of the (post)modern society places the space of aesthetics in opposition to the space of morals, I perceive the space in which art creates pictures as an indispensable delivery room for the individual *and* social majeutic: art is the midwife of morale! See Bergmann (2000b) about Bauman.

57 Further criticism of Taylor's approach is found in Brown (1989: 31f.).

58 Cf. Bergmann (2000a).

59 Rombold (1988: 262).

60 Rombold (1988: 262).

61 Rombold (1976).

62 Rombold (1980: 19).

63 Rombold (1988: 263).

64 Rombold (1988: 263f.).

65 Rombold (1988: 267).

66 Mennekes (1995: 52).

67 Volp (1980b: 31).

68 Volp (1980b: 30–34).

69 Volp (1980b: 35).

70 Schleiermacher (1812/13: 324f.): "Wenn das Bild in der Phantasie in und mit seinem Heraustreten Kunst ist, und der Vernuftgehalt im Eigentümlichen Erkennen Religion, so verhält sich Kunst zu Religion wie Sprache zum Wissen."

71 Volp (1980b: 40).

72 Volp (1984: 271).

73 In a more recent text from 1998 Volp states his view more explicitly: "Kunst ist keine Sprache" (p. 123). However, Volp wants to "compare" art to the speech events (Sprachvorgänge). Aware of the historical dominance of rhetoric over the analysis of art, he meritoriously defends the autonomous uniqueness of the visual medium and its necessary significance – albeit only functional significance – for religion. However, in my opinion, he undermines the potential of picture analysis through his semiotic, generalizing conception of culture, (p. 130), making Eco's choice universally normative for everything: the choice between either a grammar-oriented (i.e., rule-governed) or a text-oriented (i.e., interpretative) culture. I do think there are other options.

74 Heuman and Müller (1996: 11–38).

75 Müller and Heumann (1998: 7).

76 Heumann and Müller (1996: 89).

77 Müller and Heumann (1998: 10). A similar approach is found in Martland (1981: 1), who describes art and religion as "collectively created

frames of perception and meaning by which men interpret their experiences and order their lives." Pence Frantz (1998: 792), argues extensively for regarding all material culture, especially visual arts, as "an interpretation of the world (a re-presentation) that must in itself be interpreted in order for it to be viable in our constructed world of meaning," even though she gives equal status writing and image-making in a way that obscures the intrinsic quality of the visual medium.

78 Pattison (1991: xi).

79 A more philosophically grounded argumentation for the influence of aesthetics on theology and the potential of theology for aesthetics is found in Brown (1989: 36–46).

80 Pattison (1991: 9).

81 Pattison (1991: 21).

82 Pattison (1991: 28f.).

83 Pattison (1991: 54).

84 Pattison (1991: 135).

85 Pattison (1991: 153).

86 Pattison (1991: 175).

87 John Dillenberger (1986: xi).

88 John Dillenberger (1986: ch. 9).

89 Jane Dillenberger (1977, 1986, 1987, 1990).

90 Extensive interpretations of the theology of icons are found in Abel, Evdokimov, Florensky, and Iwanow Ch. 6.

91 Belting (1990: 17).

92 Bodin (1987: 14).

93 Iwanow (1995: 157).

94 About the history of the icon painting in Byzantine and medieval art, see Belting (1990: 36–41), and Abel (1989).

95 Iwanow (1995: 163).

96 Florensky (1989: 38).

97 Iwanow (1995: 164), Bodin (1987), 24, Belting (1991: 30–34).

98 Bodin (1987: 22f.).

99 Bodin (1991: 10).

100 About Florensky, see Sikojev (1989), Iwanow (1995: 164ff.), and Bodin (1987: 114–28).

101 Florensky's main text about art is "The iconostasis"; new edition "Die Ikonostase", Stuttgart 1988.

102 Iwanow (1995: 165).

103 Florensky (1989: 128).

104 Florensky (1989: 129).

105 Florensky (1989: 17f.).

106 Florensky (1989: 29).

107 Florensky (1989: 35).

108 Florensky (1989: 56).

109 Florensky (1989: 9).

110 Florensky (1989: 127).

111 Florensky (1989: 127).

112 Evdokimov (1996: 2).

113 Evdokimov (1996: 10).

114 Evdokimov (1996: 20).

115 Evdokimov (1996: 24).

116 Evdokimov (1996: 32).

117 Evdokimov (1996: 69).

118 Evdokimov (1996: 167).

119 Evdokimov (1996: 176).

120 Evdokimov (1996: 204).

121 Evdokimov (1996: 206).

122 Evdokimov (1996: 207).

123 Evdokimov (1996: 208).

124 Evdokimov (1996: 235).

125 Evdokimov (1996: 236).

126 Evdokimov (1996: 76).

127 Evdokimov (1996: 77).

128 Evdokimov (1996: 79).

129 Evdokimov (1996: 80).

130 Evdokimov (1996: 85).

131 Evdokimov (1996: 88).

132 Evdokimov (1996: 92). Bultmann's programme is not explicitly mentioned, but it is hinted at.

133 Cf. Belting (1991: 32).

134 About the model concept, see Bevans (1992: 24ff.).

135 Volp (1984: 263–67; 1990b: 322–25).

136 Henrich and Iser (1993: 18).

137 Langer (1965).

138 Cf. Jane Dillenberger (1987) and the bibliographies about Jewish and Christian art in: Adams and Apostolos-Cappadona (1987: 217–37).

139 Cf. Bergmann (1995: 459ff.).

140 Bergmann (1995: 362–65).

141 This critique is found in Bergmann (1997a: 62f.).

142 Cf. Mead (1993: 345f.).

143 Cf. Bergmann (2007a).

Chapter 4

1 Rubin (1994: 104).

2 Cf. Rubin (1994: 103f.). *Les Démoiselles d'Avignon* is a work with many complex allusions and meanings. Herding writes extensively about these. In contrast to Sundermeier, Herding (1992: 35–48) gives a more positive interpretation of Picasso's use and formation of the primitive.

3 Rubin (1994: 139f.).

4 Rubin (1994: 16).

5 The very comprehensive and much visited art exhibition of African artefacts from the entire African continent in Berlin in 1996 shows among others that this process is taking place in increasingly wider circles. See *Afrika – Die Kunst eines Kontinents*.

6 Cf. the following: Sundermeier (1998: 27–30), and Rubin (1994: 13). Klausen (1990: 177f.), also mentions Maurice Vlaminck's early contact in 1905 with the ethnographic objects of the museum as what sparked the interest in the exotic. About modernism's meeting with the exotic, see also Klausen (1977: 137–42).

7 Hiller (1993: 1).

8 Programmatically, I prefer the term and concept of "the Strange", thus avoiding the risk of projecting oneself on the screen of "the other" and "otherness". The notion "strange/r" refers to *what is strange* as well as to the stranger. For a deeper exploration of this field, see Bergmann (2007b) and (2008).

9 About the concept of primitivism in modern art, see Rhodes (1994: 13–22).

10 On exotism cf. Graham.

11 Sundermeier (1999: 18).

12 Cf. Lloyd (1991).

13 About modern artists' fascination for the exotic, see Klausen (1990: 180f.).

14 All the concepts used are problematic and reflect in themselves the unresolved tension within which, on the one hand, we find Western contemporary art and, on the other hand, we find non-Western art making. A detailed discussion of this dialectic is found in Hiller (1993: 1–4). Ströter-Bender (1991: 202), argues for the concept "Weltkunst" (world art), but she keeps the concept "Kunst aus der Dritten Welt" (Art from the third-world) for pragmatic reason. The conceptual categorization becomes even more difficult, partly because of the breakdown of the ideology and economy of the so-called "second world" and partly because of the increasing cultural pluralism in which the economically and ethnically defined inhabitants of the former third and fourth worlds have become increasingly visible in the *same* urban spaces in all regions of the four worlds.

The conceptual complexity is further increased by the emergence of the so-called neo-primitivism in the 1980s, which has spurred both interest and severe criticism among indigenous artists. Cf. Araeen. Several related phenomena are found in the neo-expressive style which has references to the ambivalent interest for the ethnical authentic of classical expressionism. About the latter, see Lloyd (1991), and about the criticism of neo-expressionism, see Hiller (1993: 284), and Tillers (1993).

B. Taylor's overview (1995: 162–65), identifies race as a central topic in the contemporary art of the 1990s which is focused on "narrative identity." The concept of "ethno-art" is affected by the same criticism as the earlier ethnography, that is, it tends to objectify and reduce the objects' context of production, function and reception. The term "regional art" is related to the (for some people) successful regionalist ideology. On the one hand, it succeeds in focusing on the art expressions outside the established power centres; however, on the other hand, it does not yet convince us that there is a direct interaction between the physical and cultural identity of the region and the art making. Also, it is not clear within the regionalist approach what criteria one should apply to define the region and how one should understand the movement across regions.

15 Cf. Bergmann (1999: 500ff.).

16 Hiller (1993, 2f.)

17 Gethmann-Siefert (1995: 8, cf. 1).

18 The material comprises (a) shorter essays/texts/expositions with detailed field and object studies with concomitant over-arching argumentation, often developed symposiums in cultural anthropology, (b) longer texts or parts of books, and (c) monographs. Three volumes from symposiums and Hiller's anthology contain occasional observations and reflections of the first category. Gregory Bateson and Clifford Geertz provide reflections over the anthropology of art within the frame of their comprehensive cultural studies. Franz Boas, Herta Haselberger, Ingrid Kreide-Damani, and Jutta Ströter-Bender have written coherent monographs on the topic. I do not organize the material according to chronology, genre or topic; rather, I organize it systematically.

19 Haselberger (1969: 9): "...künstlerische Tätigkeit der Völker geringer technischer Naturbeherrschung."

20 The term is taken from Anderson.

21 Kreide-Damani (1992: 113).

22 Kreide-Damani (1992: 113).

23 Munn (1971: 336).

24 Munn (1973).

25 Chipp (1971: 146).

26 Chipp (1971: 169). Layton (1991: 35f.), expresses a similar view, and he regards all art in small-scale communities as "frequently embedded in religion."

27 Chipp (1971: 170). Chipp's view of art in culture is a reminder of Coleman's comparison of creation and spirituality in the previous chapter.

28 Fernandez (1971: 373): "To what extent does social structure reflect aesthetic principles?"

29 Fernandez (1971: 373).

30 Forge (1971: 291).

31 Forge (1971: 294).

32 Forge (1971: 313f.). N. Thomas (1995: 34f.), aptly questions the method used in the interpretation of New Guinean art, which is based on a Western principle for representation, and Thomas points out that a striking presentation generally is more meaningful than communication or mediation of meaning.

33 Cf. Gell (1999: 17), who characterizes Forge's intention as a search for the deeper "meaning" of culture in the non-linguistic and non-natural objects of the works of art.

34 Lévi-Strauss (1971: 227f.).

35 Lévi-Strauss (1971: 234f.). Marcus and Myers (1995: 13), refer to the connection between Lévi-Strauss' analyses and the principles of surrealism for the production of collage.

36 Lévi-Strauss (1971: 237).

37 Lévi-Strauss (1971: 238f.).

38 Lévi-Strauss (1971: 239).

39 Lévi-Strauss (1971: 243).

40 Lévi-Strauss (1971: 244).

41 Lévi-Strauss (1971: 246).

42 Cf. Marcus and Myers (1995: 13).

43 Bateson (1990: 184f.).

44 Bateson (1990: 183).

45 Bateson (1990: 186).

46 Bateson (1990: 200).

47 Bateson (1990: 203). Critical points in Bateson's theory are discussed in Bergmann (1995: 294–98).

48 Bateson (1990: 204).

49 Bateson (1990: 205f.).

50 The book was based on a lecture series at the Institute for Comparative Culture Research in Oslo in 1926. Klausen (1990: 183).

51 Boas (1955: 1).

52 Boas (1955: 9f.).

53 Boas (1955: 356).

54 Boas (1955: 4).

55 Kreide-Damani (1992: 42).

56 Jonaitis (1995: 35). About Boas, cf. also Layton (1991: 18–21).

57 Krupat (1989: 144).

58 Geertz (1993).

59 Geertz (1993: 95f.); criticizing amongst others Munn.

60 Geertz (1993: 97).

61 Gell agrees to this criticism, albeit without reference to Geertz. Gell (1999: 159ff.), perceives art as a "technology of enchantment" and refers to sacralization of art which functions in a way similar to religion and hence poses special demands on the anthropology of art. In an extensive criticism of Coote's suggestion to separate between an anthropological aesthetic and an anthropology of art Gell, (1999: 215ff.), rejects the universalizing idea about the general visual aesthetic shared by all peoples at the expense of a practical study of artistic objects.

62 Geertz (1993: 99).

63 Geertz (1993: 109), by which the criticism of "the invented world" could be interpreted as directed at amongst others Lévi-Strauss.

64 Cf. Geertz (1973), and Bergmann (1997a: 112f.). See Martin (1990: 96–103), for a detailed discussion of Geertz's view on art and religion.

65 Geertz (1993: 120).

66 Cf. Harth (1996: 372f.).

67 Harth (1996: 374): "...die Frage nach dem Anderssein des Fremden."

68 Rushing (1995).

69 Lloyd (1991).

70 Rodenberg (1994).

71 Rodenberg (1994: 12).

72 Cf. the journal "Third Text."

73 Morphy (1994: 667).

74 Morphy (1994: 668).

75 Marcus and Myers (1995: 1).

76 Clifford (1985: 166). Cf. Howell (1993: 235), and Clifford (1988).

77 Marcus and Myers (1995: 10).

78 Cf. Ratcliff (1988). Even the right-wing politicizing of the art scene in the USA is scrutinized critically, Marcus and Myers (1995: 24ff.).

79 Marcus and Myers (1995: 33f.).

80 Appadurai (1986: 34): "the social life of things."

81 Marcus and Myers (1995: 34).

82 Fisher (1993: 293).

83 Price (1989: 4).

84 Price (1989: 5).

85 Kapur (1994: 48).

86 Howell (1993: 236).

87 Howell (1993: 236).

88 Araeen (1993: 181).

89 Araeen (1993: 180).

90 Durham (1994: 116).

91 Taussig (1993: 249).

92 Durham (1993). For more about Durham, see Bergmann (2000c).

93 Coote and Shelton (1992).

94 Klausen (1990: 188ff.), notices, for example, that art in modern society seems to be far more religious and sacred than we realize. The art business operates with a double valuation

system, and the role of the modern artist is similar to that of the shaman.

Chapter 5

1 T. Weimarck (1983).

2 Cf. Bjerg (1999: 171f., 176), who to his credit makes it perfectly clear that the predominant image of God throughout Christianity is that of *a seeing God*. While Bjerg (p. 193) characterizes faith as "seeing with God's eyes," which, (p. 216), creates clarity when "God's gaze interposes my gaze," I focus on the actions of the liberating God in the production and reception of the image. Should "clarity" or "liberation" become central terms for the visually enlightened soteriology?

3 Only in the practical theology and in the mission history has image creation received recognition as an autonomous expression of faith. It is time to move images from their current peripheral position into the heart of systematic theology. An early pioneer work was done by the East German mission historian Arno Lehmann, who insightfully realized the importance of "Die Kunst der Jungen Kirchen" and the ability of image creation to visualise their "own face" (1957: 22). The challenges emerging from his rather isolated endeavour were reassumed by theologians from three continents in 1996 in the symposium "Die Bilder und das Wort," see Sundermeier and Küster (1999).

4 For a comprehensive account of the contextual theology, see Bergmann (1997a).

5 Cf. Bergmann (1997a), the chapter on art and context. Hermeneutic problems in third world art is discussed in detail in Sundermeier (1999).

6 Descriptions of the creation of the work are found in B. Hjorth (1967a: 78–92), M. Hjorth (1978: 59–81), Linde (1986: 86–90), and Boström (1994: 30–36).

7 B. Hjorth (1967a: 82).

8 Cf. Boström (1994: 34f.). A detailed account of Christ images in Hjorth's work is found in Stengård (1986: 149–62).

9 According to Stengård (1986: 158f.).

10 Just like Emil Nolde, Hjorth consistently portrayed Jesus with what racists termed as Jewish, non-Arian features. With this choice he chose sides in the theological fight against the strong anti-Semitic tendencies in a Christian tradition which denied the fact that Jesus was Jewish.

11 See Jonsell (2000) for an account of Læstadius' early and original insights into the diversity of plant species in relation to topographical and climatological conditions. Even though Jonsell does not mention Alexander von Humboldt's discovery of this connection, in an historical perspective it is interesting to study the relationship between Humboldt's "physiognomic" approach and Læstadius' topological approach.

12 B. Hjorth (1967a: 79).

13 B. Hjorth (1967a: 83).

14 A group of Swedish woodcarvers inspired by the influential woodcarver Axel Petersson also called "Döderhultarn."

15 B. Hjorth (1967a: 83).

16 Stengård (1986: 161). Stengård pertinently shows how Hjorth combines the Christ identification with the "human identification," and this places Hjorth, in spite of what his critics may say, in the classic pre-Church incarnation theology tradition, in which God (according to Athanasius) became human to enable man to become God.

17 The Swedish Hymnbook 517:1,3.

18 Pappila published a comprehensive theological analysis of images and Hjorth used an excerpt of this work as his manifesto. Boström (1994: 32).

19 Pappila, in Boström (1994: 34).

20 Hjorth's first draft of this figure gave rise to huge protests, and the local people saw the image as a "ridicule of us and our Father." Hjorth altered the facial expressions and added the inscription from Læstadius' work. Further details about the controversy, including also the

hypocritical attitudes of the chapter, are found in M. Hjorth (1978: 60–69).

21 Læstadius' novel "Dårhushjonet," quotation from Jonsell (2000: 44).

22 Cf. Bergmann (1997a: 126f.).

23 Cf. Naureth (1987).

24 Cf. Danbolt (2000: 58f.).

25 Cf., e.g., Gregory of Nazianzus, *Or.o* 29.20 (in Bergmann [1995: 197]).

26 An art historical account of the cross motif is found in Mennekes and Röhrig (1994: 5–11).

27 Martin Luther, *Heidelberger Disputation 1518*, XIX.f, p. 361f.: "Non ille digne Theologus dicitur, qui invisibilia Dei per ea, quae facta sunt, intellecta conspicit... Sed qui visibilia et posteriora Dei per passiones et crucem conspecta intelligit" (translation from http://www.augustana.edu/Religion/ LutherProject/ HEIDELBU/Heidelbergdisputation.htm, 19.1.2007).

28 Gregory of Nazianzus, *Or.* 30.6.

29 *Or.* 45.25.

30 *Or.* 14.5.

31 Cf. Bergmann (1995: 341ff.).

32 Meseure (1993: 71).

33 Marc (1978: 99). Cf. Bergmann (1994b: 64).

34 Quoted from Bitter (1993: 52).

35 In agreement with Mesure (1993: 71).

36 Against Düchting (1991: 68).

37 Against Meseure (1993: 68–70), who without proper grounds declines the importance of the choice of form of the altarpiece.

38 Macke, quote from Bitter (1993: 52): "Die Zeit ist untrennbar von der Fläche." (Time cannot be separated from the surface.)

39 See Vidal (1984) for further details.

40 Schmidt (1929: 8, 102f.), regards the geographical diversity of the country as a prerequisite for the economic and social isolation of the great ancient empires of Peru.

41 Cf. Schmidt (1929: 110).

42 About "transculturation," see Pratt (1992: 6), where the term refers to selectively interpreting "transport" from one culture to the other. Syncretism normatively is a heavily laden term; for some people positively and for others negatively. In this context I use it in a fairly neutral sense as a term for an intense, lasting exchange between different cultures. The negative definition of the term syncretism presupposes a monolithic conception of culture, as if cultures can be "pure."

43 Anders (1984: 23–155), gives a thorough account of Peruvian history by several authors.

44 Cf. Schmidt (1929: 116).

45 For an overview of Andean ecology, culture and religion, especially among the Aymara and Quechua peoples, see Claros-Arispe (1996). For a general introduction to Peruvian ethnography, see Santistéban, who pays special attention to the Spanish-Andean acculturation of paintings and music, (1984: 133).

46 For a discussion of twentieth century Peru and "the fall of the nation," see Roel (1984).

47 In the introduction of his book Gutiérrez (1976) mentions specially the Indian Peruvian poet José Maria Arguedas.

48 Cf. Millones and Pratt (1990: 7).

49 Dean (1996: 181): "In colonial societies, where many ethnicities interact, visual culture is multivalent, and often dissonant. While the fine arts discussed here indicate that Andeans adopted the visual language and religion of Europeans, this is not a sign of capitulation. European art was renewed for its Andean audiences by native artists and patrons. The colonized native audience lived in a world that was simultaneously new and ancient, European and Andean, so that visual culture was necessarily created out of contradiction. That colonial art articulated personal, communal and regional pride in a language that both natives and Europeans would (at least partially) understand is its supreme accomplishment. Its paradoxical nature is the source of considerable vitality." Cf. Leicht (1944).

50 The Spanish Conquerors managed to annihilate the ritual forms for veneration of the *huacas* in Andean culture, "but they ignored the subversive nature of the ongoing reproduction of native Andean culture through its traditional structures of everyday life, including those surrounding weaving and cloth. Not grasping how the process of making an object was integrated with its use and meaning in traditional Andean society, the Spanish attempted to rid the Indians of the objects of their culture without destroying the process by which they were made. Thus, an arena of cultural identity was preserved, in the memory of its weavers, worked into the structure of the cloth." Phipps (1996: 154).

51 For a description of the pre-colonial, advanced weaving technique and the loom, see Schmidt (1929: 78–86), who also, (p. 86), emphasizes the importance of the bountiful plants and minerals resources for the rich colour scale of textile art.

52 Millones and Pratt (1990: 21, 38).

53 Ades, in the chapter *Indigenism and Social Realism* (1989: 195).

54 Author's personal archive.

55 Mosquera according to Ades (1989: 299f.). Cf. also Mosquera (1994).

56 Ades in the chapter *History and Identity* (1989: 299).

57 Cf. Smith (1996).

58 Cf. Brett (1986), who in the first chapter of his study of folk art's cultural and political relevance for social development, gives a detailed account of the production of *arpilleras* (appliquéd textile pictures) in Chile and of their wide recognition.

59 Cf. J. Thomas (1984).

60 Latin America has a long tradition of picture catechisms, starting from the sixteenth-century catechisms with a mixture of image-making and scripture. Cf. Rzepkowski (1999: 42ff.).

61 Schulte and Orzechowski (1993, 1994, 1995, 1996, 1997).

62 Santistéban (1984: 131).

63 Cf. Chapter 3, 1.2.

64 For an account of the history of apophatic theology, see Bergmann (1995: 371, 481f.).

65 Wittgenstein (1921: 115).

66 Cf. Bergmann (1995: 374f.).

67 Cf. Bergmann (1995: 375ff.).

68 LaCugna (1993: 72), expresses the prevailing Western assumption that the apophatic theology of the Cappadocians would separate the context of theology from the context of economy (the salvation history) only to reduce theology to Platonic mysticism; however, she does not provide evidence/argumentation for this. Without a basis in historical facts she purports, (p. 325), in agreement with a number of other scholars, that the apophatic theology is synonymous to the "negative theology" of the West, which is totally wrong.

69 About the transition from alterity to alienation theology, see Bergmann (2000c).

70 Bergmann (1995: 331f.).

71 Bergmann (1995: 172).

72 Zizioulas (1985). Boff (1987).

73 Bergmann (1997a).

74 Martin Luther, *Heidelberger Disputation 1518*, XX., cf. above n. 27.

75 Cf. Aulén (1965: 114ff.) and Aulén (1967: 52ff.).

76 Cf. Picht (1989: 120), who in his criticism of the limited truth concept within the natural sciences develops the thesis that the evidence is "a priori opaque, and its irresistibility resides in its opaqueness."

77 Belting (1991: 13).

78 Belting (1991: 13).

79 Belting (1991: 19).

80 Belting (1991: 24).

81 Note that Belting consistently speaks about images in the singular just as he talks about their history in the singular (sic!). Unfortunately, the

study lacks reflection about the significance of differences.

82 Jesus Christ is referred to as "the image of the invisible God" (eikon) in 2 Cor. 4:4 and Col. 1:15.

83 Jn 1:1.

84 Cf., e.g., Lüthi (1998).

85 Rombold (1993: 2, 12).

86 Schwebel (1988: 123).

87 Lüthi (1998: 66f.).

88 Also Lühti notices visual arts' ability to express sensually what the eyes cannot see. Cf. Mark C. Taylor's (1992) analyses of vague representations with no content or vigour.

89 Grözinger's criticism (1998: 37ff.), of an aesthetic which after Schleiermacher is construed as a tenet of religious experience is very fitting, because the concept of experience here accentuates the unity rather than focusing on the differences. A contextual art theology, however, attempts to use these premises as a starting point.

90 Okalla (1999: 123).

91 In the Eastern Church, the mystery of God's incarnation is described with the term "theandric."

92 Danbolt (2000: 75).

93 Bergmann (1995: 210f.).

94 Bergmann (1995: 222ff.).

95 About the spatiality of theology see Bergmann (2006) and (2007ac).

96 Cf. Bergmann (1995: 325–29).

97 Chillida (1994: 130).

98 Chillida (1994: 130).

99 Bergmann (1995: 218).

100 Auguste Rodin, quoted from Harenberg Kunst Kompaktkalender, 19 May 1999.

101 Sundermeier (1999: 9).

References

Abel, Ulf. 1989. *Ikonen: bilden av det heliga.* Hedemora: Gidlund.

Adams, Doug, and Diane Apostolos-Cappadona, eds. 1987. *Art as Religious Studies.* New York: Crossroad.

Ades, Dawn, with contributions by Guy Brett, Stanton Loomi Catlin and Rosemary O'Neill. 1989. *Art in Latin America: The Modern Era, 1820–1980.* New Haven, CT/London: Yale University Press.

Adorno, Theodor W. 1984. *Negative Dialektik.* Gesammelte Schriften, Band 6; Frankfurt am Main: Suhrkamp, 3rd edn.

— 1995 [1970]. *Ästhetische Theorie.* Frankfurt am Main: Suhrkamp, 13th edn.

Anders, Ferdinand, ed. 1984. *Peru durch die Jahrtausende: Kunst und Kultur im Lande der Inka.* Recklinghausen: Aurel Bongers.

Andersen, Troels. 1997. *Asger Jorn: En biografi, årene 1953–73.* Köpenhamn: Borgen.

Anderson, Richard L. 1989. *Art in Small-Scale Societies.* Englewood Cliffs, NJ: Prentice Hall, 2nd edn.

Apostolos-Cappadona, Diane, ed. 1985. *Art, Creativity, and the Sacred.* New York: Crossroad.

Appadurai, Arjun, ed. 1986. *The Social Life of Things: Commodities in Cultural Perspective.* Cambridge: Cambridge University Press.

Araeen, Rasheed. 1993 [1991]. "From Primitivism to Ethnic Arts." In Hiller: 158–82.

Assmann, Jan. 1999. "In Bilder verstrickt: Bildkult, Idolatrie und Kosmotheismus in der Antike." In Bernhardt and Link-Wieczorek: 73–88.

Aulén, Gustaf. 1965. *Den allmänneliga kristna tron.* Stockholm: Verbum, 6th edn.

— 1967. *Kristen gudstro i förändringens värld.* Stockholm: Verbum.

Banschbach Eggen, Renate, and Olav Hognestad, eds. 2000. *Tempel og katedral: Kunst og arkitektur som gudstroens speilbilde.* Relieff nr. 41. Trondheim: Tapir.

Bätschmann, Oskar. 1988. "Anleitung zur Interpretation: Kunstgeschichtliche Hermeneutik." In Belting: 191-221.

— 1997. *Ausstellungskünstler: Kult und Karriere im modernen Kunstsystem.* Cologne: DuMont.

Bateson, Gregory. 1990. "Stil, Grazie und Information in der primitiven Kunst." In *Ökologie des Geistes*: 182–212. Frankfurt am Main: Suhrkamp, 3rd edn [Forge, 1973].

Bauman, Zygmunt. 1994 [1989]. *Auschwitz och det moderna samhället.* Göteborg: Daidalos, 2nd edn.

— 1995. *Postmodern etik.* Göteborg: Daidalos. English edn *Postmodern Ethics*, 1993.

Baumgarten, Alexander Gottlieb. *Aesthetica.* In Schweizer 1973.

Beck, Rainer. 1984. "'Religiösität ist heute nur noch in der Kunst möglich': Ein Gespräch mit Walter Pichler." In Beck and Volp: 197–204.

Beck, Rainer, and R. Volp, eds. 1984. *Die Kunst und die Kirchen: Der Streit um die Bilder heute.* Munich: Bruckmann.

Belting, Hans. 1991 [1990]. *Bild und Kult: Eine Geschichte des Bildes vor dem Zeitalter der Kunst.* Munich: Beck, 2nd edn.

Belting, Hans, *et al.*, eds. 1988 [1985]. *Kunstgeschichte: Eine Einführung.* Berlin: Reimer, 4th edn.

Berefelt, Gunnar, ed. 1993. *Den barnsliga fantasin.* Centrum för barnkulturforskning, 22; Stockholm.

Bergmann, Sigurd. 1994a. " 'Landskapet har gått under i dammet' – Den moderna bildkonstens naturbild utmanar kulturteologin." In Bergmann and Bråkenhielm 1994: 57–90; General transl. in Bergmann 1997b: 34–70.

— 1994b. "Att genom bilder finna kors." *Vår Lösen* 6 (1994): 447–55.

— 1995. *Geist, der Natur befreit: Die trinitarische Kosmologie Gregors von Nazianz im Horizont einer ökologischen Theologie der Befreiung.* Mainz: Matthias-Grünewald-Verlag; Russian edn: Arkhangelsk 1999; English rev. edn = Bergmann 2005a.

— 1997a. *Gud i funktion: en orientering i den kontextuella teologin.* Stockholm: Verbum; English edn: *God in Context.* Aldershot: Ashgate, 2001.

— 1997b. *Geist, der lebendig macht: Lavierungen zur ökologischen Befreiungs-theologie.* Frankfurt am Main: IKO.

— 1997c. "Så främmande det lika: Den eko- och etnologiska utmaningen till bildkonsten och teologin." *Kirke og Kultur* 6 (1997): 519–41. Rev. version: *Das Fremde wahrnehmen: Die öko- und ethnologische Herausforderung der Bildkunst und Theologie.* In Müller and Heumann 1998: 96–120.

— 1999. " 'Ich bin hier mit ihnen, und dort' – Eine Verflechtung der samischen Bildwelt Ulrika Tapios mit der Reflexion der Ritualisierung, Hybridisierung und interkulturellen Kunsttheologie." In Thomas Schreijäck, ed. *Menschwerden im Kulturwandel: Kontexte kultureller Identität als Wegmarken interkultureller Kompetenz/Initiationen und ihre Inkulturationsprozesse*: 474–512. Luzern: Edition Exodus.

— 2000a. "Rättvisan och de/t främmande: En konstteologisk betraktelse av Iver Jåks' 'nagler i rom' i ljuset av Theodor W. Adornos rättvise-estetik." In Bergmann and Bråkenhielm 2000: 119–32.

— 2000b. "So fremd das Gleiche: Wie eine interkulturelle Theologie der Befreiung mit dem Fremden über die Alterität hinaus denken kann." In Sybille Fritsch-Oppermann, ed. 2000. *Das Antlitz des Anderen: Emmanuel Lévinas Philosophie und Hermeneutik als Anfrage an Ethik, Theologie und interreligiösen Dialog*: 57–97. Loccumer Protokolle 54/99; Loccum.

— 2000c. "Vilken Gud? Jimmie Durhams 'Jesus' och Iver Jåks' 'Homo Sapiens' i alienitets-teologisk belysning." In T. Jørgensen, D. Rian and O. G. Winsnes, eds. 2000. *Kropp og sjel: Festskrift til Olav Hognestad*: 203–220. Trondheim: Tapir.

— 2000d. "Transculturality and Tradition–Renewing the Continuous in Late Modernity." Contribution to the symposium "2000 Years of Christian Culture and Ethnoses of the Barents Region", Pomor State University Arkhangelsk 20–24.9.2000. Published in *Studia Theologica: Scandinavian Journal of Theology* 58.2 (2004): 140–56.

— 2004. "Makt att se, synliggöra och bli sedd: den visuella kulturens utmaning till teologin." In S. Bergmann and C. Grenholm, eds. 2004. *MAKT-i nordisk teologisk tolkning*: 99–130. Trondheim: Tapir.

— 2005. *Creation Set Free: The Spirit as Liberator of Nature.* Sacra Doctrina: Christian Theology for a Postmodern Age, 4; Grand Rapids, MI/Cambridge UK: Eerdmans.

— 2006. "Atmospheres of Synergy: Towards an Eco-Theological Aesth/Ethics of Space."

ECOTHEOLOGY: The Journal of Religion, Nature and the Environment 11.3 (September 2006): 326–56.

— 2007. "God Taking Place in Urban Space Revisioning Pneumatology in Atmospheres of Life-Giving Liberation." At the 15th Assembly of Nordic Systematic Theologians in Copenhagen, 4-7 January 2007. In J. A. Jørgensen, K. Busch Nielsen and N. H. Gregersen, eds, *Spirit and Spirituality*: 39–58. Copenhagen: University of Copenhagen.

— 2007b. " 'It can't be locked in' – Decolonising Processes in the Arts and Religion of Sápmi and Aboriginal Australia." In Sturla Stålsett, ed. 2007. *Religion in a Globalised Age: Transfers and Transformations, Integration and Resistance.* Oslo: Novus 2007.

— 2007c. "Theology in its Spatial Turn: Space, Place and Built Environments Challenging and Changing the Images of God." *Religion Compass* 1.3 (2007): 353 379, 10.1111/j.1749 8171.2007.00025.x

— 2008. "The Strange and the Self: Visual Arts and Theology in Aboriginal and Other (Post-) Colonial Spaces." In Oleg Bychkov and James Fodor, eds. *Theological Aesthetics after von Balthasar*: 201–23. Aldershot: Ashgate.

Bergmann, Sigurd, ed. 2005b. *Architecture, Aesth/Ethics and Religion.* Frankfurt am Main and London: IKO-Verlag für interkulturelle Kommunikation.

Bergmann, Sigurd, and Carl Reinhold Bråkenhielm, eds. 1994. *Kontextuell livstolkning: Teologi i ett pluralistiskt Norden.* Religio, 43; Lund: Teologiska institutionen.

— 2000. *"Man får inte tvinga någon" – autonomi och relationalitet i nordisk teologisk tolkning.* Nora: Nya Doxa.

Bernhardt, Reinholdt, and Ulrike Link-Wieczorek, eds. 1999. *Metapher und Wirklichkeit: Die Logik der Bildhaftigkeit im Reden von Gott, Mensch und Natur.* Göttingen: Vandenhoeck & Ruprecht.

Beskow, Per. 1991a. "När bilden blev ikon." In Gösta Hallonsten, ed. 1991. *Östkyrkan förr och nu: Studier i den ortodoxa traditionen*: 13–33. Religio, 34; Lund: Teologiska institutionen.

— 1991b. *Maria i kult, konst, vision.* Delsbo: Åsak, 1991.

Bevans, Stephen B. 1992. *Models of Contextual Theology.* Maryknoll: Orbis.

Bitter, Rudolf von. 1993. *August Macke.* Munich.

Bjerg, Svend. 1999. *Synets teologi.* Frederiksberg: Anis.

Blomqvist, Karin. 1999. "Gudabilder och bildteori: Dions olympiska tal i ljuset av den grekiska debatten om dyrkandet av gudabilder." In *Patristica Nordica 5: Föreläsningar hållna vid det femte Nordiska patristikermötet i Lund 20–23 augusti 1997*: 45–72. Religio, 51; Lund, 1999.

Boas, Franz. 1955. *Primitive Art.* New York: Dover.

Bodin, Per-Arne. 1987. *Världen som ikon: Åtta föredrag om den ryskortodoxa andliga traditionen.* Skellefteå: Artos.

— 1991. *Den oväntade glädjen: Sju studier i den rysk-ortodoxa andliga traditionen*, Skellefteå: Artos.

Boehm, Gottfried. 1986. "Das neue Bild der Natur: Nach dem Ende der Landschaftsmalerei." In M. Smuda, ed., *Landschaft*: 87–110. Frankfurt am Main: Suhrkamp.

— 1995. "Die Wiederkehr der Bilder." In Boehm 1995: 11–38.

— 1996. "Bildsinn und Sinnesorgane." In Stöhr: 148–165.

Boehm, Gottfried, ed. 1995 [1994]. *Was ist ein Bild?* Munich: Fink, 2nd edn.

Boff, Leonardo. 1987. *Der dreieinige Gott.* Düsseldorf.

Böhme, Gernot. 1999. *Theorie des Bildes.* Munich: Fink.

Boström, Hans-Olof. 1994. *Bror Hjorth: 1894–1968.* Stockholm: Sveriges allmänna konstförening.

Brett, Guy. 1986. *Through our Own Eyes: Popular Art and Modern History.* London: GMP.

Brown, Frank Burch. 1989. *Religious Aesthetics: A Theological Study of Making and Meaning.* Princeton: Princeton University Press.

Bryson, Norman, Michael Ann Holly and Keith Moxey, eds. 1991. *Visual Theory: Painting and Interpretation.* Cambridge: Polity Press.

Bultmann, Rudolf. 1962. *Das Evangelium des Johannes.* Göttingen: Vandenhoeck & Ruprecht, 17th edn.

Castedo, Leopoldo. 1988. *Historia del arte iberoamericano, 1: Precolombino, El arte colonial.* Madrid: Alianza.

Chillida, Eduardo. 1994. "Eduardo Chillida im Gespräch mit Friedhelm Mennekes." In Mennekes and Röhrig: 128–34.

Chipp, Herschel B. 1971. "Formal and Symbolic Factors in the Art Styles of Primitive Cultures." In Jopling: 146–70.

Claros-Arispe, Edwin. 1996. "Mensch und Natur in den Anden: Beitrag zu einem ökologischen Ethos aus der Sicht der Aymara und Quechua." In Kessler: 200–15.

Clifford, James. 1985. "Histories of the Tribal and the Modern." *Art in America* 73: 164–77.

— 1988. *The Predicament of Culture: Twentieth-Century Ethnography, Literature, and Art.* Cambridge, MA: Harvard University Press.

Coleman, Earle J. 1998. *Creativity and Spirituality: Bonds between Art and Religion.* Albany: State University of New York Press.

Coote, Jeremy. 1992. "'Marvels of Everyday Vision': The Anthropology of Aesthetics and the Cattle-keeping Nilotes." In Coote and Shelton.

Coote, Jeremy, and Anthony Shelton, eds. 1992. *Anthropology, Art, and Aesthetics.* Oxford: Oxford University Press.

Croce, Benedetto. 1969. *Estetikk som vitenskapen om uttrykket.* Oslo: Tanum; *Estetica come scienza dell' espressione e linguistica generale,* 1902.

Danbolt, Gunnar. 2000. *Det kristne bildet: Tre faser i utviklingen av den kristne kirkeutsmykning.* In Banschbach Eggen and Hognestad: 57–88.

Dean, Carolyn. 1996. "The Renewal of Old World Images and the Creation of Colonial Peruvian Visual Culture." In Fane: 171–82.

Dillenberger, Jane. 1977. *Perceptions of the Spirit in Twentieth-century American Art.* Exhibition sponsored by the Indianapolis museum of art in cooperation with the Graduate Theological Union, Berkeley; New York.

— 1986. *Style and Content in Christian Art.* New York: Crossroad.

— 1987. "Reflections on the Field of Religion and the Visual Arts." In Adams and Apostolos-Cappadona: 12–25.

— 1990. *Image and Spirit in Sacred and Secular Art.* New York: Crossroad.

Dillenberger, John. 1986. *A Theology of Artistic Sensibilities.* New York: Crossroad.

Dilly, Heinrich. 1991. "Einleitung." In Belting *et al.*: 7–16.

Durham, Jimmie. 1993. *A Certain Lack of Coherence: Writings on Art and Cultural Politics.* London: Kala Press.

— 1994. "A Friend of Mine Said That Art Is a European Invention." In Fisher: 113–19.

Düchting, Hajo. 1991. *Franz Marc.* Cologne: Dumont.

Dörries, Bernhard, and Helmut Plath, 1967 [1951]. *Alt-Hannover: Die Geschichte einer Stadt in zeitgenössischen Bildern 1500–1900.* Hannover: Feesche, 3rd edn.

Eco, Umberto. 1972. *Einführung in die Semiotik.* Munich.

— 1990 [1973]. *Das offene Kunstwerk.* Frankfurt am Main: Suhrkamp, 5th edn.

Eliade, Mircea. 1961. *Images and Symbols: Studies in Religious Symbolism.* Kansas City: Sheed Andrews & McMeel.

— 1985. "The Sacred and the Modern Artist." In Apostolos-Cappadona: 179–83.

Evdokimov, Paul. 1996 [1990]. *The Art of the Icon: A Theology of Beauty.* Redondo Beach, California: Oakwood; *L'Art de L'Icône: Théologie de la Beauté,* Paris, 1972.

166

Fane, Diana, ed. 1996. *Converging Cultures: Art & Identity in Spanish America.* New York: The Brooklyn Museum/Harry N. Abrams.

Featherstone, Mike, and Scott Lash, eds. 1999. *Spaces of Culture: City – Nation – World.* London: Sage.

Fernandez, James W. 1971. "Principles of Opposition and Vitality in Fang Aesthetics." In Jopling: 356–73.

Fisher, Jean. 1993. "Unsettled Accounts of Indians and Others." In Hiller: 292–313.

Fisher, Jean, ed. 1994. *Global Visions: Towards a New Internationalism in the Visual Arts.* London: Kala Press.

Florenskij, Pavel. 1989. *Die umgekehrte Perspektive: Texte zur Kunst.* Munich: Matthes & Seitz.

Forge, Anthony, 1971. "Art and Environment in the Sepik." In Jopling: 290–314; originally published 1965.

Forge, Anthony, ed. 1973. *Primitive Art & Society.* London: Oxford University Press.

Frank, Hilmar. 1995. *Joseph Anton Koch, Der Schmadribachfall: Natur und Freiheit.* Frankfurt am Main: Fischer.

Freire, Paulo. 1972 [1970]. *Pedagogik för förtryckta.* Stockholm: Gummessons.

Förster, Eckart, and Michael Rosen, trans. and eds. 1993. *Opus Postumum.* Cambridge: Cambridge University Press.

García-Rivera, Alejandro. 1999. *The Community of the Beautiful: A Theological Aesthetics.* Collegeville, MN: The Liturgical Press.

Gardiner, Michael. 1999. "Bakhtin and the Metaphorics of Perception." In Heywood and Sandywell: 57–73.

Geertz, Clifford. 1973. "Religion as a Cultural System." In *The Interpretation of Cultures*: 87–125. New York.

— 1993. "Art as a Cultural System." In: *Local Knowledge: Further Essays in Interpretive Anthropology*: 94–120. London: Fontana.

Gell, Alfred. 1999. *The Art of Anthropology: Essays and Diagrams.* London/Brunswick, NJ: Athlone.

Gethmann-Siefert, Annemarie. 1987. *Einführung in die Ästhetik.* Munich: Fink, 1995.

Goodman, Nelson. 1973. *Sprachen der Kunst.* Frankfurt am Main.

—1993. "Kunst und Erkenntnis." In Henrich and Iser: 569–91.

Graham, Huggan. 2001. *The Postcolonial Exotic: Marketing the Margins.* London/New York: Routledge.

Grözinger, Albrecht. 1998. "Gibt es eine theologische Ästhetik?" In Müller and Heumann: 35–43.

Gutiérrez, Gustavo. 1976. *Theologie der Befreiung.* Munich: Mainz, 2nd edn.

Harries, Richard. 1993. *Art and the Beauty of God.* London: Mowbray.

Harth, Dietrich. 1996. "Das Gedachtnis der Kulturwissenschaften und die Klassische Tradition: Erinnern und Vergessen im Licht interdisziplinärer Forschung." *International Journal of the Classical Tradition* 2.3: 414–42.

Haselberger, Herta. 1969. *Kunstethnologie: Grundbegriffe, Methoden, Darstellung.* Vienna and Munich: Schroll.

Hegel, Georg Wilhelm Friedrich. 1952 [1807]. *Phänomenologie des Geistes.* Hamburg, new edn.

Heidegger, Martin. 1960. *Vom Ursprung des Kunstwerkes.* Stuttgart.

Hellemo, Geir. 1999. *Guds billedbok: virkelighetsforståelse i religiøse tekster og bilder.* Oslo: Pax.

Henrich, Dieter, and Wolfgang Iser, eds. 1993. *Theorien der Kunst.* Frankfurt am Main: Suhrkamp, 4th edn.

Herding, Klaus. 1992. *Pablo Picasso, Les Demoiselles d´Avignon: Die Herausforderung der Avantgarde.* Frankfurt am Main: Fischer.

Hermerén, Göran. 1988. *The Nature of Aesthetic Qualities.* Lund: Lund University Press.

Heumann, Jürgen, and Wolfgang Erich Müller. 19996. *Auf der Suche nach Wirklichkeit: Von der*

(Un-)Möglichkeit einer theologischen
Interpretation der Kunst. Frankfurt am Main:
Peter Lang.

Heywood, Ian. 1999. " 'Ever More Specific':
Practices and Perception in Art and Ethics." In
Heywood and Sandywell: 198–217.

Heywood, Ian, and Barry Sandywell, eds. 1999.
Interpreting Visual Culture: Explorations in the
Hermeneutics of the Visual. London/New York:
Routledge.

Hiller, Susan. 1993 [1991]. The Myth of
Primitivism: Perspectives on Art. London/New
York: Routledge.

Hirn, Yrjö. 1964 [1913]. Det estetiska livet.
Stockholm: Prisma.

Hjorth, Bror. 1967a. Mitt liv i konsten.
Stockholm: Bonniers.

— 1967b. "Om primitiv skulptur." In Bror
Hjorth: 17–21. Moderna museets
utställningskatalog, 71; Stockholm: Moderna
museet.

Hjorth, Margareta. 1978. Närbild av Bror: Bror
Hjorth 1950–1968. Stockholm: Rabén &
Sjögren.

Howell, Signe. 1993. "Art and Meaning." In
Hiller: 215–37.

Iser, Wolfgang. 1993.
"Interpretationsperspektiven moderner
Kunsttheorie." In Henrich and Iser: 33–58.

Iwanow, Wladimir. 1995. Russland und das
Christentum. Theologie Interkulturell, Band 8;
Frankfurt am Main: Verlag für interkulturelle
Kommunikation (IKO).

Jay, Martin. 1993. Downcast Eyes: The
Denigration of Vision in Twentieth-Century
French Thought. Berkeley, CA: University of
California Press.

Jeffner, Anders. 1972. The Study of Religious
Language. London: SCM.

Jonaitis, Aldona. 1995. "Introduction: The
Development of Franz Boas' Theories on
Primitive Art." In Jonaitis, ed. A Wealth of
Thought: Franz Boas on Native American Art:
3–37. Seattle/London/Vancouver/Toronto:
University of Washington Press/Douglas &
McIntyre.

Jonsell, Bengt. 2000. "Den okände Læstadius." In
Forskning & Framsteg 1: 40–45.

Jopling, Carol F. 1971. Art and Aesthetics in
Primitive Societies: A Critical Anthology. New
York: Dutton.

Kandinsky, Vasily. 1965. Über das Geistige in der
Kunst. Bern, 8th edn.

Kant, Immanuel. "Opus Postumum." In
Gesammelte Schriften. Akademieausgabe
Band 21.

— 1977. "Beantwortung der Frage: Was ist
Aufklärung?" In Werkausgabe (ed. by Wilhelm
Weischedel); Frankfurt am Main: Suhrkamp.

Kapur, Geeta. 1994. "A New Inter Nationalism:
The Missing Hyphen." In Fisher: 39–49.

Kemp, Wolfgang, ed. 1985. Der Betrachter ist im
Bild: Kunstwissenschaft und Rezeptionsästhetik.
Cologne: DuMont.

Kessler, Hans, ed. 1996. Ökologisches Weltethos
im Dialog der Kulturen und Religionen.
Darmstadt: Wissenschaftliche Buchgesellschaft.

Kieffer, René. 1987. Johannesevangeliet 1–10.
Kommentar till Nya Testamentet, 4A; Uppsala:
EFS.

Kiilerich, Bente, and Hjalmar Torp. 1998.
Bilder og billedbruk i Bysants: trekk av tusen års
kunsthistorie. Oslo: Grøndahl Dreyer.

Klausen, Arne Martin. 1977. Kunstsosiologi.
Oslo: Gyldendal.

— 1990. "Samtidskunst og det eksotiske: Et
antropologisk perspektiv" (Contemporary Art
and the Exotic: An Anthropological Perspective).
Terskel and Threshold 1: 177–91.

Kreide Damani, Ingrid. 1992. KunstEthnologie:
Zum Verständnis fremder Kunst. Cologne:
DuMont.

Krupat, Arnold. 1989. The Voice in the Margin:
Native American Literature and the Canon.
Berkeley, CA: University of California Press.

Kurtén, Tage. 1982. Vetenskaplig teologi och dess
samhällsrelation. Åbo.

Lacan, Jacques. 1995. "Was ist ein Bild/ Tableau?" In Boehm: 75–89.

LaCugna, Catherine Mowry. 1993. *God for Us: The Trinity & Christian Life.* San Francisco: Harper.

Langer, Susanne K. 1965. *Philosophie auf neuem Wege: Das Symbol im Denken, im Ritus und in der Kunst.* Frankfurt am Main.

Layton, Robert. 1991 [1981]. *The Anthropology of Art.* Cambridge: Cambridge University Press, 2nd edn.

Leicht, Hermann. 1944. *Indianische Kunst und Kultur: ein Jahrtausend im Reiche der Chimu.* Zürich: Orell Füssli.

Lehmann, Arno. 1957. *Die Kunst der Jungen Kirchen.* Berlin: Evangelische Verlagsanstalt, 2nd enlarged edn.

Lévi-Strauss, Claude. 1966. "The Science of the Concrete." In Jopling: 225–49; originally edited in *The Savage Mind,* 1966.

Linde, Ulf. 1967. "Till Bror Hjorth." In *Bror Hjorth*: 7–15. Moderna museets utställningskatalog, 71; Stockholm: Moderna museet.

— 1986. "Volymens hemlighet." In *Möte med Bror Hjorth*: 7–29. Stockholm: Bildförlaget Öppna ögon.

Lloyd, Jill. 1991. *German Expressionism: Primitivism and Modernity.* New Haven, CT: Yale University Press.

Luther, Martin. 1883. "Heidelberger Disputation 1518." In WA, Band 1; Weimar.

Lüthi, Kurt. 1998. "Tendenzen zeitgenössischer Kunst – eine Kunst des Bilderverbots?" In Müller and Heumann: 56–68.

Marc, Franz. 1978. *Schriften.* Ed. by Klaus Lankheit; Munich.

Marcus, George E., and Fred R. Myers. 1995. *The Traffic in Culture: Refiguring Art and Anthropology.* Berkeley, CA/Los Angeles/ London: University of California Press.

Marcuse, Herbert. 1980. *Den estetiska dimensionen: Bidrag till kritik av en marxistisk estetik.* Göteborg: Röda bokförlaget (*Die Permanenz der Kunst.* 1977. Munich).

Martin, James Alfred. 1990. *Beauty and Holiness: The Dialogue between Aesthetics and Religion.* Princeton: Princeton University Press.

Martland, Thomas R. 1981. *Religion as Art: An Interpretation.* Albany: State University of New York Press.

Mead, George H. 1993. *Ästhetische Erfahrung.* In Henrich and Iser: 343–55.

Mennekes, Friedhelm. 1995. *Künstlerisches Sehen und Spiritualität.* Zürich/Düsseldorf: Artemis/Winkler.

—2000. "Between Doubt and Rapture – Art and Church Today: The Spiritual in the Art of the Twentieth Century." *Religion and the Arts* 4.2: 165–83.

Mennekes, Friedhelm, and Johannes Röhrig. 1994. *Crucifixus: Das Kreuz in der Kunst unserer Zeit.* Freiburg: Herder.

Mertin, A., and H. Schwebel, eds. 1988. *Kirche und moderne Kunst: Eine aktuelle Dokumentation.* Frankfurt am Main.

Meseure, Anna. 1993. *August Macke 1887– 1914.* Cologne: Benedikt.

Millones, Luis, and Mary Louise Pratt. 1990. *Amor Brujo: Images and Culture of Love in the Andes.* Syracuse University.

Mitchell, W. J. T. 1994. *Picture Theory: Essays on Verbal and Visual Representation.* Chicago/ London: The University of Chicago Press.

Molander, Bengt, ed. 1995. *Mellan konst och vetande: Texter om vetenskap, konst och gestaltning.* Göteborg: Daidalos.

Morphy, Howard. 1991. *Ancestral Connections: Art and an Aboriginal System of Knowledge.* Chicago: The University of Chicago Press.

— 1994. "Art: The Anthropology of Art." In Tim Ingold, ed. *Companion Encyclopedia of Anthropology, Humanity, Culture and Social Life*: 648–85. London/New York: Routledge.

— 1998. *Aboriginal Art.* London: Phaidon.

Mosquera, Gerardo. 1994. "Some Problems in Transcultural Curating." In Fisher: 133–39.

Mueller von der Haegen, Anne. 1998. *Giotto di Bondone, about 1267–1337*. Cologne: Könemann.

Müller, Wolfgang Erich, and Jürgen Heumann, eds. 1998. *Kunst-Positionen: Kunst als gegenwärtiges Thema evangelischer und katholischer Theologie*. Stuttgart: Kohlhammer.

Munn, Nancy D. 1971. "Visual Categories: An Approach to the Study of Representational Systems." In Jopling: 335–55.

— 1973. "The Spatial Presentation of Cosmic Order in Walbiri Iconography." In Forge: 193–220.

Mädler, Inken. 1997. *Kirche und bildende Kunst der Moderne: Ein an F. Schleiermacher orientierter Beitrag zur theologischen Urteilsbildung*. Tübingen.

— 1998. "Direktiven – Perspektiven: Die Kunst der Moderne im Horizont theologischer Bestimmungen." In Müller and Heumann: 18–34.

Nauerth, Claudia. 1987. "Bilder zum Naturfrieden." In Rau, Ritter and Timm: 111–41.

Nida-Rümelin, Julian, and Monika Betzler, eds. 1998. *Ästhetik und Kunstphilosophie von der Antike bis zur Gegenwart*. Stuttgart: Kröner.

Nobel, Agnes. 2000. "Handen och lärandet: Om betydelsen av handens skolning i vår tid." *Tvärsnitt* 22.3: 28–39.

Nørredam, Mette. 1986. "Primitivisme i dansk kunst." In *Louisiana Revy* 26.3 *Den globale dialog: primitiv og moderne kunst*: 16–26.

Ocvirk, Otto G., Robert E. Stinson, Philip R. Wigg, Robert O. Bone and David L. Cayton. 1994. *Art Fundamentals: Theory & Practice*. Madison/Dubuque: WCB Brown & Benchmark, 7th edn.

Okalla, Joseph Ndi, 1999. "Hermeneutik schwarzafrikanischen Sehens: Betrachtungsweise im Spannungsfeld von Kultfunktion, Sozialfunktion und Ästhetik." In Sundermeier and Küster: 107–23.

Ouspensky, Leonid, and Vladimir Lossky. 1982. *The Meaning of Icons*. Crestwood NY: St Vladimir's Seminary Press.

Paillard, Jean. 1987. *Du skickade en salamander: Kristus som djur i modern svensk litteratur*. Stockholm: Alba.

Palmer, Michael F. 1984. *Paul Tillich's Philosophy of Art*. Berlin: De Gruyter.

Pattison, George. 1991. *Art, Modernity and Faith: Towards a Theology of Art*. New York: St Martin's Press.

Pence Frantz, Nadine. 1998. "Material Culture, Understanding, and Meaning: Writing and Picturing." *Journal of the American Academy of Religion* 66.4: 791–815.

Phillips, Tom. 1996. *Afrika – Die Kunst eines Kontinents*. Exhibition catalogue Köln: DuMont.

Phipps, Elena J. 1996. "Textiles as Cultural Memory: Andean Garments in the Colonial Period." In Fane: 144–56.

Picht, Georg. 1989. *Der Begriff der Natur und seine Geschichte*. Stuttgart: Klett Cotta.

— 1990a [1986]. *Kunst und Mythos*. Stuttgart: Klett Cotta, 3rd edn.

— 1990b. *Kants Religionsphilosophie*. Stuttgart: Klett Cotta, 2nd edn.

Pratt, Mary Louise. 1992. *Imperial Eyes: Travel Writing and Transculturation*. London/New York.

Price, Sally. 1989. *Primitive Art in Civilized Places*. Chicago/London: The University of Chicago Press.

Ratcliff, Carter. 1988. "The Marriage of Art and Money." *Art in America* 76: 76–84, 145–47.

Raters, Marie-Luise. 1998. "Art. Benedetto Croce." In Nida-Rümelin and Betzler: 180–84.

Rau, Gerhard. 1987. " 'Sollen Wolf und Schaf beieinander weiden?' Frieden in der Schöpfung – eine Einführung." In Rau, Ritter and Timm: 7–19.

Rau, Gerhard, A. Martin Ritter and Hermann Timm, eds. 1987. *Frieden in der Schöpfung: Das Naturverständnis protestantischer Theologie*. Gütersloh: Mohn.

Rhodes, Colin. 1994. *Primitivism and Modern Art*. London: Thames & Hudson.

Rice, David Talbot. 1993 [1963]. *Art of the Byzantine Era*. London: Thames & Hudson.

Ringbohm, Sixten. 1970. *The Sounding Cosmos: A Study in the Spiritualism of Kandinsky and the Genesis of Abstract Painting*. Åbo.

Rodenberg, Hans-Peter. 1994. *Der imaginierte Indianer: Zur Dynamik von Kulturkonflikt und Vergesellschaftung des Fremden*. Frankfurt am Main: Suhrkamp.

Roel, Virgilio. 1984. "Peru im 20. Jahrhundert." In Anders: 120–25.

Rombold, Günter. 1976. *Kunst: Protest und Verheißung*. Linz.

— 1980. "Transzendenz in der modernen Kunst." In Schmied: 14–27.

— 1988. *Der Streit um das Bild: Zum Verhältnis von moderner Kunst und Religion*. Stuttgart: Katholisches Bibelwerk.

— 1993. "Bilderverbot und Gottesbilder." *Kunst und Kirche* 1.

Rorty, Richard M., ed. 1992. *The Linguistic Turn: Essays in Philosophical Method*. Chicago: University of Chicago Press.

Roters, Eberhard. 1984. "Die Bildwelt der Kunst als Herausforderung der Kirche." In Beck and Volp: 13–24.

— 1995. *Jenseits von Arkadien: Die romantische Landschaft*. (Art in Context). Cologne/London: DuMont/Calmann & King.

Rubin, William. 1994. "The Genesis of 'Les Demoiselles d'Avignon.'" In W. Rubin, H. Seckel and J. Cousins, *Les Demoiselles d'Avignon*: 13–144. Studies in Modern Art, 3; New York: The Museum of Modern Art.

Rushing, W. Jackson. 1995. *Native American Art and the New York Avant-Garde: A History of Cultural Primitivism*. Austin: University of Texas Press.

Rzepkowski, Horst. 1999. "Die Bedeutung der einheimischen christlichen Kunst für die Evangelisierung: Historische Perspektiven." In Sundermeier and Küster: 27–47.

Sandqvist, Tom. 1994. *Från hieroglyfen till flasktorkaren: Bilden är i bilden II*. Stockholm/Stehag: Symposium.

Sandström, Sven. 1988. "Fyra aspekter på konstbilden." Unpublished, Institutionen för konstvetenskap, Lund.

— 1993. "För fantasin står alla dörrar öppna: om förnuftets komplementaritet och kreativitet." In Berefelt: 85–119.

— 1995. *Intuition och åskådlighet*. Stockholm: Carlssons.

Santistéban, Fernando Silva. 1984. "Die Ethnographie von Peru." In Anders: 126–32.

Scheer, Brigitte. 1997. *Einführung in die philosophische Ästhetik*. Darmstadt: Wissenschaftliche Buchgesellschaft.

Schleiermacher, Friedrich. 1812–13. "Die Entwürfe zu einem System der Sittenlehre (Ethik)." AW II.

Schmidt, Max. 1929. *Kunst und Kultur von Peru*. Berlin: Propylän.

Schmied, Wieland. 1984. "Spiritualität in der Kunst des 20. Jahrhunderts." In Beck and Volp: 112–35.

Schmied, Wieland, ed. 1980. *Zeichen des Glaubens, Geist der Avantgarde: Religiöse Tendenzen in der Kunst des 20. Jahrhunderts*. Stuttgart: Klett Cotta.

— 1990. *Gegenwart Ewigkeit: Spuren des Transzendenten in der Kunst unserer Zeit*. Stuttgart: Cantz.

Schoell-Glass, Charlotte. 1998. *Aby Warburg und der Antisemitismus: Kulturwissenschaft als Geistespolitik*. Frankfurt am Main: Fischer.

Schulte, Berna, and Cristy Orzechowski, eds. 1993. *Manual De Fiestas Santiago de Pupuja*. Ed. Bartolomé de Las Casas; Cusco, Peru.

— 1994. *Donde Hay Dos O Tres.* Tomo 1 de la serie "Que venga tu Reino"; ed. Abya Yala; Quito, Ecuador.

— 1995. *Tu Palabra Nos Da Vida.* Tomo 2 de la serie "Que venga tu Reino"; ed. Abya Yala; Quito, Ecuador.

— 1996. *Iglesia Peregrina De Dios.* Tomo 3 de la serie "Que venga tu Reino"; ed. Abya Yala; Quito, Ecuador.

— 1997. *Y El Verbo Se Hizo Arte: Arte y teología de los pequeños de Diós, Communidades Cristianas de Santiago de Pupuja.* Tomo 4 de la serie "Que venga tu Reino"; Adveniat Essen, Alemania.

Schwebel, Helmut. 1980. "Die Christus-Identifikation des modernen Künstlers." In Schmied: 67–79.

— 1998. "Bildverweigerung im Bild: Mystik – eine vergessene Kategorie in der Kunst der Gegenwart." In Mertin and Schwebel: 113–23.

Schweizer, Hans Rudolf. 1973. *Ästhetik als Philosophie der sinnlichen Erkenntnis: Eine Interpretation der "Aesthetica" A.G. Baumgartens mit teilweiser Wiedergabe des lateinischen Textes und deutscher Übersetzung.* Basle: Schwabe.

Sebeok, Thomas A. 1994. *An Introduction to Semiotics.* London: Pinter.

Shield, Peter. 1995. "Naturens orden – fra non-sens til intetsteds." *Louisiana Revy* 35. 2 *Asger Jorn*: 44–52.

— 1998. *Comparative Vandalism: Asger Jorn and the Artistic Attitude to Life.* Aldershot, Brookfield Vermont/Copenhagen: Ashgate/Borgen.

Sikojew, André. 1989. "Pavel Florenskij." In Florenskij: 157–68.

Sjölin, Jan-Gunnar. 1993. *Att tolka bilder: bildtolkningens teori och praktik med exempel på tolkningar av bilder från 1850 till idag.* Lund: Studentlitteratur.

Smith, Michael L. 1996. "An Andean Nation in the Making." In Insight Guides *Peru*: 89–99. Ed. Tony Perrott; Hong Kong: APA.

Soskice, Janet Martin. 1987 [1985]. *Metaphor and Religious Language.* Oxford: Oxford University Press.

Stengård, Elisabeth. 1986. *Såsom en människa: Kristustolkningar i svensk 1900-talskonst.* Stockholm: Verbum.

Stock, Alex. 1990. "Ist die bildende Kunst ein locus theologicus?" In A. Stock, ed., *Wozu Bilder im Christentum? Beiträge zur theologischen Kunsttheorie*: 175–81. St Ottilien: EOS Verlag.

— 1998. "Die Bilder, die Kunst und die Theologie." In Müller and Heumann: 11–17.

Stöhr, Jürgen, ed. 1996. *Ästhetische Erfahrung heute.* Cologne: DuMont.

Ströter-Bender, Jutta. 1991. *Zeitgenössische Kunst der "Dritten Welt."* Cologne: Dumont.

Sundermeier, Theo. 1996. *Den Fremden verstehen: Eine praktische Hermeneutik.* Göttingen: Vandenhoeck & Ruprecht.

— 1998. "Fremd – Vertraut." In D. Lüddeckens, ed., *Begegnung mit der Fremde: Begegnung von Religionen und Kulturen*: 19–34. Dettelbach: J. H. Röll.

— 1999. "Bild und Wort: Hermeneutische Probleme der christlichen Kunst in der Dritten Welt." In Sundermeier and Küster: 9–26.

Sundermeier, Theo, and Volker Küster, eds. 1999. *Die Bilder und das Wort: Zum Verstehen christlicher Kunst in Afrika und Asien.* Göttingen: Vandenhoeck & Ruprecht.

Tapies, Antoni. 1974. *L'art contra l'estètecia*, Barcelona; *Kunst kontra Ästhetik.* St Gallen: Erker, 2nd edn 1994 [1983].

Taussig, Michael. 1993. *Mimesis and Alterity: A Particular History of the Senses.* New York/London: Routledge.

Taylor, Brandon. 1995. *Kunst heute.* (Art in Context). Cologne: Dumont.

Taylor, Mark C. 1992. *Disfiguring: Art, Architecture, Religion.* Chicago: University Press.

Tertullianus. 1994. "Adversus Marcionem." In *Sources chrétiennes*: 399. Paris: Cerf.

Thomas, Jorge. 1984. "Peruanische Volkskunst der Gegenwart." In Anders: 203–207.

Thomas, Nicholas. 1995. *Oceanic Art*. London: Thames & Hudson.

Tillers, Imants. 1993. "Locality Fails." In Hiller: 314–25.

Tillich, Paul. 1985 [1961]. "Art and Ultimate Reality." In Apostolos-Cappadona: 219–35.

— 1987. *On Art and Architecture*. New York: Crossroad.

Tuchman, Maurice, ed. 1993 [1986]. *Spiritual in Art: Abstract Painting, 1890–1985*. Abbeville, new edn.

Vidal, Javier Pulgar. 1984. "Land und Menschen." In Anders: 16–22.

Vilks, Lars. 1995. *Konstteori: Kameler går på vatten*. Nora: Nya Doxa.

Virilio, Paul. 1995. *Fluchtgeschwindigkeit*. Frankfurt am Main: Fischer; *La vitesse de liberation*. Paris, 1995.

Volp, Rainer. 1980a. "Art. VII. Das Bild als Grundkategorie der Theologie." In *Art. Bild*, TRE, 6: 357–568. Berlin/New York.

— 1980b. "Die Metamorphose der Bildwelt – eine Herausforderung an die Religion." In Schmied: 29–41.

— 1984. "Kunst als Gestaltungskompetenz: Zur Ästhetik kirchlicher Praxis." In Beck and Volp: 259–73.

— 1990a. "Art. Kunst und Religion VII: Vom Ausgang des 18. bis zum Ende des 19. Jahrhunderts." In TRE 20: 292–306.

— 1990b. "Art. Kunst und Religion VIII: Das 20. Jahrhundert." In TRE 20: 306–29.

Wallenstein, Sven-Olov. 1996. "Det utvidgade fältet – från högmodernism till konceptualism." In Konsthögskolan and Raster. *Konsten och konstbegreppet*: 117–86. Kairos, vol. 1;

Stockholm: Royal University of Fine Arts/Raster.

Weimarck, Ann-Charlotte. 1995. *Joseph Beuys och sökandet efter den egentliga livskraften*. Stockholm/Stehag: Symposium.

Weimarck, Torsten. 1983. "Konst är det som håller gudabilden levande när den är död som gudabild: om idoler och bilder, gudabilder och avgudabilder." In Vetenskapssocieteten i Lunds årsbok.

— 1992. *Nya borddansen: en essä om det bildskapande bordet*. Stockholm/Stehag: Symposium.

— 1999. *Some Aspects of Image, Mimesis and Representation and the Roles of Studium and Punctum in Interpretation*. Contribution to the Symposium on the Methodology of Art History, Stockholm 14–16.4.1999.

Welsch, Wolfgang. 1996. *Grenzgänge der Ästhetik*. Stuttgart: Reclam.

— 1999. "Transculturality: The Puzzling Form of Cultures Today." In Featherstone and Lash: 194–213.

Wentinck, Charles. 1979. *Modern and Primitive Art*. Oxford: Phaidon.

Wittgenstein, Ludwig. 1973 [1921]. *Tractatus logico-philosophicus: Logisch-philosophische Abhandlung*. Frankfurt am Main: Suhrkamp, 9th edn.

— 1971 [1958]. *Philosophische Untersuchungen*. Frankfurt am Main: Suhrkamp [Oxford, 1958].

Zaloscer, Hilde. 1997. *Visuelle Beschwörung, autonomes Kunstwerk, Ideograph: Eine Begriffsklärung*. Vienna: Böhlau.

Zeindler, Matthias. 1993. *Gott und das Schöne: Studien zur Theologie der Schönheit*. Göttingen: Vandenhoeck & Ruprecht.

Zizioulas, John D. 1985. *Being as Communion: Studies in Personhood and the Church*. New York.